ENCOURAGING COOPERATION AMONG COMPETITORS

Tariffs published during three months of 1981–1982 by the Eastern Central Motor Carriers Association (one of the ten major motor carrier rate bureaus).

Encouraging Cooperation among Competitors

THE CASE OF MOTOR CARRIER DEREGULATION AND COLLECTIVE RATEMAKING

WILLIAM B. TYE

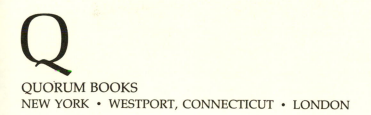

QUORUM BOOKS
NEW YORK • WESTPORT, CONNECTICUT • LONDON

Library of Congress Cataloging-in-Publication Data

Tye, William B.
  Encouraging cooperation among competitors.

  Bibliography: p.
  Includes index.
    1. Trucking—United States—Rates. 2. Trucking—
Government policy—United States. I. Title.
HE5623.T94 1987   388.3'24   86-25554
ISBN 0-89930-246-7 (lib. bdg. : alk. paper)

Library of Congress Catalog Card Number: 86-25554
ISBN: 0-89930-246-7

First published in 1987 by Quorum Books

Greenwood Press, Inc.
88 Post Road West, Westport, Connecticut 06881

Printed in the United States of America

∞

The paper used in this book complies with the
Permanent Paper Standard issued by the National
Information Standards Organization (Z39.48-1984).

10 9 8 7 6 5 4 3 2 1

Copyright Acknowledgments

The excerpt from an address by Alexander Gerschenkron, reprinted here as a
prologue, was originally published in *The Public Interest* (Winter 1970):
118–19, and has been reprinted with permission.

7155960

To my father,
"For no evil can come to a good man"

Prologue

Your trouble is that you have not studied the literature of the subject. I am not going to give you a long reading list, but I must summarize for you one single item on that reading list. This is a fairy tale by Hans Christian Andersen, a fairy tale which, in the dark days of the Nazi occupation, the Danes used so subtly and so effectively. That fairy tale is called "The Most Unbelievable Thing." There was a kingdom, and in the kingdom there was a king, and he had a princess, and he was interested in the progress of the arts. And at a certain point he announced that he would give the princess in marriage to the man who would accomplish the most unbelievable thing.

And there was great excitement and tremendous competition in the land. Finally, the great day came when all those prepared works had to be presented for judgment. There were many marvelous things, but towering high above them was a truly wonderful thing. It was a clock, a clock produced by a handsome young man. It had a most wonderful mechanism, showing the calendar back and forth into the past and into the future, showing the time, and around the clock were sculptured all the great spiritual and intellectual figures in the history of mankind.

And whenever the clock struck, those figures exercised most graceful movements. And everybody, the people and the judges said that yes, to accomplish a thing like that was most unbelievable. And the princess looked at the clock and then looked at the handsome young man, and she liked them both very much. And the judges were just about to pronounce their formal judgment, when a new competitor appeared, a lowbrow fellow. He, too, carried something in his hand, but it was not a work of art, it was a sledgehammer. He walked up to the clock and he swung out and with three blows he smashed up the clock and everybody said, why, to smash up such a clock, this is surely the most unbelievable thing, and that was how the judges had to adjudge.

And this is relevant to the present situation at Harvard.

It is now 100 years since President Eliot started converting what after all was an ancient but rather obscure college into a great university, the greatest university in the land. What has taken 100 years to create can be destroyed in as many weeks. This university, like the clock in the story, like all great works of art, is a frail and fragile creation, however beautiful, and unless you do something about it, and unless you let the administration do something about it, this wonderful work of art will be destroyed, and the guilt will be yours.

Alexander Gerschenkron, Professor of Economic History,
Harvard University, in his address to the assembled faculty
on the subject of SDS occupation of University Hall,
as quoted in *The Public Interest* (Winter 1970): 118–19.

Contents

Contents   xi

Tables

Figures

Preface

Like most young transportation economists, I began my research on collective ratemaking in the trucking industry with the presumption that nothing good could come from this type of regulation. Having read and contributed to the literature on the economics of regulation, which taught us that economic regulation of trucking caused substantial losses of economic welfare, I presumed that the same must be true for collective ratemaking. After all, price fixing was supposed to be *per se* illegal.

But like other young transportation economists whose learning on the subject came mostly from reading what other transportation economists had written, I actually knew very little about tariffs and how trucking rates were established. These sorts of things were not on the special exams for a Ph.D. at places like Harvard. I do remember seeing my father poring over all those tariffs in his office, but it all seemed needlessly complicated—or at least that was what we were told—when compared to how it would be once the golden age of deregulation was achieved.

During the period of administrative regulatory reform at the Interstate Commerce Commission, the elimination of most of the regulatory constraints in the industry was expected shortly. But the new Motor Carrier Act of 1980 did not promise to dismantle the antitrust immunity for the collective ratemaking process in the motor carrier rate bureaus. I remember hearing the regrets over this omission expressed by the Washington, D.C., contingent of economists who had made a career out of being the scourge of the motor carrier industry. They felt quite sure that the retention of collective ratemaking would be a major impediment to the development of price competition in the motor carrier industry.

About the same time I received a call from the late Daryl Wyckoff of the Harvard Business School about joining him in participating in a marketing study for a large regional motor carrier. My subsequent experience in management consulting in the motor carrier industry provided information quite different from the perceptions in Washington. Had I gotten up in front of my motor carrier clients and suggested that the answer to the raging price war and to their deteriorating financial condition was to call Vernon Farriba at the Southern Motor Carrier Rate Conference and ask him to do his job and stop the price cutting, I would have been laughed out of the room. Yet transportation economists in Washington thought this was how things worked in the industry. By then I had moved to a neutral position on collective ratemaking. But if motor carrier rate bureaus were not fixing prices, what were they doing?

Only later did I begin to learn why an institution almost uniformly scorned by the academic economists who knew little about it was so overwhelmingly supported by the people who knew the most about it— carriers and traffic managers and the organizations representing their interests. I was soon approached by the late John Fessenden, an attorney who represented motor carrier rate bureaus, and Dabney Waring of the Motor Common Carrier Association. Would I conduct a study of price competition in the industry for the newly formed Motor Carrier Rate-making Study Commission? And was there a role for rate bureaus in enhancing efficiency in the new environment of permissive regulation? I was fairly sure of the answer to the first question but quite unsure of the second. The rationale for rate bureaus in this new environment would be quite different from that under the prior regime of strict regulation. A recent paper by Donald Dewey of Columbia was said to be highly pertinent. The result was a massive study which I submitted to the Motor Carrier Ratemaking Study Commission in 1982.

Over the next several years I began to see that the problem of collective ratemaking in trucking is a special, albeit extreme, case of a more general problem. The problem is that individual firms in the transportation industries provide service only over limited portions of a network, but customers' demands extend over the entire network. The necessity of providing through freight service from any origin to any destination requires cooperation among firms who are also expected to compete in the new environment of regulatory reform. These industries had been regulated in part precisely to deal with the "interconnect" and "competitive access" issues. But the antitrust laws generally presume that firms should compete, not cooperate.

Sensing that motor carrier collective ratemaking was both a topic of interest in its own right and a case study of the more general problem in the transportation industries, and feeling confident that it was at least a topic that I knew something about, I embarked on the writing of this book. James Harkins of the Regular Common Carrier Conference and the managers of the major motor carrier rate bureaus agreed to provide much appreciated typing and editorial assistance, while I agreed to provide my weekends and evenings. Toward the end Dabney Waring remarked that "a work of art is never finished—only abandoned."

The results that follow reflect many discussions with the above-mentioned persons and countless others who have participated in the literature and debates over collective ratemaking in recent years. Their help is gratefully acknowledged.

Introduction 1

[Y]ou have already heard—and will continue to hear—all of the arguments for and against rate bureaus that have ever been made. I am quite aware that there is little new to be added to the decades of discussion of these institutions.

> GEORGE W. WILSON, Graduate School of Business, Indiana University, *Testimony before the Motor Carrier Ratemaking Study Commission*, Boston, 19 March 1982.

Collective ratemaking in the motor carrier industry is undoubtedly the most poorly understood issue in the literature on economic regulation. While strongly held opinions are commonplace, real knowledge of the collective ratemaking process and of how trucking tariffs are constructed is scarce.

Collective ratemaking is an institution whereby groups of motor carriers discuss, agree on, and then publish collective tariffs which establish the price and terms for motor carrier service under antitrust immunity granted by the Reed-Bulwinkle Act.[1] A rate bureau is a nonprofit organization established by the carriers and authorized by the Interstate Commerce Commission (ICC) to conduct meetings of member carriers and to provide ancillary services such as publishing collectively established tariffs.[2] Ten major general freight regional rate bureaus publish tariffs applying to various geographic regions while another collective organization (the National Motor Freight Traffic Association) is responsible for nationwide commodity classification. Because the carriers' participation in rate bureau activity relates directly or indirectly to price, these activities would ordinarily be a cause for action under the antitrust laws without an express antitrust immunity.[3]

Collective ratemaking is significant primarily in the less-than-truckload (LTL) intercity freight sector of the trucking industry, the so-called general freight common carrier. (Roadway Express and Consolidated Freightways are two well-known examples of the larger carriers.) These LTL carriers ordinarily have hundreds or even thousands of employees operating a highly sophisticated network of terminals to pick up and deliver less-than-truckload shipments via consolidation of such individual shipments into truckloads for movement over regular routes among terminals. LTL carriers must be distinguished from the truckload (only) (TL) operator, who provides a door-to-door service for TL shipments without the need for terminals to consolidate small shipments. The TL carrier often operates at a much smaller scale—sometimes a single employee (the owner/operator). The LTL sector of the trucking industry is nevertheless widely regarded as unconcentrated when compared to the typical scale of United States industry.[4]

In addition, specialized carriers, such as armored car services or chemical haulers, meet a specialized need, often with specialized equipment, and contract carriers do not hold themselves out to offer common carrier service. Both common and contract carriers are distinguished from private carriers, who principally serve the transportation needs of their owners but have more recently been authorized to sell their services to other shippers. Also, there are small parcel carriers such as United Parcel Service who provide a specialized motor carrier service. Each of these types of carriers has evolved into a highly specialized market segment with different marketing, pricing, and service strategies.

The LTL intercity transportation market is distinguished by two important attributes which make the collective ratemaking issue significant to buyers and sellers of its services. First, motor carriers hold themselves out as common carriers in their service territories of virtually any nonbulk commodity not requiring specialized handling (such as explosives or cement). When the commodities range from bowling balls to flagpoles to packing materials designed scientifically to minimize weight, a cost-oriented pricing structure for serving such diverse traffic can become complex very quickly.

In contrast to the breadth of commodities handled, only a few general commodity carriers offer nationwide service. Most specialize geographically to a greater or lesser degree depending on the specific carrier. However, they are able to provide nationwide services by using agreements with other carriers to handle "joint-line" or "interline" traffic. LTL carriers generally distinguish themselves as long-haul, regional, or local/short haul. Because of operational differences in the services, they rarely try to compete in more than one of these markets simultaneously. Even when a carrier is authorized to conduct nationwide service, as most major carriers now are, it will engage in convenience interlining rather than serving all movements via single-line service. This combination of almost exhaustive commodity and specialized geographic coverage is accomplished by an extremely complex pricing system (specified in multilateral rate bureau tariffs and extensive bilateral agreements among carriers on the terms by which service will be jointly provided).

After a long and bitter debate,[5] much of the rigid regulatory structure of entry, rate, and service controls that had characterized the interstate motor carrier industry was repealed by the Motor Carrier Act of 1980 (hereafter MCA).[6] The economic case for regulatory reform was predicated on several important assumptions about market structure in the trucking industry: (1) trucking markets are characterized by many specialized shipper needs that would (in the absence of regulatory restraint) be served by diverse companies with no clear optimal size; (2) while individual market segments might be relatively concentrated, concentration at the national and regional levels was expected to be low; and (3) the absence of significant scale economies (relative to the size of the relevant market) together with low fixed costs and relatively easy entry and exit implied that free-market competition would be sufficient to protect against anticompetitive abuses without regulatory constraint.

In contrast to the more radical changes in economic regulation of rates and entry, Congress elected to make only limited changes in the practice of collective ratemaking in the MCA. Rather, the MCA established a Motor Carrier Ratemaking Study Commission (hereafter Study Commission or MCRSC) to advise Congress on policy for the antitrust immunity for collective ratemaking.

The ensuing debate over the proper role of collective ratemaking in the trucking industry was marked by fluctuating fortunes of the participants.[7] Fresh from their success with Congress and the Interstate Commerce Commission in reducing regulation of the trucking industry, the opponents of collective ratemaking started the year 1982 on the intellectual offensive. Time was on their side because the MCA prohibited single-line collective ratemaking (subject to a number of conditions and exceptions discussed below) after a date as early as 1 January 1984, but no later than 1 July 1984.[8] Outspoken academic economists[9] and government agencies (U.S. Department of Transportation [DOT], Federal Trade Commission [FTC], and U.S. Department of Justice [DOJ]) united in opposition to any form of collective ratemaking in the trucking industry. New appointees to the ICC began to signal their distaste for enforcing even the minimal regulatory provisions of the MCA and perceived continued exercise of collective ratemaking as an obstacle to total deregulation. Many reasonable but uninformed outsiders instinctively assumed that no good could ever come from a motor carrier rate bureau, which, after all, sanctioned activities that might otherwise be unlawful. Supporters of collective ratemaking, on the other hand, seemed to be obstructing the trend toward deregulation in an environment in which both the trucking industry (the Teamsters labor union in particular) and price fixing lacked credibility. In arguing for the continuation of the antitrust immunity, the trucking industry was regarded by critics as simply making a self-serving set of foot-dragging arguments much like the ones already rejected by Congress in passing the MCA.[10]

By the second half of 1982, however, the trucking industry and shipper organizations had arrayed an impressive list of supporters of collective ratemaking, including many respected academic economists who had not been previously heard from on the subject. During the hearings before the Study Commission, shipper organizations were virtually unanimous in their support of continued collective ratemaking in the trucking industry.[11] The government agencies and academic economists who opposed the antitrust immunity had presented an anemic case in comparison, especially in the context of their vehement opposition to the antitrust immunity.

The activism of the supporters of collective ratemaking during the hearings contrasted sharply with that of the opponents of collective ratemaking. After an initial salvo against collective ratemaking at the first hearing of the Study Commission—relying almost entirely on old data and studies done prior to the MCA—the opposition was amazingly quiet in the remaining hearings. There was an occasional disgruntled shipper or disaffected academic, but no new evidence was provided at the hearings on the post–1980 experience to support the charges that were heard in the early hearings. As the Study Commission was concluding its hearings, the opponents of collective ratemaking were clearly on the defensive.

Indeed, the year 1982 marked a dramatic shift in the tone of the case against collective ratemaking. At the first hearing of the Study Commission on 18 November 1981, spokesmen for DOT, DOJ, and the FTC claimed that motor carrier rate bureaus were a "government-enforced cartel"; that rate bureaus suppressed price competition; that the right of Independent Action (IA)[12] was an illusion; that collective ratemaking discouraged ratemaking innovations and rate/service options, raised prices, created monopoly profits, and induced excessive service competition.

During the course of the hearings of the Study Commission, it became clear that these assertions could not be supported by the evidence. Critics who called for the abolition of collective ratemaking had disregarded the dramatic changes which had taken place in the trucking industry since administrative regulatory reform was initiated by the ICC prior to the MCA.[13] The contention that motor carrier rate bureaus were acting as government-enforced cartels was considered laughable by knowledgeable shippers and carriers. In reality there was a major price war under way via an avalanche of Independent Actions by carriers in addition to the widespread use of individual carrier tariffs. This activity involved substantial and widespread rate cuts, particularly in the form of discounts off rate bureau tariffs.[14] *The New York Times* described the resulting situation as a "a price war that makes the competition between airlines seem like light-hearted jousting among friends."[15]

In fact, there was no regulatory or rate bureau obstacle to rate-cutting through individual carrier initiative.[16] Nor did carriers perceive any meaningful federal regulatory restrictions on their territory, operations, or service options. Regulation of motor carrier rates and entry by the ICC had become substantially more permissive than it was prior to the MCA.

One of the more interesting cases of the revisionism in light of this new evidence seems to have occurred at the Federal Trade Commission. At the initial hearing of the Study Commission, the then chairman James C. Miller of the FTC strongly opposed the antitrust immunity, relying on a study by Denis A. Breen of the FTC staff.[17] At a much later date, a second Breen study[18] differed substantially from those early statements. The later paper recanted most of the earlier assessment by the FTC. For example, the first Breen study claimed that motor carrier rate bureaus served as a government-enforced cartel. The second Breen study largely discredited this and many other accusations. It represented an important restatement of the argument against collective ratemaking after evaluation of the record of many months of hearings before the Study Commission. Breen later concluded that in the motor carrier industry, "the welfare gains from successful prosecution of horizontal-restraint cases are likely to be slight . . . ; the *per se* standard seems inappropriate here if horizontal agreements among carriers create efficiencies that could not be achieved in a less restrictive manner."[19] The change could not have been more dramatic. Nevertheless, some critics of collective ratemaking testified before the Study Commission, saying that "by and large, trucking is still pretty much 'business as usual.' "[20]

As the initial case against rate bureaus lost credibility, critics took a curious turn. When it became evident that the initial charges against collective ratemaking were no longer valid in light of the rate war and the permissive regulatory environment, some opponents elected to make charges against the rate bureaus exactly the opposite of the ones offered initially to the Study Commission. The new argument was that collective ratemaking now played an inconsequential role in the industry and could be eliminated as a relic of a bygone era. Curiously, no benefits or costs were claimed from elimination of collective ratemaking under this "revisionist" case for the opposition.[21] Alternatively, the efficiency benefits of collective ratemaking were conceded to be so great that carriers would find a way to achieve them even without the antitrust immunity.[22]

The revisionist case against collective ratemaking produces some interesting paradoxes.[23] If the services provided by rate bureaus would not be missed, there are no benefits waiting to be realized by dismantling the rate bureaus and the remnants of regulation left by the MCA. In the areas of entry, price/service options, and price competition, revisionists did not identify any specific opportunities for improved efficiency from the abolition of collective ratemaking which were not already available.

Why then were the revisionists so insistent that the antitrust immunity be revoked? One began to wonder what the dispute was all about.

From the weakening of the opposition case, it might be supposed that the collective ratemaking issue would fade into obscurity. Supporters of regulatory reform, it would appear, were entitled to declare the victory won and write their memoirs. The testimony before the Study Commission had shown that much of the rhetoric against the rate bureaus uttered in the early hearings was false. Critics had failed to consider the regulatory reforms in the MCA, the greatly changed competitive environment in the industry resulting from administrative regulatory changes, and the appalling recession in the industry.[24] More important, many previous opponents of collective ratemaking were becoming neutral and even conceding that rate bureaus provided important efficiency gains to carriers and shippers.

This optimism, however, was short-lived. The Study Commission, in a six to four vote, issued an unequivocal majority report condemning all collective ratemaking and recommending the total elimination of the antitrust immunity.[25] Despite the fact that the analysis of the collective ratemaking process based on pre–1980 data was shown to be no longer valid, the Study Commission's majority report repeated the old arguments.[26] Where new data showed that the old complaints about collective ratemaking were invalid, these were taken as evidence that the functions of collective ratemaking had become obsolete. Supporters of collective ratemaking had won the battle of the facts in the hearings, but the Study Commission majority seemed not to be listening.

The virtual unanimity that characterized the position of carriers and shippers on the collective ratemaking issue before the Study Commission was shattered by developments at the ICC shortly after the Study Commission report. During the hearings of the Study Commission, all of the major shipper organizations had strongly supported collective ratemaking.[27] Opponents of collective ratemaking (particularly free-market enthusiasts) found themselves in the awkward position of explaining why an economic institution strongly supported by both buyers and sellers was somehow contrary to the public interest.[28]

The trouble started with the shippers. Coincidental with controversy over the report of the Study Commission, the Interstate Commerce Commission began what can only be described as a deliberate decision to renounce its responsibilities to enforce the MCA. This decision occurred during a period of increased rate discounting (often in the form of what were termed "allowances" off existing collective tariffs, i.e., rebates unilaterally established by the carriers).

The net result was a series of general rate increases that were routinely approved by the ICC in the midst of an accelerating rate war. But in this rate war the largest shippers benefited most.[29] Some argued that the result was the rate restructuring in favor of the large shipper at the expense of the small that was predicted by the opponents of deregulation. Carriers maintained that the increases were necessary to offset previous underpricing of these shipments induced by regulation.[30] But to the smaller shippers and the shippers of smaller consignments and their representatives, the results looked like the rate war to secure the traffic of the large shippers was being financed by unjustified general rate increases permitted by unsupervised antitrust immunity. What was worse, shippers perceived that a permissive ICC was signaling that it had no intention of seriously considering either rate level or rate structure issues being raised by these pricing trends. The ICC seemed to be warning shippers to expect no regulatory protection against potential abuses of the antitrust immunity.[31] A more cynical policy to destroy the carrier/shipper consensus for collective ratemaking could not be imagined.

The National Small Shipments Traffic Conference (NASSTRAC) was the first to act.[32] As the Study Commission report was completed, NASSTRAC changed its long-standing position of support for collective ratemaking.[33] In response to the NASSTRAC request in June 1983, the ICC opened a proceeding[34] to determine whether antitrust immunity for collective setting of rates for small shipments should be revoked. Shortly afterward, the National Industrial Transportation League (NITL) also reversed its long-standing support for collective ratemaking.[35] By the time the ICC dismissed the proceeding,[36] the damage to the consensus on collective ratemaking was complete.

Subsequent events were also to undermine motor carrier use of the collective ratemaking process. As a result of the Study Commission's recommendations and the failure of Congress to act, the restrictions on collective ratemaking for single-line rates (as provided for in the MCA of 1980) went into effect at the end of June 1984. After a flurry of tariff-reform activity prior to this date, collective ratemaking activities quieted considerably as many carriers feared to use their remaining rights for collective ratemaking.[37] At the same time, many larger carriers were completing the installation of private tariff systems that avoided direct use of collective ratemaking procedures for much traffic. Since the cumulative effects of collectively established tariffs remained until an individual carrier actively cancelled its participation, the result was a relatively inactive period for collective ratemaking, with the notable exception of general rate increases.

These trends also marked a particularly divisive period for the motor carrier industry.[38] The industry was being torn apart by the rate war and the bankruptcies that resulted. The ICC's enforcement of its regulatory powers had atrophied to the point that some were questioning whether it had any further role to play.[39] Even one carrier executive expressed skepticism about the rate bureaus for the first time.[40]

Meanwhile, the Rocky Mountain Motor Tariff Bureau, one of the largest rate bureaus, filed a request in April 1983 for nationwide authority. Approval of this and similar proposals for other rate bureaus in the proceeding that resulted (*Ex Parte* No. 297 [Sub-No. 7]) would have put them in competition with one another rather than in the historical situation of having exclusive geographic franchises. This proposal was strongly opposed by the smaller regional carriers who felt that their influence in collective ratemaking decisions would be reduced if the regional rate bureaus lost in a competitive struggle among rate bureaus for survival. The ICC decided to take no action on the proposals in a vote on 20 May 1985, but once again the damage to the previous consensus was evident. Meanwhile, renewed calls for the total elimination of even the standby potential for rate regulation by "sunsetting" the ICC and the institutions of collective ratemaking were being heard.[41]

These events suggest that regardless of the merits of the issues, the debate may already have run its course. Most interested parties have already made up their minds, if there was ever any serious consideration of the evidence one way or another. The discussion that follows, however, is based on the belief that, like Mark Twain, the death of the collective ratemaking issue is greatly exaggerated, and the outcome will have profound results for the trucking industry and regulation reform more generally. These issues go beyond the specialized concerns of the motor carrier industry, because the dilemmas of encouraging both cooperation and competition are found to a degree among all firms in industries undergoing a transition to deregulation and operating over a service network. The motor carrier industry offers an excellent opportunity for illustrating these issues, particularly the application of the newly emerging theory that cooperation among competitors in competitive markets can enhance efficiency.

The study first defines a new set of standards for evaluating the antitrust exemption in Chapter 2. Based on these standards, data on recent structure and performance of the trucking industry are examined in Chapter 3. The following two chapters examine the efficiency-enhancing features of collective ratemaking and evaluate various policy options. The final chapter closes with conclusions and recommendations.

Overview of Issues Raised
by Collective Ratemaking
in the Motor Carrier Industry

> I was and continue to be a strong advocate of deregulation of the transportation industry. I have a pro-deregulation record of which I am proud. I want to explain why I consider that record to be consistent with my vote in the Ratemaking Study Commission.
>
> If I could boil down my views to a simple explanation, it would be this: When I began working on the issue of promoting competition in the trucking industry, I started with the notion that entry was 90 percent of the problem. After more hearings and study than I care to remember, and after observing the results of the Motor Carrier Act of 1980, I have come to the conclusion that I was wrong. Entry was 99 percent of the problem.
>
> ...[L]ook at the trucking industry since 1980. How can one explain the unprecedented rate competition among trucking firms since July 1980? Has this been the direct result of the elimination of antitrust immunity? Of course not. The motor carrier industry continues to have the same degree of immunity from the antitrust laws that it has had since 1948. The difference is entry—liberalized entry....
>
> In this kind of environment, unless there are *regulatory* constraints on entry, it is virtually impossible to restrict price competition. In fact, this is probably more true for trucking than most other industries....How could companies "fix" prices in such an environment? The simple answer is that they can't.
>
> Statement of former senator HOWARD W. CANNON,
> 8 April 1983, in Study Commission *Report*, pp. 64–67.

The issue of collective ratemaking was the most controversial of any considered by Congress in the Motor Carrier Act of 1980, as evidenced by the decision to create the Motor Carrier Ratemaking Study Commission to conduct an independent inquiry into the controversy. In addition, the Motor Carrier Act specifically directed that the Interstate Commerce Commission (ICC) was not to dismantle the collective ratemaking process unilaterally and postponed the implementation of the proposed restrictions on collective single-line ratemaking until after receiving the recommendations of the Motor Carrier Ratemaking Study Commission.

The reluctance of Congress to make any major changes in the collective ratemaking process was undoubtedly based on the fact that bureau ratemaking was the least understood aspect of the motor carrier regulatory process. Collective ratemaking involves the obscure and highly specialized world of tariffs, classifications, and rates. Prior to the sunshine provisions which made rate bureau meetings open to the public, outsiders were never really quite sure what was going on in these meetings.

Antitrust exemption for the collective ratemaking process does not readily lend itself to compromise or to making gradual changes at the margin, as does, say, the policy on motor carrier entry. The quantum nature of proposed changes in collective ratemaking goes beyond reform of regulation and has the effect of dismantling the rate bureaus and the vestiges of regulation. It is widely recognized that changes in collective ratemaking can be used to induce irreversible changes in market structure and regulation in the trucking industry. Consequently, opinions on collective ratemaking are often governed by reference to a hidden agenda (such as making the task of regulation impossible) rather than with an objective assessment of the real dilemmas of the problem. As the positions harden, new facts are treated either as irrelevant or necessarily confirming already entrenched positions. The unfortunate results are strong positions on the subject of collective ratemaking, often based on an incomplete knowledge of either the collective ratemaking process or the consequences of changing it.

Also clouding the discussion is the legacy of past debates. During the period of strict rate and entry regulation by the ICC, defenders of rate bureaus almost seemed to argue that collective ratemaking suppressed ruinous price competition in the public interest.[42] Not only was this an unacceptable rationale for collective ratemaking in an era of regulatory reform, it also happened to be untrue. Nevertheless, critics of collective ratemaking usually proceed first by assuming that restrained price competition results from the antitrust immunity and then arguing that price fixing is obsolete and undesirable in the new era. Their answer is therefore to abolish collective ratemaking.[43]

But simply treating collective ratemaking as a relic of a bygone era fails to consider whether rate bureaus provide additional functions in a permissively regulated or deregulated market and thereby actually promote the new goals of transportation policy. A fresh examination of the benefits and costs of collective ratemaking in the context of the new competitive environment is needed.

THE TENSION BETWEEN ANTITRUST AND REGULATION

The existence of economic regulation does not, as a matter of law, necessarily preempt the enforcement of the antitrust laws. Legal doctrine has traditionally held that the antitrust laws will apply in full force to regulated industries without an explicit constitutional or statutory exemption, unless there is a "plain repugnancy." However, the courts have considered the special circumstances of regulation in a particular industry in evaluating the reasonableness of a business practice. This tension has created substantial uncertainty over the legality of many activities of regulated firms.[44] Furthermore, as a practical matter, there are many circumstances where regulation and antitrust principles are mutually exclusive in their practical application.[45] In other cases, they are alternative means of accomplishing the same ends, and the two institutions stand side by side in an uneasy struggle over jurisdiction.

In transportation, there is certainly a strong tendency for changes in antitrust and regulatory policy to be synchronized. For example, the Motor Carrier Act partly deregulated new proposals for "released rates" (tariffs that provide for reduced rates in consideration of a limitation in liability for loss and damage), required such rates to be negotiated and filed as Independent Actions by carriers, eliminated antitrust immunity for any discussion or collective setting of such rates at the bureaus, and specifically provided for the application of the antitrust laws. This is a clear case where regulation and collective ratemaking were set aside in favor of increasing the domain of the antitrust laws. However, recent developments in economic theory now question whether economic efficiency might justify restriction of the application of the antitrust laws even in a permissively regulated or deregulated, highly competitive market, to which we now turn.

THE "NEW LEARNING" ON COOPERATION AMONG COMPETITORS

Collective ratemaking in the trucking industry is an issue that simply refuses to die. The reasons go beyond the emotions that have often obscured the facts and confused the discourse. If it were a simple matter of the interests of motor carriers against the interests of the public, the problem would have been disposed of long ago. Collective ratemaking continues to pose meaningful issues for transportation policy because it challenges traditional assumptions of antitrust law and economics and has far-reaching implications for issues beyond those in the trucking industry.

The broadest of these issues is an ongoing dispute about the antitrust laws—whether the laws themselves, and more specifically recent enforcement policy, on balance make a net contribution to economic welfare.[46] Skeptics are not only challenging certain decisions under the rule of reason, but also the most fundamental precept, the *per se* prohibition on price fixing. Mindful of OPEC's recent failure to stabilize prices, scoffers question whether even unregulated cartels can fix prices in a competitive market. Price-fixing conspiracies may simply fall of their own weight.[47]

This "new learning" goes beyond simply a permissive attitude toward price fixing. It further contends that cooperation among competitors can actually be procompetitive and efficiency enhancing. That otherwise illegal agreements on price among competitors have certain public benefits is certainly not a new proposition in the regulated transportation industries.[48] However, a belief that collusion over price is *per se* inefficient is an article of faith in the antitrust law and forms the consensus of support for the *per se* prohibition against price fixing in antitrust law. Yet respectable economists are now offering articulate objections to such beliefs.[49] These doubts of the conventional wisdom are being reinforced by recent court cases that are applying a rule-of-reason test to activities closely associated with collusive price fixing,[50] while new legislation has been passed or proposed to allow more direct cooperation among competitors.[51]

As the transportation industries emerged from regulation to the greater scrutiny of the antitrust laws and as antitrust attorneys and transportation industry experts familiarized themselves with the other's expertise, economic practices in transportation posed unique antitrust issues. These new concerns often arose from the fact that service over an integrated transportation system necessitated a high degree of co-ordination among nonintegrated suppliers, despite the fact that those same carriers were horizontal competitors in the same or in other markets.[52] Carriers were told to compete vigorously in the new environment, while it was implicitly assumed that desirable cooperative arrangements would be left undisturbed. The new ability of carriers to withdraw that cooperation unilaterally raised important new antitrust issues, most disturbingly when a carrier's joint service in coordination with another carrier competed directly with its own single-line service. Permissible behavior under the antitrust laws was not so obvious, especially when the cooperation of the vertically integrated carrier was absolutely essential for the nonintegrated carrier to compete with the alleged "bottleneck carrier" in the marketplace.[53]

A NEW TEST FOR POLICY EVALUATION BASED ON MARKET STRUCTURE

Suppose one were to observe car manufacturers publishing sticker prices, but actual sales took place at substantial discounts from these list prices. The inferences are that such list prices serve merely as a reference price for negotiations and that they increase efficiency by providing information to customers, even if they do not serve as a posted price (a price offer not generally considered subject to negotiation).

Given the lack of standardization in the products being purchased, the buyer is able to judge the reasonableness of a particular price by comparing the discount with the typical discount on other trades. (This reference price provides a rationale for the legal requirement that auto manufacturers attach a sticker price to all new cars.) If, on the other hand, substantial trades took place at the posted price, one would conclude that the reduced transactions and information costs of avoiding the need to negotiate were responsible for the use of this pricing system in a competitive market.[54]

Now suppose we observed that in the first situation auto manufacturers consulted one another in designing the format of the list prices and even the price levels (assume away the problems raised by the legality of such information exchanges). What would one then infer about the practice? As long as there are substantial discounts from list prices and no evidence of collusion in establishing the discounts from the list price, the logical inference is that there must be an efficiency gain in setting the collective list price. No other explanation for the practice of collusion seems credible if anticompetitive establishment of the actual price to the consumer is ruled out.

Now suppose that the collectively established sticker prices are found to be discounted substantially for most transactions but also serve as posted prices in a minority of other cases. Considering only these limited data, the proper inference is no longer as clear as in the first case. Collusion to establish the posted price in this example might be construed as justified by efficiency gains or by efforts to extract a monopoly profit on sales at the list price, or both. Once again, the answer would have to come from a study of the competitiveness of the market. If one could conclude that the market structure and behavior were sufficiently competitive, both the posted and negotiated prices would be deemed competitively established.

Even in the above example, however, the presence of active discounting suggests constraints on the use of collusion to extract monopoly profits. The higher the price established by cooperation, the less its creditability as a posted price and the greater the incentive of buyers and sellers to incur the negotiating costs of agreeing on a discount. The fewer the trades at a high list price, the less value it has as a posted price—and the greater the certainty of buyers that they are being "had" if they pay the list price. This threat, plus the loss of efficiency in using a posted price, thus constrains to some degree sellers' incentives to raise the list price to monopoly levels.

The preceding hypothetical example points to the dangers of applying a naive, illegal *per se* label to cooperation among competitors once the possibility of efficiency gains is considered a credible explanation for cooperative behavior. From a strictly economic (if not necessarily a legal) perspective, it would be appropriate to apply a rule of reason to the facts at hand to evaluate the dangers of price fixing and the potential efficiency gains from cooperation.

If the dangers of anticompetitive pricing and the likelihood of efficiency gains were both credible, the choice of whether to permit collusion would be more difficult. One would have to decide whether the benefits of collective ratemaking offset the costs and whether strict regulation were needed to minimize the costs.[55] In any event, the dispute would turn on the amount of discounting, the degree of competition, and the efficiency gains from collusion over the price—not whether whitewall tires should be standard equipment or whether price fixing *per se* leads to economic inefficiency.

A difficult tradeoff could be avoided, however, if it could be established that the dangers of anticompetitive pricing were *de minimis*. This would be particularly true if the *a priori* case for the efficiency gains were credible.

The typical basis for a complaint about collective ratemaking does not proceed in this manner. It starts with (1) an observation about allegedly undesirable market performance in the trucking industry, is followed by (2) a value judgment about the desirability of the market structure that is alleged to be the cause of the performance, and ends with (3) the conclusion that collective ratemaking is responsible for both the undesirable performance and market structure and should be abolished by eliminating the antitrust immunity. An example of this syllogism is as follows: (1) motor carrier rate structures are overly complex; (2) this complexity arises from the incentive to use collective ratemaking procedures to implement overly complex, industrywide, value-of-service rate structures instead of simple rate schedules offered independently by individual carriers; and thus (3) elimination of collective ratemaking would eliminate the offending barrier to implementation of these efficient pricing schemes. Opponents then attempt to demonstrate the syllogism by suggesting alternative pricing schemes, showing how they have been used in other markets, and contending that the elimination of collective ratemaking is the only obstacle standing in the way of their adoption.

The dispute over the desirability of permitting collective ratemaking as an option thus proceeds in the guise of a debate over the economic efficiency of alternative pricing schemes. Reformers offer their ideas of how the best system should be designed and attribute all discrepancies between their alternatives and the current system to collective ratemaking. In turn, defenders of the rate bureaus find fault with the innovative proposals, point to the fact they are nothing new and are, in fact, already in use, or note that there is plenty of incentive for the carriers to adopt these proposals today if they were more efficient.

At other times, the dispute takes the character of a debate over de-regulation itself. The collective ratemaking issue is treated as another chapter in the debate over regulatory reform, and any argument against regulation is treated as a body blow to collective ratemaking. If the prior regime of strict regulation is no longer valid, it is concluded that the collective ratemaking that supported it must serve no further valid public policy.[56]

Some critics even argue that a particular market practice is undesirable *per se* if it is the result of a collective decision process. They start with the fundamental conviction that antitrust immunity and economic regulation are inherently inefficient. The consequences of their proposals in terms of market structure, conduct, and performance may be only vaguely identified. Their goals are defined in terms of means, where the increased role of antitrust and elimination of collective ratemaking equate to an improved industry performance. In this mindset, it does not really matter how things turn out with the loss of collective rate-making because the results will in any event be considered economically justified as consonant with free-market principles. At times, this mentality has taken on the mark of a holy war against the antitrust immunity.

These approaches to the collective ratemaking issue have had several undesirable results for the debate on motor carrier antitrust policy. First, they have generated a fair amount of high-minded cant which has not been helpful in producing objective information. Second, they have obscured a basis for common agreement over the goal of promoting efficiency and competition in the motor carrier industry, despite seeming differences over means.

The tone of the debate has also served to confuse outsiders who lack knowledge of the trucking industry. The debate has encouraged a wide-spread belief that policymakers must first reach decisions on the best performance for the trucking industry with regard to a host of complex technical issues unknown outside the trucking industry and understood only by industry experts. Only then, it is believed, may the lay person draw conclusions about the desirability of collective ratemaking. Finding it impossible to resolve all these matters on an item-by-item basis, there is an understandable tendency to resolve the dispute in favor of competition, which is equated to the elimination of antitrust immunity for collective ratemaking.

The following chapters represent an effort to reorient the fundamental approach to these problems. The new approach calls for encouragement of an industry structure for the motor carrier industry that promotes competition, economic efficiency, and innovation. An efficient industry structure that permits a variety of structural alternatives, rather than some outsider's imposed vision of desirable industry practices, should govern the choice of policy.[57] Examination of disputes over practices is useful only in clarifying disputes over the preferred industry structure, but not in using a decision over the most desirable practice to infer the desirability of suppressing certain structural alternatives.

Emphasis on identifying and eliminating structural market imperfections and encouraging competition among structural alternatives on equal terms rather than relying on preordained conclusions on desired industry practices leads to an entirely different perspective on the issues raised by antitrust immunity for collective ratemaking. The first step is to recognize that cooperation among competitors in the trucking industry can produce efficiency gains, particularly in setting industry standards, minimizing information costs to buyers and sellers, and reducing transactions costs.[58] Cooperation among competitors to achieve efficiency gains is particularly likely in providing certain industrywide or multifirm services for which there are substantial economies of scale. Not only will multilateral solutions provide efficiency gains, but they will also prevent control of these services by individual firms—a situation that can increase the minimum efficient scale required to become an effective competitor in the industry.

A strong case is made in the following pages that the benefits of cooperation are significant in the trucking industry and not fully appreciated by the critics of collective ratemaking. The benefits are chiefly the following:

1. Reduced transactions cost among carriers in providing coordinated joint-line (or interline) service by providing a list price or a benchmark rate structure, which serves either as a fallback (or posted) price or a starting point for bilateral negotiations;
2. Providing a similar service in reducing transactions and information costs for carrier/shipper communications and negotiations; and
3. Thereby reducing minimum efficient scale, promoting efficient carrier specialization, and preserving an unconcentrated market structure necessary to achieve a more competitive industry.

The pages that follow demonstrate that the level of coordination required among motor carriers to accomplish these efficiencies presents antitrust issues unique to the trucking industry, although they are present to a lesser degree in other transportation networks.

The possibility of efficiency gains is credible enough to provide a sufficient rationale for collective ratemaking even in the absence of a motive for noncompetitive pricing. Examination of the efficiency gains from collective ratemaking is a useful exercise, but not because their measurement is crucial to the choice of appropriate public policy in a highly competitive pricing regime. The crucial issue is whether the present market structure of trucking would permit collective ratemaking to be abused. If the danger of anticompetitive abuse is *de minimis* and the benefits are reasonably credible, the burden of proof shifts to the opponents to show the following:

1. The present collective ratemaking system has defects which are significantly injurious to the public interest;
2. Those defects are clearly attributable to the collective ratemaking process and not readily corrected by other, less radical, means;
3. Elimination of antitrust immunity will correct the defects without creating other more significant ones; and
4. There are no offsetting public-interest benefits from the collective ratemaking process.

It is thus not necessary to conclusively prove the presence of significant efficiency gains from collective ratemaking, although they are material, in order to allow the practice, if the anticompetitive dangers are *de minimis*,[59] as indeed they are. Potential anticompetitive objectives of cooperation among competitors are nearly impossible in an industry that is characterized by numerous competitors, unrestrained individual pricing actions, no means to restrict output or enforce adherence to a collectively established price schedule, and the absence of entry barriers to either the collective decision process or the industry itself. This is the very industry structure in trucking previously cited by opponents of collective ratemaking in their justification for total deregulation of the industry.[60] But even if there were some doubt, proponents of vigorous antitrust enforcement must still demonstrate that the benefits of reduced anticompetitive pricing would offset the administrative and regulatory costs of antitrust enforcement.

If anticompetitive objectives for cooperative behavior are not credible, then the only rationale for cooperation becomes the desire for efficiency gains. Since there are significant administrative and transactions costs to the carriers from participating in collective action, the existence of collective ratemaking institutions suggests that the efficiency gains are tangible. If they were not, there would be no explanation of why carriers bothered to participate in the first place. Without efficiency gains, collective ratemaking would simply fall of its own weight. A market test thus answers the claims of scoffers that efficiency gains are *de minimis*.

As for the contention that noncollusive, bilateral solutions to the coordination problem would produce efficiency gains of even greater magnitude, the market test would demand of skeptics a credible explanation: Why would not buyers and sellers be highly motivated to seek those efficiency gains exclusively for themselves by abandoning the collective process for the freely available and purportedly more efficient bilateral alternative?

Indeed, if efficiency gains explain collective ratemaking in a regime of vigorous competition, the real question becomes the motivation of carriers to participate if they are unable to earn excessive profits. When the efficiency gains are easily appropriable by a nonmember of the collective ratemaking process, a "free rider" problem potentially emerges because every carrier has an incentive to let the other carriers incur the transactions costs of providing the benefits of collective ratemaking.[61] This incentive to be a free rider would, of course, be enhanced by placing a "tax" on the collective process by exposing the participants to a *per se* or even a rule-of-reason antitrust test.

STUDY APPROACH

The study provides data and information on the structure of and recent behavior in the motor carrier industry, relying on two major sources. The first is a review of the evidence in the substantial literature on collective ratemaking and antitrust as it applies to the transportation industries. Numerous studies of the economics of competition in trucking as well as the complete testimony and transcript before the Motor Carrier Ratemaking Study Commission were examined and evaluated. Second, new data and information on the impact of the Motor Carrier Act and related regulatory changes implemented by the ICC were compiled. This research included extensive interviews with motor carrier[62] and railroad executives, rate bureau personnel, shippers, and individuals knowledgeable about developments in ratemaking in the transportation industries. I attended several rate bureau meetings to observe firsthand how collective ratemaking is working under the MCA.

The proposed methodology contrasts sharply with that of the Study Commission in reaching its finding to recommend abolishing all forms of collective ratemaking. The Study Commission tested whether or not the ratemaking goals of the prior regulatory regime were legitimate and, if so, whether collective ratemaking was successful in achieving those objectives in an environment of competition. Since the report rejected the goals of the prior regulatory regime at the outset, collective ratemaking naturally failed the test. Most of the evidence considered by the Study Commission—the fact that shipper participation in collective ratemaking was limited,[63] the argument that the ICC provides little supervision of individual rates,[64] the contention that rates under deregulation are not stabilized,[65] the fact that ratemaking has recently become more competitive and relies less on collective tariffs based on industry averages,[66] the fact that small shipments (shippers)[67] and service to small communities and shippers are not being cross-subsidized,[68] and so forth[69]—is either not directly relevant to the new era or must be reevaluated in terms of current regulatory goals.[70] The possibility that these data contradict the report's fundamental conclusion that collective rate-making inflates rate levels was not even considered by the Study Commission.

The role of antitrust immunity for collective ratemaking should be evaluated in light of its contribution to the goals of economic performance in the trucking industry and not on the basis of a visceral opposition to antitrust immunity. The Motor Carrier Act sought to reform the substance of economic regulation of the motor carrier industry by increasing the role of competition while leaving much of the institutional structure of regulation intact. This compromise is an acceptable means of accomplishing regulatory reform while retaining the institutional safeguards desired by carriers and shippers to prevent potential abuse to the antitrust immunity. The Motor Carrier Act has resulted in a combination of vigorous competition, permissive economic regulation, and antitrust immunity. This combination is producing reasonable results in the marketplace. In short, the proponents of motor carrier deregulation have already won their objectives. Having accomplished their objectives, they should quit and write their memoirs.

Although the study approach will emphasize the existence of price competition, the collective ratemaking issue raises a host of questions on industry performance for which answers will also be attempted along the way:

Cooperation versus competition

1. Too much standardization of pricing and service discourages price competition and service innovation. Is a nationwide integrated system of motor carrier service facilitated by a multilateral system of pricing and service standards (which are frequently departed from on a unilateral and bilateral basis) a good thing? Or is it a sign of collusion and suppressed competition to be discouraged in favor of a proliferation of bilateral arrangements which would produce increased diversity? What is the proper balance of the tension between cooperation and competition in the motor carrier industry?

Effects of collective ratemaking

2. Are motor carrier rate bureaus, in conjunction with the ICC, acting as government-enforced cartels to stifle rate competition, making the right of Independent Action an illusion? Is the potential for anticompetitive behavior, which is inherent in any collective pricing arrangement, being abused? Is the result an unduly rigid rate structure with too much uniformity of prices, not enough rate/service options, wasteful service competition, and protection of inefficient carriers?

3. What is the significance of the rate war going on in the motor carrier industry today? How does the present combination of collective rate-making and widespread use of Independent Action and individual carrier tariffs affect the rate level and the rate structure? Are there impediments to carriers in using cost-based ratemaking? Are there any restrictions today on carriers pricing any way they want?

Effects of abolishing collective ratemaking

4. Would today's trucking market (not an irrelevant hypothetical ideal of strict regulation) be more or less competitive after the loss of the antitrust immunity? Would the abolition of collective ratemaking open up any opportunities for more competition that do not exist right now?

5. Is it possible to replace the present multilateral system of collective ratemaking with a bilateral system without encountering a fundamental dilemma of the two alternative outcomes, those being (1) an excessive diversity of tariffs and service, which would mean a Tower of Babel to carriers and shippers; or (2) a consistent, workable, nationwide system which might be construed as evidence of forbidden behavior under the antitrust laws?

6. Motor carriers compete directly with their single-line services, but they also are joint venturers for interline services under joint rates. Is there any principle of economics or law that would permit carriers to meaningfully employ antitrust immunity for joint-line collective rate-making while applying the full force of the antitrust laws to their pricing behavior for the competing single-line service? How would the courts apply the existing law on tacit collusion and parallel action to joint-line rates with and without antitrust immunity for joint-line rates?

7. What is a single-line rate as defined by the MCA, and what exactly did Congress intend to prohibit by the restrictions on single-line rates? Is it possible to construct a "Chinese Wall" between single-line rates and joint-line rates from the point of view of antitrust immunity? Could broad joint-line tariffs be constructed to meet this requirement?

8. Suppose the courts enforced an end-to-end test of anticompetitive behavior on joint-line ratemaking so that carriers could not engage in joint-line ratemaking with their competitors. Could carriers use broad tariffs for joint-line rates, or would there be joint-line rates only for certain shippers in narrowly defined geographic areas where carriers were not in direct competition?

9. In an atmosphere with severe risks of antitrust liability, how would carriers choose among the options—publication of a benchmark rate structure without immunity, ossification of the rate structure, use of combination rates, mergers, and the assumption of ratemaking leadership by a few large carriers who would unilaterally set the standards—

to meet the needs now satisfied by collective ratemaking? What effect would these alternatives have on the level of competition and the structure of the industry?

10. What can we learn about the likely effects of abolishing collective ratemaking from the experience we have gained since the Motor Carrier Act abolished collective ratemaking for "released rates"?

11. How do the transactions costs of the present multilateral system compare with the proposed bilateral alternative? Since computerized tariff information systems require common agreement on classification, points groupings, and other parameters of ratemaking, how would these services function if they were required to play the role of rate bureaus in standardization of tariffs rather than merely providing information storage and retrieval? What scale economies would these services enjoy? Would small carriers and shippers be disadvantaged?

12. Would the application of the antitrust laws do a better job of implementing national transportation objectives for the motor carrier industry than a continuation of the present policy of intense competition and permissive regulation?

13. Would motor carrier management continue to incur the expense of supporting the rate bureaus and a nationwide system of interconnected service under joint-line rates in an environment of uncertain antitrust enforcement, or would they elect to play it safe and allow the system to collapse?

14. If collective ratemaking were abolished, exactly what institutions would replace it? What would the rate structure look like? How would freight be classified? Would the ratemaking system be totally different from today's system, or would today's system be frozen forever because nobody could change it unilaterally without antitrust immunity?

Evaluation of the Structure and Performance of the Trucking Industry under the Motor Carrier Act of 1980　3

> We were being called by shippers every day, sometimes several times a day, asking us to meet the rates of our competitors. If we hadn't cut prices, I would not be talking to you now. Before we used to sell service, now we have to be marketers as well. We have cut back our staff everywhere except salesmen. But even the salesmen have had to be retrained. They have to be skilled traffic specialists who can go out and explain the maze of new rates we have and tailor them to the customer's freight. It's just like the airlines.
>
> Spokesman for Overnite Transportation Company
> in *The New York Times*, 24 January 1982.

Motor carrier rate bureaus have been a source of controversy for many years. The economic argument against the rate bureaus generally goes something like the following. Motor carrier rate bureaus, abetted by the ICC, exhibit cartel behavior in their attempt to fix prices and restrict entry. The results of this restraint on competition are high and inflexible rates, an unduly complex rate structure with too much discriminatory value-of-service pricing, too much uniformity of prices and not enough rate and service options, wasteful service competition and operating practices, protection of inefficient carriers, and unreasonably high profits.

With antitrust immunity, an important prerequisite for a cartel is present. Missing, however, is an enforcement mechanism for deterring price competition and service expansion by bureau members and preventing entry in the industry, all of which would be highly motivated by monopoly prices but would undermine cartel profits. According to critics, this is where regulation by the ICC comes in. By restricting entry and price competition at the behest of the rate bureaus and their members, the ICC allegedly completes the picture of a cartel.[71]

When the Motor Carrier Ratemaking Study Commission began its deliberations, critics of collective ratemaking stated that "there is little new to be added to the decades of discussion of these institutions. . . . A rate bureau is essentially a price-fixing organization."[72] "Collective ratemaking is inherently anticompetitive and inevitably leads to higher rates than would be established in its absence . . . Even if entry into trucking were to remain relatively free, the existence of collective rate-making would continue to foster rates higher than competitive rates."[73]

Industrial organization theory often proceeds by means of a structure-conduct-performance paradigm.[74] The logic is that elements of industry structure such as barriers to entry, scale economies, sunk costs, and concentration all strongly influence conduct, which consists of output, price, and product variety decisions. These decisions in turn can be evaluated for their performance in terms of economic welfare.

The present study applies the paradigm to the trucking industry by assuming the position of critics of collective ratemaking: that nonpredatory price competition is desirable in the trucking industry and that firms should be allowed to pursue cost-minimizing strategies without regulatory constraint. In this chapter, data on the structure of the industry are examined in detail. However, the principal conclusion, that fears of anticompetitive pricing from collective ratemaking are unfounded, ultimately rests on actual evidence of price competition and the absence of collusive attitudes or actions that would raise questions about the achievement of the price competition goal. The data on price competition are given special consideration for two other reasons. First, many of the strictly economic elements of industry structure in the motor carrier industry are not seriously debated. Second, the existence of a strong link between structure and conduct is not widely agreed upon in the industrial organization literature. An examination of recent industry conduct on price competition in response to the changed structural elements of economic regulation goes right to the heart of the critics' complaints.

After a brief survey of industry structure and recent financial performance in the trucking industry, the chapter next examines the changed role of ICC regulation in the motor carrier industry. Evidence of the economic performance of the trucking industry since 1980 confirms that the Motor Carrier Act of 1980 has been highly successful in accomplishing its objectives of eliminating unnecessary and harmful regulation and encouraging a more competitive trucking industry. The evidence shows an industry with few, if any, effective regulatory restraints on operating practices and entry. Simply put, the government-controlled cartel theory no longer holds because the Interstate Commerce Commission is no longer exercising any meaningful regulatory constraints on price and entry of motor carriers.

Next comes an examination of the degree of price competition that has ensued as a result of these regulatory reforms. The evidence shows that numerous innovative rate and service options have arisen. The motor carrier industry has endured the biggest price war in recent history, one that has approached a blood bath. Rate bureaus have certainly failed to enforce price discipline since 1980, if they tried at all. Finally, the chapter ends with an examination of the theory that collective ratemaking has resulted in inflated rate levels. The complaint that collective ratemaking has resulted in an unduly complex rate system is postponed to Chapter 5.

MARKET STRUCTURE IN THE INTERCITY GENERAL FREIGHT MOTOR CARRIER INDUSTRY

Analysis of industry structure in the motor carrier industry is plagued by the absence of current data, particularly on the unregulated trucking sector. The deregulation debate of the late 1970s spurred a great deal of data collection and analysis, but this mostly dried up after the passage of the MCA. The last *Census of Transportation* was in 1977, and much of the data collection efforts that were ancillary to economic regulation are now beginning to atrophy.

Nevertheless, a reasonably consistent picture emerges: at the onset of regulatory reform, regulated motor carriers represented less than half of intercity truck motor freight, which of course also competes with other modes of transportation in many market segments (depending on price and service requirements). Within the regulated trucking markets, the truckload (TL) sector is extremely unconcentrated because of minimum investment levels dictated by the absence of terminals and a network of service. The less-than-truckload (LTL) market is more concentrated, but still unconcentrated relative to the scale of American industry.

Regulatory reform has resulted in a substantial number of new entrants, almost all in the truckload sector of the business. The diversion of truckload business from the regular route carriers, the continuing rate war, and the decline in LTL business (in part caused by the recession) have bankrupted a number of carriers and threaten to increase industry concentration substantially in the LTL sector.

Table 1 shows one estimate of the relative shares of the carrier types during the period of strict rate regulation and entry requirements. According to that source, ICC-regulated trucking represented less than half of the total intercity motor carrier ton-miles in 1972. According to another source, ICC-regulated carriers in 1980 still represented less than half of total intercity freight trucking tonnage,[75] and the figure remained at around 44 percent of revenue and 40 percent of the tonnage in 1984.[76] General freight carriers moved 10 percent of the tons and represented 61 percent of the revenues of the larger regulated motor carriers.[77] As shown in Table 2, another source estimated a somewhat higher share of tonnage for regulated general freight common carrier interstate service

Table 1
Intercity Truck Traffic by Type of Carrier (1972)

	All Carriers	For Hire Regulated Carriers		Uncertificated Carriers (exempt traffic only)	Private Carriage
		Interstate	Intrastate		
Ton Miles (Billions)	470.0	197.9	4.7	70.5	196.93
Percentage of Ton Miles	100.0	42.1	1.0	15.0	41.9

Source: William B. Tye, et al., "Load Factors of Motor Carriers in the Interstate Highway System: Consequences for Regulatory Policy," in *Motor Carrier Economic Regulation* (Washington, D.C.: National Academy of Sciences, 1978): 549.

Table 2
Structure of the Motor Carrier Industry (1979)

	Dollars (Billions)	Tons (Millions)	Ton-Miles (Billions)
Total Motor Carrier	142.7	2240.0	628.0
of which:			
Regulated Motor Carrier	--	1278.2	363.0
of which:			
Regulated General Freight Common Carriers (Interstate)	24.4	314.1	--
of which:			
Collective Tariffs	15.4	144.9	81.4
of which:			
Class Rated	11.3	93.2	45.9

Source: MAC Group, "Statistical Overview of the Trucking Industry" (August 1982)—derived from other sources.

(14 percent). Surprisingly, more than a third of the revenue and even more of the tonnage was moving under private tariffs for the regulated general freight common carriers prior to the MCA.

Despite entry restrictions by the ICC, general freight carriers showed surprisingly low levels of market concentration prior to regulatory reform even when the relevant markets were defined at the lowest possible levels of aggregation (LTL freight for city pairs). Russell Cherry's analysis of traffic data supplied by the eight largest rate bureaus in Table 3 shows a minimum of 16 average carriers in each of the length-of-haul market segments. The Herfindahl Index, favored by the Justice Department as a measure of industry concentration, falls within the range defined as moderately concentrated (where the increase in concentration from a merger would have to be in the middle range for antitrust concerns to arise),[78] even at these very low levels of market definition. The LTL industry trade association, the Regular Common Carrier Conference, represents the interests of about 2,500 firms.

More recent data[79] on overall concentration within the LTL sector suggest increased concentration since 1980.[80] Figure 1 shows that LTL tonnage began a decline in 1978 that was not arrested until 1983. Truckload traffic handled by these carriers declined disastrously with no recovery. Operating revenues declined as a result of the rate war, and all measures of profitability followed suit (see Figure 2 and Figure 3). The market share of the 10 largest carriers increased steadily with no signs of abating, as shown in Figure 4.

Indeed, all indications are that the trend will continue. The 10 largest LTL carriers in 1984 earned 61.2 percent of the total LTL industry operating income,[81] and the most profitable 10 carriers earned 86 percent of the total.[82] After some reduction in the operating ratio[83] as the country moved out of recession, this key indicator has increased again in the most recent period.[84] This poor economic performance in the context of the cumulative effects of past inadequate financial returns forecasts substantial insecurity for the LTL general commodity carriers. A statistical analysis of the general freight industry as of 1983 projected that about 32 percent would fail and another 27 percent would fall in the zone of uncertain economic viability.[85]

THE GOVERNMENT-ENFORCED CARTEL THEORY

The economic theory of cartels and evidence of price-fixing conspiracies[86] suggest several factors required for successful cartelization of an industry:

1. High entry barriers, either legal, physical, or economic
2. Relatively few firms, so that communication and the dynamics of reaching shared goals and implementing agreements are facilitated

Table 3
Measures* of Carrier Concentration in 442 of the Largest Origin-Destination
Pairs in the United States (1976)

	Less Than 1,000 Miles	1,000– 1,499 Miles	1,500– 1,999 Miles	Over 2,000 Miles
Average Number of Carriers per Origin-Destination Pair	21	17	16	16
Four-Firm Ratio**	.615	.643	.663	.650
Herfindahl Index+	.146	.136	.155	.150
Average Mileage	518	1199	1698	2388

*All measures are averages weighted by the numbers of ton-miles in each of the 442 origin-destination pairs.

**Market share of the largest four firms.

+The Herfindahl or Herfindahl-Hirshman Index is the sum of squared market shares in the relevant market.

Source: Compiled by the MAC Group, "Statistical Overview of the Trucking Industry" from Russell Cherry, "Rate Effects of Collective Ratemaking and the Meaning of Concentration in Regulated Motor Carriage," Arthur D. Little, Inc., Cambridge, MA (July 1982).

Figure 1
Tons of Freight Carried: General Freight Motor Carrier Industry (1978 = 100)

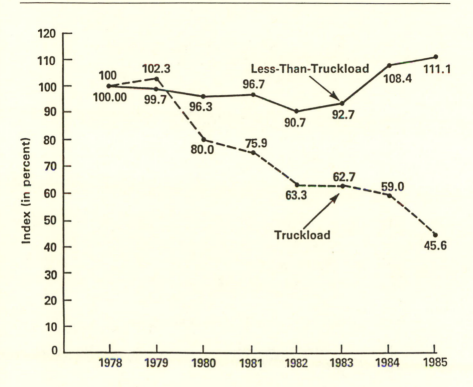

Source: Irwin H. Silberman, *Statement before Surface Transportation Subcommittee*, U.S. House of Representatives, Washington, D.C., 6 November 1985.

3. The ability to detect and punish in some effective way those who violate the agreement; this preferably involves some legal sanction

4. A standardized product to make pricing decisions easy and cheating difficult[87]

Two fundamental propositions underlie the government-enforced cartel theory advanced by the opponents of collective ratemaking. The first is the notion that cartels are inherently unstable:

[A]s a practical matter, a successful cartel is very difficult to create and maintain [footnote omitted]. It requires tight control over supply. Otherwise the oversupply will put pressure upon the firms to bid down the price to clear the market. Supply can be enlarged either by existing firms or new entrants, perhaps attracted by the cartel's high prices. Secondly, there must be relatively tight discipline that prevents members of the cartel from cheating by shaving prices or increasing service in order to get a bigger piece of the pie. It is in each firm's

Figure 2
Annual Operating Revenues, Net Carrier Plant and Equipment, and
Profitability: General Freight Motor Carrier Industry

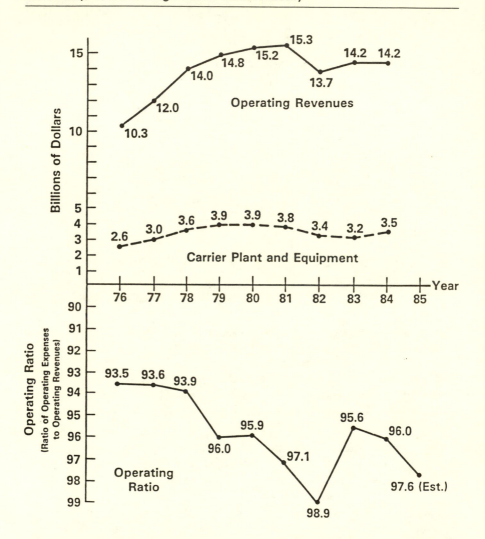

Source: Irwin H. Silberman, *Statement before Surface Transportation Subcommittee*, U.S. House of Representatives, Washington, D.C., 6 November 1985.

Figure 3
**Rates of Return on Equity: General Freight Motor Carrier Industry and Value
Line Industrial Composite**

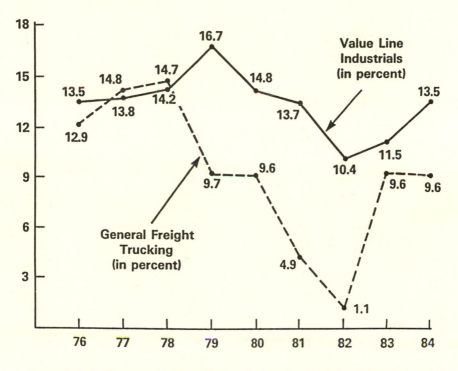

Source: Irwin H. Silberman, *Statement before Surface Transportation Subcommittee*, U.S.
House of Representatives, Washington, D.C., 6 November 1985.

individual interest to cheat on the agreement, so long as others are complying.
There must also be relative uniformity of product. Significant variations will
disrupt standardized pricing necessary to police the cartel. Communication
among the cartel must be very good in order to produce agreement upon policy
and prompt response to changing situations.[88]

Second, it is generally agreed that in an unconcentrated industry such
as trucking, with no private enforcement mechanisms, only strong government regulation can overcome these competitive forces within the
cartel.[89] Motor carrier rate bureaus are alleged to rely on the following
ICC enforcement mechanisms to offset the inherent instability of the
cartel:

1. Entry controls;
2. Rate regulations, including:

Figure 4
Share of General Freight Motor Carrier Industry Revenues Accounted for by
10 Largest Carriers

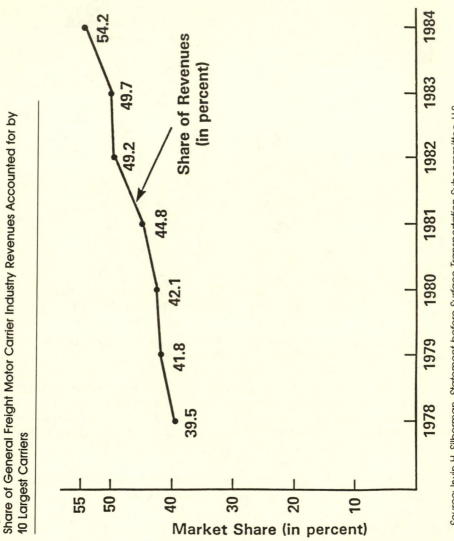

Source: Irwin H. Silberman, *Statement before Surface Transportation Subcommittee,* U.S.
House of Representatives, Washington, D.C., 6 November 1985.

a) The right of carriers to protest competitors' proposed rate cuts, and

b) ICC power to grant antitrust immunity to rate bureaus;

3. Requirements that tariffs be published, filed, and kept open to public inspection, and adhered to;

4. ICC power to set minimum rates; and

5. ICC power to suspend, investigate, and reject proposed rate cuts.[90]

The validity of the government-enforced cartel theory therefore turns on the strength of regulatory restrictions on motor carriers in the post–1980 environment.

CHANGES IN THE REGULATORY POWERS OF THE ICC IN THE MOTOR CARRIER ACT OF 1980

Whether the ICC historically did not encourage a sufficient amount of rate competition in the motor carrier industry is a matter for historians of motor carrier regulatory policy. What is important today is that the ICC, in *Ex Parte* No. 297 and in a series of other administrative decisions prior to 1980, and Congress in the MCA of 1980 fundamentally changed competitive conditions in the motor carrier industry.[91] To begin with, the MCA of 1980 made a significant change in motor carrier regulatory policy by adding the word *competitive* to the list of desired attributes for the motor carrier regulatory structure. The MCA marked a new era of greater reliance on competition, as evidenced by the amendment to national transportation objectives:

[W]ith respect to transportation of property by motor carrier, to promote competitive and efficient transportation services in order to [A] meet the needs of shippers, receivers, and consumers; [B] allow a variety of quality and price options to meet changing market demands and the diverse requirements of the shipping public; [C] allow the most productive use of equipment and energy resources; [D] enable efficient and well-managed carriers to earn adequate profits, attract capital, and maintain fair wages and working conditions; [E] provide and maintain service to small communities and small shippers; [F] improve and maintain a sound, safe, and competitive privately-owned motor carrier system; [G] promote greater participation by minorities in the motor carrier system; and [H] promote intermodal transportation.[92]

Chief among the more important changes[93] to accomplish these objectives were:

1. A substantially *more permissive entry policy*: Section 5 of the MCA of 1980 changed the burden of proof for and tightened restrictions on protesting operating authority applications. Combined with the ICC's prior policy of liberal grants of authority, regulatory restrictions on entry have been reduced

enormously, and most carriers have whatever operating authority they need. Almost immediately after the passage of the act, the results were impressive:

From July 3, 1980, to June 2, 1981, 2,932 new carriers applied to the Commission for operating authority. In addition, over 36,000 new certificates have been served during that same 11 month time frame. Of these, 11,300 were authorities granted on applications filed under the new statute. The balance represent the successful disposition of a 24,700 case backlog made up of pre-Act applications which were pending at the time of enactment. . . .

While the increase in the number of grants of operating authority is dramatic, it understates the actual increase in the rate of entry that has taken place, because requests for and grants of authority are broader now than they were prior to passage of the Act. In response to the congressional mandate against narrow and restrictive certificates, the Commission has strongly encouraged the filing of applications broad in commodity and geographic scope.[94]

2. The *elimination of meaningful operating authority restrictions*: Section 6 of the MCA of 1980 provided for elimination of gateway restrictions, circuitous routings, and other geographic and commodity restrictions on carriers, thereby automatically opening up new markets to existing carriers.

3. The encouragement of Independent Actions (IA's) by carriers:

   a) The institution of a Zone-of-Rate-Freedom (ZORF) that permitted IA's that, within a certain zone, could be protested or suspended only under very restricted conditions and to which the antitrust laws apply (Section 11);

   b) The institution of no-notice IA's (*Ex Parte* No. 297 [Sub-No. 5]);[95]

   c) The prohibition of protests of IA's of any motor carrier by rate bureaus before the ICC (Section 14 [b] [3] [B] [iii]);

   d) The elimination of collective ratemaking for released rates (Section 12).

4. The substantial reduction or elimination of regulatory restrictions on competing forms of truck transport, such as contract (Section 10), private (Section 9), and exempt (Section 7) motor carriers, agricultural cooperatives (Section 24), rail piggyback services (deregulated by the ICC under provisions of the Staggers Rail Act in *Ex Parte* No. 230 [Sub-No. 5]), and owner-operators.[96]

These changes in the law were soon implemented by the ICC as liberally as possible. The results were profound. For example, control over entry and carrier operating authority is widely agreed to be the critical ingredient in any governmental regulation of trucking.[97] Without strong controls on entry, the government-enforced cartel theory falls apart, a finding even its proponents would accept.[98] Yet the ICC was inviting new entrants to enter the industry without meaningful regulatory restrictions.

Changes in the method of exercising the right of IA through the bureaus implemented by the ICC in *Ex Parte* No. 297 (Sub-No. 5) had a comparable effect on motor carrier pricing. As a result of these changes, carriers were able to make it considerably more time-consuming for their competitors to "flag in," or join, an IA. The consequence was to enhance the competitive appeal of the IA procedure at the rate bureaus. Combined with the dearth of traffic, the result was an avalanche of IA activity almost immediately after the Motor Carrier Act was passed.

Prior to the Motor Carrier Act, the ICC had already prohibited rate bureaus from protesting IA's of their own members and voting collectively to join IA's. It also prohibited any form of discrimination in fees, docketing,[99] and publishing IA's. In the notice of proposed rulemaking in *Ex Parte* No. 297 (Sub-No. 5), the ICC flatly prohibited advance docketing of IA's, thereby requiring that there be no notice of IA's prior to filing the tariff with the Commission. Upon reconsideration, the Commission voted to give the carrier the option of providing prior notice to shippers and other carriers. In addition, the Commission's practice has been to grant five-day emergency permission (rather than the usual 30-day public notice after filing with the Commission) only to leaders in rate cutting, but not to flagging into a rate cut to meet competition.[100] The ICC's intention was to encourage more assertive use of IA's, and the intended effect has certainly been realized.[101]

When a carrier proposed an IA for its account prior to the ICC decision, the bureau automatically provided notice of the IA to competitors and to shippers through docketing the proposal. Docketing allows other carriers 10 to 15 days to join the IA if they desire, with the same effective date as the original proponent. The ICC required the bureaus to eliminate this advance notice at the proponent's discretion. The decision provided for no docketing of the action at all (an "absolutely no-notice IA"), docketing prior to filing with the Commission (a "notice IA"), or docketing simultaneously with filing (a "no-notice IA"). The ICC stated that "the right of independent action requires independent actors to have exactly the same publication options under a bureau agreement as they have with respect to proposals published totally apart from the bureau." The intended effect was to encourage IA's by enhancing the competitive advantage to the proponent by making it more difficult for competitors to flag in that tariff change with the same effective date as the original proponent. Individual carriers may, of course, join an IA at a later time once they have been notified.

To see how the collective ratemaking process was changed by the Motor Carrier Act and the ICC's implementation of *Ex Parte* 297, it is useful to compare Figure 5, a flow chart of existing practice, with Figure 6, a flow chart of the prior procedures at the Eastern Central Motor Carriers Association (ECMCA), a major motor carrier rate bureau. In addition to the new no-notice IA procedure, regular docket proposals are now automatically published unless they are appealed to the General Rate Committee (GRC) by a member carrier. This change obviously has

Figure 5
Alternative Paths for Proposing and Publishing Tariffs Open to Motor Carriers

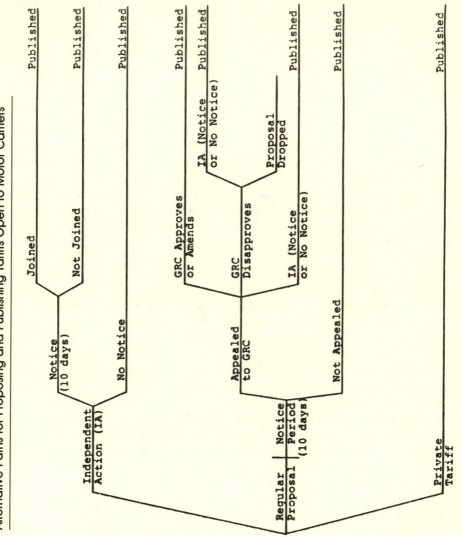

Figure 6
Collective Ratemaking Process Prior to the Motor Carrier Act of 1980

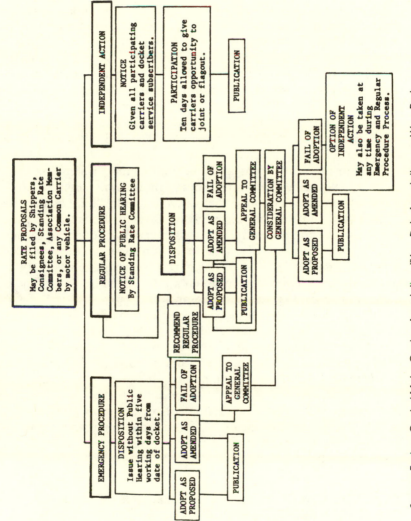

Source: Eastern Central Motor Carriers Association, "Your Rate Association and You: Partners for Progress," Akron, Ohio, n.d.

the effect of streamlining the process and encouraging rate actions by the carriers. Furthermore, the Standing Rate Committee, composed only of bureau employees, no longer makes an initial determination on the proposal, as it once did. By sending all appealed dockets directly to the GRC, and only on appeal, the regular docketing process has been streamlined.[102]

Figure 5 illustrates the timing factor which often motivates a carrier's choice of the no-notice IA. A notice IA and an unappealed regular proposal generally take the same time to implement. In the case of the former, there is a notice period to allow carriers who wish to join the IA. The same length of time is afforded member carriers to appeal a regular proposal. If the regular proposal is appealed by a member, delays are incurred while the GRC hears the docket. Both the notice period and the hearing period can be avoided by use of the no-notice proposal, which saves 10 to 15 days over a notice IA, and even more time over an appealed regular docket.

The sunshine provisions and the elimination of standing rate committees have made the entire process more transparent. In the past, shippers sometimes claimed that carriers would "hide behind the rate bureau" and not bargain forthrightly. Bureau recalcitrance was often blamed for voting down dockets negotiated by individual carriers and shippers. Whatever may have happened in the past, carriers are clearly negotiating seriously today for rates. If the carrier expects that the General Rate Committee will turn down a rate, the shipper usually expects the carrier to get that rate through an IA.

Public notice is accomplished through a *Docket Bulletin*, which lists the new rate proposals for the regular procedure and IA's, and a *Docket Status Register* to permit interested parties to determine the exact status of any particular docket item. In addition, bureaus may publish a *Tariff Watching Service* to keep their member carriers aware of tariff activities of nonbureau carriers or competing modes of transport. Bureau carriers also engage in a substantial amount of private tariff publishing (i.e., a tariff applicable to only one carrier), and these nonagency tariffs are also reported. In fact, many member carriers use the bureaus as printing agencies for private tariffs.[103]

ICC REGULATION OF RATES AND THE EXISTENCE OF PRICE COMPETITION UNDER THE MOTOR CARRIER ACT OF 1980

ICC regulation today clearly provides a very feeble structural mechanism for enforcing cartel behavior among motor carriers. A second test is conduct. Does one see the results of a highly competitive process in the motor carrier industry today?

On the alleged illusion of the right of Independent Action

If a cartel cannot effectively control the rates of its membership, the collusive arrangement will eventually be broken in a market structurally conducive to competition. Attempts to establish cartel rates will be fruitless because they will generate excess supply that will cause "shading the cartel price" to become even more profitable. In the motor carrier industry, opportunity for such shading comes in the form of IA's, discounting, and private tariffs. Critics of collective ratemaking, however, have routinely discounted the effectiveness of the carrier's right to Independent Action.[104]

Since the Reed-Bulwinkle Act, carriers have always had the undisputed legislative right to Independent Action. This right has been upheld and reinforced by the Interstate Commerce Commission and the Motor Carrier Act of 1980 as noted above. Anyone who doubts that carriers have any reluctance to utilize this pricing vehicle in a completely unrestrained manner should examine a *Docket Bulletin* of any motor carrier rate bureau soon after the ratemaking reforms of the MCA. There is absolutely no evidence to support the innuendos that the collective ratemaking process intimidates and coerces carriers from taking independent action.[105]

The avalanche of IA's that occurred soon after passage of the MCA literally tested the bureaus' capacity to print the tariff pages required to implement the carriers' rate actions.[106] Tables 4 and 5 illustrate the publishing problem from one bureau's point of view. Although 1980 represented a substantial increase in tariff activity over 1979 for the Eastern Central Motor Carriers Association (ECMCA), tariff publishing almost doubled in October and November 1981 as compared with a comparable period from the previous year. Furthermore, there was a precipitous drop in regular procedure dockets and a corresponding meteoric increase in IA's, particularly no-notice IA's.

Motor carrier pricing decisions were firmly in the domain of individual carrier management, certainly not smoke-filled rooms at the bureau. While ECMCA carriers were initiating 1,736 total IA's during the October-November 1981 period, only 21 regular procedure dockets went before the General Rate Committee (GRC), and most of them were either adopted in modified form or approved. During October and November of 1981, the GRC rejected seven out of 1,736 dockets proposed by ECMCA carriers, including both regular dockets and IA's. In that same period, carriers elected to use the IA procedure nine times either before or after the regular docket was referred to the General Rate Committee.[107] Whether the seven rejected proposals were ultimately adopted as an IA by the proponent is not known, but it is possible that most were. Table

Table 4
Carrier Choice of Rate Publishing Procedure: Eastern Central Motor Carriers
Association (October 1980 and November 1981)

	1980	1981
Regular Procedure Dockets	373	130
Published without GRC referral	239	81
Approved by GRC	15	6
Rejected by GRC	24	7
Modified by GRC	25	8
Other (withdrawn, etc.)	70	28
Independent Action on Regular Procedure Dockets*	63	9
IA – Prior Notice	532	674
IA – No Prior Notice	0	923
ZORF (Zone-of-Rate-Freedom)	0	0
Total	968	1,736

Includes only docketed rate proposals and does not include other carrier instructions to the bureau, such as joining IA's.

*Carrier elects IA procedure after appeal to GRC or after GRC rejects docket.

Source: Eastern Central Motor Carriers Association.

5 shows that this trend away from collective procedures to independent actions has continued through more recent periods at Eastern Central.

Other major rate bureaus reported similar experience during this time frame. Table 6 shows the experience for the Southern Motor Carriers Rate Conference. The yearly aggregates do not fully convey the acceleration of the trend toward no-notice IA's immediately after the MCA of 1980, which is shown in Tables 7 and 8. Other bureau data are shown in Tables 9 through 13 and also confirm this same trend away from regular dockets to no-notice IA's, and Table 14 provides summary data for all major bureaus through 1982.

Virtually all these IA's represent downward price adjustments to the class rate structure.[108] While every bureau was inundated by a substantial increase in IA's, this form of rate cutting does not begin to tell the whole

Table 5
Carrier Choice of Rate Publishing Procedure: Eastern Central Motor Carriers Association (1980–1985)

PROCEDURE	1980 6 mo. (7/1 through 12/31)	1981 Entire Year	1982 Entire Year	1983 Entire Year	1984 6 mo. (1/1 through 6/30)	1984 6 mo. (7/1 through 12/31)	1985 6 mo. (1/1 through 6/30)
Regular Procedure Dockets	863	1319	893	723	101	20	41
Published without GRC referral	542	830	744	578	51	1	3
Approved by GRC	50	61	12	62	29	13	0
Rejected by GRC	61	81	12	3	0	1	0
Modified by GRC	76	100	86	62	20	0	37
Other (Withdrawn, etc.)	134	247	39	18	1	5	1
Independent Action of Regular Procedure Dockets*							
IA-Prior Notice	113	124	3	1	0	0	0
IA-No Notice	1564	4252	2085	618	71	129	248
ZORF (Zone-of-Rate-Freedom)	0	2501	5737	3517	846	412	277
	0	0	0	0	0	0	0
TOTAL	2540	8196	8718	4859	1018	561	566

Includes only docketed rate proposals and does not include other carrier instructions to the bureau, such as joining IA's.

*Carrier elects IA procedure after appeal to GRC or after GRC rejects docket.

Source: Eastern Central Motor Carriers Association.

Table 6
Carrier Choice of Rate Publishing Procedure: Southern Motor Carriers Rate
Conference (Calendar Years 1980 and 1981)

	1980	1981
Regular Proposal	3,872*	3,883
Published without GRC Referral	2,885	3,147
Approved by GRC	284	206
Rejected by GRC	185	127
Modified by GRC	386	319
Other (withdrawn, etc.)	132	84
IA – Prior Notice	6,116	7,459
IA – No Prior Notice	0	5,777
ZORF (Zone-of-Rate-Freedom)	0	0
Total	10,180	17,119

Includes only docketed rate proposals and does not include other carrier instructions to the bureau, such as joining IA's.

*The 3,872 figure for 1980 does not comport with the 4,064 figure in the following table. The bureau explains that the discrepancy results from the particular method of assigning proposals to "Bulletin Weeks" which may result in year-end discrepancies in the two data sources.

Source: Southern Motor Carriers Rate Conference.

story. Further cuts have occurred through carrier private tariffs, many of them in the form of across-the-board discounts off bureau rates.[109]

Discounts soon became the rule rather than the exception.[110] Hausman's study[111] showed an accelerating portion of total traffic moving at a discount off the collective bureau tariff soon after the inauguration of regulatory reform. As shown in Table 15, the discounting was heaviest for class rated traffic (as opposed to commodity rated traffic which applies only to certain types of commodities and limited groups of shippers), less-than-truckload, and single-line traffic. Hausman concluded from his analysis of the data that the inability of rate bureaus to maintain prices during falling demand was evidence "significantly at odds" with the cartel theory of rate bureaus. Other data presented by Hausman showed that the largest discounts at this time were being offered by the smaller regional carriers—the ones as we shall see with the most to lose if antitrust immunity were revoked.

Table 7
Carrier Choice of Rate Publishing Procedure: Southern Motor Carriers Rate Conference (Monthly Totals, 1980 and 1981)

Bulletin Weeks	Regular Proposals		Notice IA's		No-Notice IA's	
	1980	1981	1980	1981	1980	1981
1 - 4	223	281	203	462	--	--
5 - 8	260	442	343	653	--	1
9 - 12	296	383	366	684	--	53
13 - 16	298	432	373	747	--	402
17 - 20	280	379	482	668	--	400
21 - 24	273	306	596	582	--	301
25 - 28	266	250	625	681	--	530
29 - 32	244	249	628	586	--	714
33 - 36	326	215	557	550	--	611
37 - 40	301	257	408	516	--	516
41 - 44	423	266	419	449	--	615
45 - 48	400	234	544	445	--	748
49 - 52	338	189	572	436	--	826
53	136		221			
Total	4,064	3,883	6,116	7,459	0	5,777

Includes only docketed rate proposals and does not include other carrier instructions to the bureau, such as joining IA's.

Source: Southern Motor Carriers Rate Conference.

Table 16 shows that the ICC took an extremely permissive attitude toward suspending proposed rate cuts implemented by carriers after the passage of the MCA. Although the ICC has occasionally suspended and investigated general rate *increases*, the regulatory deterrent to rate cutting is virtually nonexistent.[112] After the ICC refused to suspend Roadway's cuts of up to 50 percent on some traffic, it was clear to everyone that the ICC was going to stand aside and do nothing about the rate war.

Had the Motor Carrier Act not been passed at the onset of a severe recession in the trucking industry, we might not have had good evidence on just how susceptible the motor carrier ratemaking system was to price competition. The post–1980 recession provided a test of the system's ability to accommodate the incentives for price competition when

Table 8
Carrier Choice of Rate Publishing Procedure: Southern Motor Carriers Rate
Conference (Calendar Years 1984 and 1985)

	1984 Jan.–June	1984 July–Dec.	1985 Jan.–June
Regular Proposals	586	76	23
Published without GRC Referral	181	22	8
Approved by GRC	242	5	7
Modified by GRC	5	3	3
Other (Withdrawn, etc.)	14	47*	2
IA – Prior Notice	72	79	26
IA – No Prior Notice	2,904	2,050	2,789
ZORF (Zone-of-Rate-Freedom)	0	0	0
TOTAL	3,562	2,205	2,838

*This figure includes 41 obsolete dockets which were withdrawn due to expiration of the 120-day limit.

Source: Southern Motor Carriers Rate Conference.

Table 9
Carrier Choice of Rate Publishing Procedure: Middle Atlantic Conference

Year	Regular Proposals	Percent	Notice IA's	Percent	No-Notice IA's	Percent	Total
1977	2,791	66.0	1,438	34.0	--	--	3,951
1978	2,439	61.7	1,512	38.3	--	--	3,343
1979	2,152	64.4	1,191	35.6	--	--	
1980	2,665	56.8	2,031	43.2	--	--	4,696
1981	2,193	32.3	3,116	45.8	1,488	21.9	6,797
1982	1,051	10.5	3,203	32.0	5,755	57.5	10,009
1983	741	6.3	2,693	22.8	8,397	70.9	11,831
1984							
1st Half	86	1.8	1,650	35.5	2,916	62.7	4,652
2nd Half	67	1.7	1,294	33.6	2,490	64.7	3,851
1985							
1st Half	53	.9	2,028	35.9	3,570	63.2	5,651

Source: Middle Atlantic Conference.

45

Table 10

Carrier Choice of Rate Publishing Procedure: Rocky Mountain Motor Tariff Bureau

	1980	1981	1982	1983	1-1 through 6-30 1984	7-1 through 12-31 1984	1-1 through 6-30 1985	7-1 through 12-31 1985
Regular Proposal	8243	8763	4700	4614	3150	177	129	8
Published without RC Referral	2,178	4,763	1,482	1,808	768	0	20	95
Approved by RC	3,330	2,544	2,398	1,854	1,875	94	67	2
Rejected by RC	586	359	151	198	308	35	11	0
Modified by RC	1,056	776	358	393	85	16	8	3
Other (withdrawn, etc.)	553	411	311	361	114	32	23	3

	1980	1981	1982	1983	1-1 through 6-30 1984	7-1 through 12-31 1984	1-1 through 6-30 1985	7-1 through 12-31 1985
IA – Prior Notice	1,510	3,728	370	56	78	0	0	1
IA – No Prior Notice	0	10,743	8,582	4,030	1,682	1,441	1,137	583
ZORF (Zone-of-Rate-Freedom)	0	0	0	0	0	0	0	0
TOTAL	1,510	14,021	8,962	4,086	1,760	1,441	1,137	584
Total Independent Action and Regular Proposals	9,753	22,784	13,652	8,700	4,910	1,618	1,266	592

Table 11

Carrier Choice of Ratemaking Procedure: Pacific Inland Tariff Bureau (Interstate)

	1980	1981	1982	1983	1984	1985 (8 Mos.)
Regular Docket Procedures*	623	670	889	872	214	15
Approved	523	573	808	621	197	15
Not Approved	41	30	32	39	2	–
Withdrawn	59	67	49	212	15	–
Independent Action – No Notice	138	255	333	196	121	135

*Includes GRC meetings and Interim Bulletin.

Source: Pacific Inland Tariff Bureau.

Table 12
Carrier Choice of Rate Publishing Procedure: Central States Motor Freight Bureau

YEAR	REGULAR PROCEDURE	PERCENT	NOTICE IA'S	PERCENT	NO-NOTICE IA's	PERCENT	TOTAL
1978	1,086	32.5	2,259	67.5	....	....	3,345
1979	887	27.7	2,317	72.3	....	....	3,205
1980	749	21.6	2,722	78.4	....	....	3,471
1984							
1st Half	580	23.5	7	0.3	1,884	76.2	2,471
2nd Half	14	1.2	2	0.2	1,153	98.6	1,169
TOTAL	594	16.3	9	0.3	3,037	83.4	3,640
1985							
1st Half	318	28.4	2	0.2	800	71.4	1,120

Includes only docketed rate proposals and does not include other carrier instructions to the bureau, such as joining IA's.

Source: Central States Motor Freight Bureau.

Table 13
Carrier Choice of Rate Publishing Procedure: Niagara Frontier Tariff Bureau

	1978	1979	1980	1981	1982	1983	1984 First Half	1984 Second Half	1985 First Half
REGULAR PROPOSALS	1,271	1,232	1,647	1,866	NA	NA	402	44	17
Published without GRC referral	949	904	1,336	1,632	NA	NA	356	35	5
Reported by GRC (or SRC)	221	209	145	60	NA	NA	3	0	0
Approved by GRC	72	69	167	241	NA	NA	13	4	3
Modified by GRC					NA	NA	23	5	4
Other (withdrawn etc.)	30	51	38	40	NA	NA	7	0	5
IA -- Prior notice	1	1	39	92	NA	NA	785	500	509
IA -- No prior notice	0	0	0	6	NA	NA	1,438	1,801	1,868
ZORF (Zone-of-Rate-Freedom)	0	0	0	0	NA	NA	0	0	0
TOTAL	1,272	1,233	1,686	1,964			2,625	2,345	2,394

Source: Niagara Frontier Tariff Bureau, Inc.

Table 14
Bureau Rate Filings: Selected General-Freight Bureaus

Year	Month	Collective Proposals	Notice Independent Actions	No–Notice Independent Actions	Total
1976*		25,217	9,261	0	34,478
1977*		27,382	8,950	0	36,332
1978		30,722	28,784	0	59,506
1979		28,106	28,870	0	56,976
1980	Jan thru June	19,602	30,341	0	49,403
1980	July	2,023	5,242	0	7,265
	Aug	2,260	5,245	0	7,505
	Sept	2,062	5,509	0	7,517
	Oct	2,659	6,783	0	9,442
	Nov	2,351	4,508	0	6,859
	Dec	2,114	5,171	0	7,285
	TOTAL	32,531	62,799	0	95,320
1981	Jan	2,473	7,201	10	9,684
	Feb	2,652	5,601	200	8,453
	Mar	2,930	7,026	491	10,447
	April	2,566	6,314	1,473	10,353
	May	2,136	8,037	2,513	12,721
	June	2,186	7,176	2,156	11,518
	July	1,688	8,071	3,916	13,675
	Aug	1,682	6,486	4,014	12,182
	Sept	1,424	6,320	3,560	11,304
	Oct	1,688	6,973	5,220	13,881
	Nov	1,189	5,496	5,993	12,678
	Dec	1,632	5,355	4,831	11,538
	TOTAL	23,979	80,091	34,377	138,434
1982	Jan	1,024	5,310	5,009	11,343
	Feb	1,268	4,394	4,857	10,519
	Mar	1,120	4,210	5,489	10,819
	April	1,762	3,063	5,283	10,108
	May	1,488	4,259	4,692	10,439
	TOTAL	6,662	21,236	25,330	53,228

*Does not include Middlewest Motor Freight Bureau.
Source: Rate Bureau Submissions to the MCRSC.

Table 15
Eastern Central Motor Carriers Association: Rate Experience by Shipment
Type (1980–1981)

| Category | Percent of Total (Percent of Shipments Discounted) | | | | |
	1980	1981	January 1981	July 1981	December 1981
Total	100.0	100.0	100.0	100.0	100.0
	(7.9)	(17.2)	(13.3)	(18.5)	(24.4)
Class	69.2	68.9	67.9	68.6	70.4
Shipment	(4.8)	(17.4)	(12.9)	(19.1)	(27.7)
Commodity	27.4	27.5	28.8	28.1	25.5
Shipment	N/A	(1.0)	(0.5)	(1.5)	(3.5)
LTL Class	57.9	59.5	57.8	59.6	61.2
	(4.3)	(19.0)	(13.8)	(19.1)	(30.1)
Single Line	80.8	83.2	82.0	84.0	85.5
	(8.3)	(18.6)	(14.8)	(19.8)	(27.1)

Does not include "off-bill" discounts that apply to a shipper's total traffic and do not therefore appear on the freight bill.

Source: Hausman, "Information Costs," p. 385. Used with permission.

the trucking industry faced excess capacity. Rate cutting during that time was pervasive and virtually unrestrained. Whether the rate cutting was (1) always latent and simply waiting for a deep recession, or (2) unleashed by the ICC's changed stance on regulation and the Motor Carrier Act's new emphasis on competition does not matter. What does matter is that price competition is a reality in today's trucking marketplace.

The disparate pattern of rate cutting makes it difficult to judge the magnitude of the revenue erosion from discounting.[113] Every carrier seems to have a different discount plan and is constantly changing it to meet changing competitive circumstances. Carriers generally maintain data on the cost of their discounts but may be overestimating their revenues because of future claims for discounts. Through the Continuous Traffic Study (CTS), bureaus are aware of the discounts which show up on the freight bills, but a special effort is required to compute discounts which do not show up on the freight bills, especially when they are not filed through bureau tariffs. All this is confused by the fact that carriers are constantly revising their discounts.[114] For individual shipments, the discounts range from zero to, say, 50 percent.[115]

Table 16
Freight Motor Carrier Tariff Publications

	FY 1980	FY 1981	FY 1982
Publications Filed	427,006	516,304	739,602
Rejections	2,864	4,784	7,911
Suspension Cases (i.e., protests)	408	288	276
Suspended (in full)	131	88	28
Suspended (in part)	9	2	1
Investigated	4	2	1
Informal Complaints (via Tariff Integrity Board)	51	10	0
Formal Complaints	37	37	57

The numerical increase in tariff rejections has been attributed to the increase in the number of tariff filings since the Motor Carrier Act of 1980, and, more particularly, to the increase in the number of Independent Actions which have been filed by carriers inexperienced with the intricacies of ICC regulation. It is expected, however, that the number of tariff rejections will decrease as carriers gain more experience with rate filing requirements. In fact, it should be noted that the number of tariff rejections slowed in the last three quarters of fiscal year 1982. In the first quarter, the ICC rejected 3,437 of the 134,145 tariffs filed. In the last three quarters, it rejected only 4,474 of the 605,457 tariffs filed.

Source: Interstate Commerce Commission, as quoted by Study Commission, *Report*, p. 226.

While no data base presently exists on the magnitude of discounting off the bureau tariffs, the data from Table 17 for the Rocky Mountain Bureau (involving long-distance traffic nationwide) is instructive. The data show increasing effective discount rates in all traffic categories over time and the biggest discount rates for class-rated traffic. These data actually underestimate the effective rates of discount because many of the discount programs require the shipper to file a claim periodically, and thus do not show up on the freight bill which is sampled in the CTS. Furthermore, proprietary tariffs have replaced commodity tariffs to a large extent (note the decline in use of commodity tariffs).

Table 18 shows that overall rates seemed to be increasing for the larger regulated carriers, both TL and LTL, as shown in column 1. Column 2, however, shows overall revenue/hundredweight (for TL and LTL) for general commodity carriers to be increasing, but this statistic is undoubtedly reflecting the loss of TL freight and of course does not reflect

Table 17
Rocky Mountain Motor Tariff Bureau: Percentage of Revenue and Effective
Rate of Discount Allowances*

	Year 1980	Year 1981	Year 1982	Year 1983	Year 1984
Total Bureau Traffic	100.00	100.00	100.00	100.00	100.00
Effective Discount Rate	None	40.03	6.87	13.58	23.79
Minimum Charge Traffic	7.46	8.26	8.95	9.72	9.44
Effective Discount Rate	None	N/A	5.73	11.46	19.42
Class Rated Traffic:					
Less than 10,000 lbs.	56.44	60.93	68.07	73.28	75.56
Effective Discount Rate	None	N/A	7.61	14.93	25.42
10,000 lbs. and Over	13.40	11.47	9.77	9.05	10.45
Effective Discount Rate	None	N/A	6.67	13.21	22.63
Commodity Rated Traffic	22.70	19.34	13.21	7.95	4.55
Effective Discount Rate	None	N/A	1.30	2.72	2.67

*Does not include allowances not stated on freight bills.
Source: Rocky Mountain Motor Tariff Bureau.

Table 18
Reported Pricing Trends in Truck Transportation

Year	Class I Trucking * Cents/Ton-mile	Revenue/Hundred- weight (General ** Freight Carriers)	LTL Revenue per Hundredweight (East. + Central Frame Carriers
1977		$ 3.14	
1978		3.46	$ 7.07
1979		3.91	7.73
1980	18.00	4.92	9.19
1981	20.00	5.61	10.32
1982	20.77	6.00	11.28
1983	21.01	6.19	12.23
1984	22.16	6.58	11.85
1985			12.04

Source: Transportation Policy Associates, *Transportation in America*, November 1985, p. 11.

**Source*: Harkins, Table 2.

***Source*: Silberman, "Statement," 6 November 1985. p. 15.

distance or other elements of the service. Column 3 shows a decline in revenue/hundredweight for Eastern Central Carriers for 1984 with revenue/hundredweight in 1985 at levels less than 1983. All of these statistics do not reflect changes in the mix of freight and therefore should not necessarily be taken as accurate indices of actual price levels.

The development of new service and rate options

Supporters of collective ratemaking have historically pointed to the substantial amount of competition to bureau carriers in the form of non-member carriers, contract carriers, private carriage, nonprofit shipper cooperatives, and other modes, especially piggyback. They also pointed to extensive use of the IA process.[116] In the past, competition has resulted in a vast proliferation of special tariff provisions, such as exception ratings and commodity rates, designed to reduce transportation costs below those that would be produced by the class-rate structure. While such departures were not unknown under strict regulation, they have certainly accelerated. Examples of innovative tariffs include:

1. Exception ratings taking precedence over the classification rating (and classification changes);

2. Column and point-to-point commodity rates;

3. Loading and unloading allowances;

4. Multiple pickup and shipment discounts and aggregate weight and revenue discounts;

5. Allowances in lieu of pickup or delivery service; and

6. Discounts based on a minimum threshold revenue over a given period of time for all shipments tendered.

The new ratemaking environment has generated a plethora of new service/rate options for shippers. While some carriers have departed from bureau tariffs through IA's, others have even gone their own way with private tariffs[117] for on-line traffic. Some of these involve simplified tariff systems that use zip codes rather than traditional bureau point and distance computations.[118] Two early examples of this were AAA Cooper and Georgia Highway Express (now Transus).[119] These carriers implemented a new rate scale for small shipments as an alternative to the class-rate structure. This decision is relevant not only because it illustrates that the right of independent action is hardly illusory. It also illustrates that even carriers who do not adopt bureau ratemaking standards fully for their on-line traffic often employ the collective ratemaking and classification system for interline traffic.[120]

The lack of collusive attitudes in the trucking industry

Apart from the concrete actions of motor carriers in the area of rate competition, a fundamental change has occurred in the attitude of motor carrier pricing executives since 1980. In the months that followed Overnite's across-the-board 10 percent discount soon after the passage of the MCA of 1980, some motor carriers hung back, hoping that the discounting would go away. But everyone quickly realized the price cutting would not abate as the rate cutters caused serious erosion of the traffic of the timid carriers. Carriers, many of whom had never considered pricing at out-of-pocket costs to be a major competitive weapon, began to change their pricing strategy to compete on the basis of low rates. The previous relative stability of pricing gave way to a frenzy of rate slashing. Everybody complained about everybody else, but nobody could stop it. Carrier management realized that the more stable pricing arrangements of the pre–1980 period were in jeopardy, and the survival of their companies was at stake. The industry's collective interest was to hold the line, but individually, carriers realized that their companies would lose market share and be seriously harmed if they did not join the rate cutting.

Motor carriers also cited a changed attitude on the part of shippers.

The chairman of the ICC and administration officials were promising billions in savings in the costs of trucking as a result of regulatory reforms. Shippers learned that substantial rate cuts were there for the asking. Carriers were desperate for traffic and willing to meet those demands.

Quantitative information on the level of ratemaking activity is not sufficient to capture the spirit of the changes now going on in the motor carrier industry. Carrier management has been challenged by an adverse operating environment of rate cutting and volume losses. Major changes are occurring in management practices and attitudes, and these changes increase the emphasis on pricing, marketing, and corporate planning. This change in attitude provides a litmus test of the consequences of regulatory reform.

There is little doubt that motor carrier management is irrevocably committed to the changes in the motor carrier industry envisaged by the MCA of 1980. Commonly accepted maxims of the industry are being discarded in favor of new approaches. While there is no one indicator of this change in attitude, the signs are evident:

1. An increased role of pricing, modern marketing concepts, and corporate strategic planning in an industry traditionally dominated by an orientation toward operations;
2. Traffic departments that are flooded with requests by sales representatives for rate actions;
3. A substantial increase in interest in costing systems and a greater reliance on individual carrier cost information in ratemaking and traffic solicitation;[121]
4. Changes in price/service options, operational policies, and service territories;
5. Introduction of innovative rate structures;
6. Development of management information and decision systems that permit a carrier to respond far more quickly to competitors' actions;
7. A noticeable lack of interest in the regulatory process as a means of advancing corporate interests and in increased reliance on the carrier's service and pricing decisions; and
8. A "siege mentality" at times, in which carriers make decisions on the basis of very short-run corporate interests.[122]

The present system contains powerful competitive forces driving carrier pricing decisions. Motor carrier rate bureaus cannot ignore these forces. The price war attests to that fact.

The significance of the ZORF provision

Under the Zone-of-Rate-Freedom (ZORF) provisions of the MCA of 1980, motor carriers were to be allowed a "yo-yo" provision which permitted them an upward or downward rate flexibility free from rights of protest and suspension. This provision was designed to give the carriers rate-making freedoms without fear that the ICC would restrain carrier ratemaking initiatives within this zone.

Under the ZORF provision, the carrier may elect to increase or decrease a rate by 15 percent above or below the rate in effect one year earlier. The Commission cannot suspend the rate on grounds of unreasonableness, although it can be challenged on the grounds that it is discriminatory, unduly preferential or prejudicial, or predatory. If the carrier elects to use the ZORF, the rates are established outside the scope of antitrust immunity although it can publish the ZORF rate through a rate bureau.

Since the Motor Carrier Act was passed, one carrier has used the ZORF. One critic claimed that "few carriers have availed themselves of the zone, leading us to believe that carriers continue to huddle together under antitrust immunity."[123] The "ceiling price" effect of collective ratemaking, however, shows why the ZORF has become redundant. On the up side, individual carriers have limited power to raise rates unilaterally since they would lose significant traffic to their competitors. On the down side, there appear to be no constraints on rate reductions. The use of the ZORF automatically removes the carrier's antitrust immunity and gains it nothing, so why bother?

Conclusion

The prerequisite factors for successful cartelization are simply not operative in the motor carrier industry today. The same traffic executives for motor carriers who socialize at rate bureaus go back to their offices and slash prices if it serves individual carrier interests. Indeed, in many companies, pricing decisions are being made by those higher up in the carrier organization than the attendants of bureau meetings.

It all comes down to whether Breen's five enforcement mechanisms[124] are being used to sustain cartellike behavior. This list really boils down to two elements: control on entry and the power of the ICC to suspend and reject rate cuts.[125] Cartels break down when they cannot control pricing and output, both inside and outside the cartel.

The present entry standards afford no protection whatsoever to incumbent motor carriers.[126] Most carriers have helped themselves to whatever operating authority they pleased. Indeed, many found that unwanted operating authority was thrust upon them by the ICC's policy of expanding the scope of requests for authority.

On the question of pricing, rate bureaus are powerless to "identify and punish cheaters," even if they wanted to. The bureaus have no mechanisms to enforce pricing standards; they cannot protest bureau members' IA's or any motor carrier's rates; they cannot restrain IA's by their members in any way; and they cannot act on rate proposals. Far from enforcing a cartel, as a result of the restrictions on their rights to protest members' IA's, they have fewer rights before the ICC than an ordinary citizen.

EFFECTS OF COLLECTIVE RATEMAKING ON RATE LEVELS

Motor carrier general rate increases using the antitrust immunity conferred by the MCA of 1980 have become increasingly controversial. The ICC has routinely approved them while larger shippers have negotiated large discounts. Representatives of certain shipper groups charge that these general rate increases were being used to finance a rate war for the benefit of larger shippers, and this belief has recently undermined the widespread support by shippers for collective ratemaking.

While the loss of shipper support is a recent phenomenon, critics of antitrust immunity have always charged that collective ratemaking results in rate levels above those that would prevail in a deregulated market.[127] They have also charged that regulation and collective ratemaking result in unnecessarily complex and discriminatory rate structures.

The resulting rate structure is claimed to cause economic inefficiency arising from incorrect price incentives for shippers. Uneconomic rate structures arising from the influence of collective ratemaking allegedly cause "misallocation of traffic" among modes and economic costs in the form of a deadweight loss.[128] Critics, however, argue two exactly opposite consequences of the allegedly higher rates for costs and service.

James C. Miller, former chairman of the FTC, stated before the Study Commission that collective ratemaking and regulation have held trucking prices too high and *service too low*:

When price is held above a competitive level, as numerous studies show the case to be for trucking, shippers are denied additional units of trucking service which they value more highly than what it would cost society to produce. This artificial restriction on output imposes a deadweight welfare loss on society . . . my colleagues and I on the Commission have reviewed the arguments for and against collective ratemaking. We find that collective ratemaking imposes substantial costs on the U.S. economy in terms of higher rates and restrained service.[129]

Another critic, Denis Breen, took the opposite view that the government-enforced cartel in trucking is imperfect, resulting in "wasteful service competition" and *too much regulation-induced trucking service*.[130] Indeed, Miller also endorsed this opposite view when he complained that shippers may have gotten too much service at too high a price under regulation with bureau ratemaking:

There is some evidence that, overall, the trucking industry presents shippers with inefficient price-quality offerings. That is, rates tend to rise above the levels that would obtain under competition and then (in certain markets) carriers compete away the potential excess profits by adding more service, increasing sales expense, *et cetera*. The result that while in certain instances shippers get better service than they would under competitive conditions, the value of this increased service is not worth its additional cost. Also, while there is a variety of specialized services, the menu may be more limited than it would be under conditions of competition.[131]

Critics offer inconsistent theories of whether the sign of the effects of collective ratemaking on service levels and capacity is positive or negative, but are united in concluding that there is an effect, and it is undesirable. This inconsistency reflects a more fundamental, underlying difficulty in the theory of how collective ratemaking and rate regulation allegedly affect the equilibrium level of trucking, rates, costs, and service. Apparently the discrepancy starts with a confusion between the effects of entry constraints (which presumably restrict output) and the effect of rate regulation (which allegedly increases output of incumbents given the alleged effect of the regulation of rates).

The easiest case to deal with for the present purposes is the case where prices are fixed by regulation but not service or cost levels. The "imperfect cartel" theory says that since the ICC controlled entry of new carriers and price levels but did not control capacity or service levels, excessive profits resulting from high rates were dissipated by carriers attempting to compete on the basis of service, resulting in excessive empty mileage, and so on. The present situation of free entry and rate wars makes these claims of wasteful service competition out of date. And even before the Motor Carrier Act was passed, the economics profession had largely recanted the more extreme positions taken by critics who earlier had estimated large economic efficiency losses in trucking on the demand side resulting from uneconomic price structures.[132]

Miller's "withheld service" theory is not so easily addressed as his "excessive service" theory. By its very definition, an economically inefficient high price produces excess supply unless quantity as well as price is fixed. Thus the charge that collective ratemaking inflates rate levels must address both the mechanism by which rates are said to be increased above competitive levels and the procedures used to suppress the excess supply necessarily elicited as a result of the inflated price.

Critics offer three mechanisms to explain how, even in the current absence of a government-controlled cartel, collective ratemaking would inflate rate levels: (1) grouping carriers' costs for establishing general rate increases protects inefficient carriers by making collective rates depend on the average, not the most efficient, carrier;[133] (2) collective ratemaking encourages excessive wages by making it possible to pass on higher wages negotiated in an industrywide bargaining agreement through the collective process;[134] and (3) any collusive arrangement, even with free entry and no regulatory restraints on price, is *per se* anticompetitive and inherently leads to higher prices.[135]

None of these arguments withstands scrutiny in the new competitive environment of trucking. The conclusion that collective ratemaking protects inefficient carriers and inflates costs has nevertheless gained widespread credibility, if only by constant repetition.

Collective ratemaking allegedly protects inefficient carriers

The "inefficient carrier" argument was initially phrased in its most naive form: under collective ratemaking the costs of the most inefficient carrier in the rate bureau determine the rate level and all other carriers earn excess profits. Both the Senate and House reports on the MCA of 1980 apparently accepted the most extreme version of the inefficient-carrier argument:

The clear advantage of the rate bureau process is that it provides a certain predictability in the rate structure and is a system that shippers and truckers have learned to live with over the years. The disadvantage is that the system inherently tends to result in rates that will be compensatory for even the least efficient motor carrier participating in the rate discussions. When this happens, consumers lose the benefit of price competition that would occur if more efficient carriers were able to offer more attractive rates.[136]

These arguments were originally offered to describe the situation where the collective tariff sets the actual price and clearly do not apply where competition forces carriers to undercut the collective rate level. But even if regulators were to prevent price competition, the argument that collective rate levels were set to keep the least efficient carrier in business makes no sense. Group ratemaking neither bails out the inefficient nor penalizes the efficient, by definition of the averaging process. When rate bureaus file for general rate increases, the cost data represent weighted average costs of carriers in the bureau. Some carriers are more efficient, and others are less so. By definition of the process, a collective ratemaking system based on weighted average costs will cause more than half the carriers to do worse than the weighted average[137] and cannot be said to establish rate levels based on the costs of the least efficient carrier. An inefficient carrier, who by definition has higher than average costs and is not making a return necessary to stay in business, cannot possibly be protected by rates that only cover the costs of the weighted average carrier. By definition, the inefficient carrier does worse than the weighted average and will fall by the wayside if it consistently earns less than its cost of capital.[138]

When the crudest form of this argument was turned aside, it was next reformulated as a somewhat more sophisticated argument that group ratemaking eliminates the normal incentive of individual company management to contain costs.[139] But this claim also fails. Under a process where rates are based on weighted average costs, each carrier has a strong incentive to "beat the averages" because it retains virtually every cent of cost savings (ignoring the relatively small impact of an individual carrier's cost reductions on the group average).[140] The argument that collective ratemaking somehow eliminates the incentives normally found in company management to enhance efficiency simply does not withstand scrutiny.

The latest effort to reformulate the theory is by the Motor Carrier Ratemaking Study Commission. The Study Commission's report concluded that collective rate levels (equal to the costs of the weighted average firm) are above competitive levels because economic theory states that prices are set by the most efficient firm in a competitive market.[141] This conclusion is a distortion of the theory of competitive markets.[142] Obviously if prices were set in a competitive equilibrium to equal costs of the most efficient firm, all other firms would be unable to cover their costs and would eventually drop out of the market. If there were permanent differences in costs among firms, the most-efficient-firm theory would lead to monopoly as the equilibrium industry structure. A major premise of the Ratemaking Study Commission's conclusion is based on economic logic that simply cannot be sustained.

Economic theory, in fact, posits the exact opposite. It is the costs of the least efficient source of supply which is marginally competitive in the long-run equilibrium, not the most efficient source, that equates to price in the long run in a competitive market. According to the classical theory of "economic rent,"[143] in the long run, competitive firms of above average efficiency bid up the prices of their unusually productive resources and create economic rents, thereby raising their costs to the level of less efficient firms. Owners of competitive firms cannot permanently enjoy the benefits of more productive input resources than their competitors, and the costs of all firms will tend to rise to meet those of the highest-cost firm at the margin (which determines the long-run equilibrium price).[144] The extra profit generated by more productive resources in the short run is captured in the long-run competitive equilibrium by the owner of the more efficient resource. This economic rent cannot be extracted by customers without monopsony market power. In competitive markets, only the power of the government to tax can be used to extract the rents arising from superior productivity from their owners.[145] Or the government can attempt to confer a monopoly upon another resource, such as labor in the form of unions, to attempt to extract the economic rent. In the latter case, labor's success will depend on the elasticity of the demand for the final product, the possibilities for substitution among productive resources, and the elasticity of supply of such substitutes.[146]

There will always be a least-efficient supplier struggling at the margin in a competitive market and barely surviving. It is the long-run marginal cost of this competitor that determines the price in a competitive market, and more efficient suppliers earn economic rent. There is no evidence that collective ratemaking somehow uses a cost standard for ratemaking that is conceptually above that in a competitive market. Indeed, the reverse is true.

Collective ratemaking allegedly encourages excessive wage levels

The effect of collective ratemaking on wage levels becomes the remaining basis for the Study Commission's conclusion that collective ratemaking inflates rate levels. But the Study Commission's conclusion that rates reflect costs, "dollar for dollar,"[147] becomes circular—rates determine costs and vice versa. What then limits both?

In reality, the problem the Study Commission was struggling with was the combined effect of industrywide labor agreements reinforced by regulatory constraints on entry, not collective ratemaking.[148] What allegedly made the process work to raise wages prior to regulatory reform is the fact that higher rates could not elicit entry, not that the mechanism for the rate increase was a collective proposal to the ICC for a general rate increase. The alleged direction of causation, despite the timing of events, was the effort of organized labor to appropriate for itself the benefits of restrictions on competition, both entry and service.[149] In citing the proof before deregulation, the Study Commission referred to it as "only scattered evidence."[150] Once the benefits to the incumbent carriers of restricted entry and rate competition were eliminated, the theory states that there is nothing left for labor to extract—indeed, labor would be forced into a give-back strategy despite the continuation of collective ratemaking.

This interpretation has been confirmed by events in the post–1980 era, which has been characterized by "concessionary bargaining" by the Teamsters union,[151] despite the fact that carriers can continue to propose collective rate increases to the ICC. The loss of traffic, bankruptcies, and rate wars have produced tremendous pressures on motor carriers to reduce wages and fringes and to increase productivity. The result has been a breakdown of the national labor agreement to bargaining at the regional, local, or firm-specific level. Entry and expansion by nonunion carriers have encouraged "double breasting" (i.e., creation of nonunion divisions of unionized carriers) and "employee stock ownership plans" (ESOPs) to transfer ownership to employees in exchange for wage cuts.

Asserting an indirect effect of collective ratemaking on rate levels through effects on wages makes little sense in a world of permissive regulation. The most logical variant of the theory states that the wage gains would be approved because carriers believed they could be absorbed or passed on because of high rates engendered by collective ratemaking. This in turn raises the real issue, whether collective ratemaking works via the third alleged mechanism to raise prices.

Collective ratemaking allegedly increases rates *per se*

Even after rejecting all the possible explicit mechanisms by which collective ratemaking is alleged to have generated excessively high rates, critics cling to the feeling that the collective setting of rates has a tendency to produce rates that are inherently higher than competitive levels.[152] Unfortunately, critics merely assert these effects without clearly demonstrating how such a noncompetitive equilibrium could be achieved in the presence of free entry, low market concentration, and unrestrained right of independent action. The lack of a specific model that explains how collective ratemaking *per se* leads to higher rates is troubling because it is difficult to test and evaluate the critical assumptions.

These beliefs fail to confront the fundamental problem they raise: What happens to the industry disequilibrium of excess supply that the theory predicts?[153] In a market with numerous incumbents where prices are alleged to be in equilibrium above competitive levels, there must be some force that prevents firms from entering, expanding output, and forcing prices back to competitive levels. The problem for the *per se* theory is to specify exactly what force sustains the equilibrium at rates above competitive levels. The required force is not specified by the proponents, but some possible explanations can be supplied by examining the underlying economic theory of oligopoly and price fixing.

It is useful to start with the competitive model of atomistic competition. The familiar model is shown in Figure 7. The equilibrium is "noncooperative" in that every firm chooses its profit-maximizing output given the market price. This results in the familiar condition that price equals marginal cost when price is P_2 and quantity is Q_2. The market is therefore in equilibrium. If P_1 is temporarily the price, the output is Q_3. Since price is above average cost, excess profits exist temporarily. But entry

Figure 7
Price and Quantity under Competition and Alleged under Collective
Ratemaking

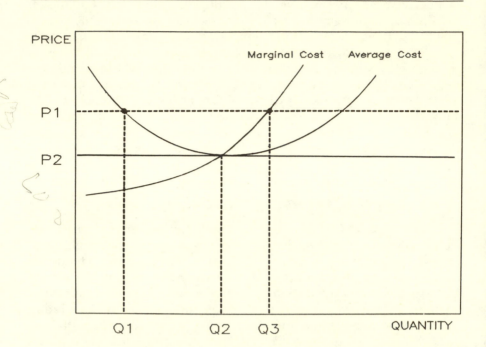

of new firms drives price to P_2, where all firms price at marginal cost, and no excess profits exist.

The figure illustrates various mechanisms by which collective rate-making could allegedly work to achieve an anticompetitive equilibrium. Suppose carriers use the collective ratemaking process to establish a rate of P_1. The problem for the *per se* theory then is to identify how output and entry might be controlled to prevent competitive forces from forcing rates back down to P_2 in an unconcentrated market. Such constraints on output and entry are generally categorized as noncooperative (oligopolistic) or cooperative (genuinely collusive) in the theory of industrial organization.

The oligopolistic version of the theory assumes that each carrier perceives that its decisions on price and service will affect the price and service decisions of competitors. The noncooperative equilibrium "means simply that economic agents cannot rely upon any agreement being binding on other agents."[154] Although firms are assumed not to conspire *per se*, a reasonably high degree of communication (or at least understanding) is required among participants because each seller's "conjectures" about its competitors' responses to its price and quantity are crucial to the equilibrium. The noncooperative oligopoly equilibrium is enforced by mutually reinforced assumptions by each incumbent that any individual effort to change output and prices will be responded to by competitors in a way that eliminates the profit that would otherwise result from a unilateral change under perfect competition. A noncooperative oligopoly is a market structure where, in equilibrium, each firm voluntarily restricts output below competitive levels because of a belief that an increase in its output invokes output decisions of competitors in ways adverse to its interests (as measured by the "conjectural variation").[155] According to the theory, output will be less and prices will be higher than the competitive result, yet no firm has an incentive to expand output even though price exceeds marginal cost. This result is based entirely on perceptions by the firms as to the strategic interaction of their decisions and those of competitors.[156] As these perceptions of competitors' responses change, perhaps in response to experience, so will the noncooperative equilibrium.

One possible basis for the *per se* theory is that collective ratemaking somehow facilitates a noncooperative oligopoly outcome at capacity levels lower and rate levels higher than under perfect competition despite free entry. Brander and Spencer,[157] in fact, offer a generalized theoretical model of how such a noncooperative oligopoly equilibrium would be achieved. Their model assumes free entry into an industry where each incumbent believes that an expansion of its output (i.e., service) will be responded to by all other incumbents with an expansion of output. Each incumbent therefore perceives a noncollusive punishment by other incumbents of individual expanded output. New entrants join these firms whenever industry excess profits are positive, believing that their entry will have a negligible effect on total industry profits because of the large number of firms.

An imperfectly competitive oligopoly equilibrium is established where price equals average cost above each firm's minimum cost point (say at P_1 and Q_1 in Figure 7), but each firm is unable to profitably expand output because of a belief that the decision will invoke an output response of competitors that eliminates the profit.[158] Because the achievement of an inefficient high price in the noncooperative equilibrium is completely dependent on each firm's perception of competitors' responses to its own output decision, any mechanism such as collective ratemaking that improves communication could possibly help support the mutual expectations necessary to motivate noncollusive enforcement of the output-restricting equilibrium.

Brander and Spencer's chief contribution is to show just how dubious are the assumptions required to achieve an inefficient yet zero-profit, noncooperative oligopoly outcome under free entry. The entire model is based on an extreme dichotomy between the responses of competitors to entry decisions of newcomers and to output expansions of incumbents. Firms in the model are unreasonably assumed to believe that other incumbents respond strongly via output expansion to increased output of a single incumbent firm, but entry by any number of new firms invokes zero response. Or put another way, a new entrant must believe that its entry has a negligible effect on incumbents; but after it has entered, it then believes its output decisions invoke a substantial response by incumbents. It is ordinarily far easier to monitor and detect entry decisions than output decisions and to respond accordingly, but the model assumes just the opposite. The incongruity of the required assumptions, even within the context of the theoretical model, is obvious.

Even apart from reservations about the internal consistency of the model as a theoretical construct, examination of the sufficient assumptions to produce such an outcome suggests that the trucking industry is not a particularly good candidate. The nature of the collective rate-making process, the large number of firms in the industry, and the difficulty of defining output in a complex service industry make the trucking industry a poor candidate for a Cournot/Nash equilibrium where inefficiently high prices are sustained by mutually reinforcing expectations of output decisions of each competitor.[159]

The formation of the necessary conjectural variations on output decisions is at variance with the reality of trucking operations. In the model, each carrier is assumed to operate voluntarily at an inefficiently low scale because a decision to expand service is deterred by competitor's threats of output expansion. But in the trucking industry, service is provided over a complex network, and it is virtually impossible to define the quantity that is being offered, much less measure it as a strategic interaction variable.[160] The current rate war strongly suggests that a noncooperative, inefficient oligopoly is a highly unlikely candidate to solve the excess capacity allegedly created by inflated prices instigated by rate bureaus.

Brander and Spencer's model is also implausible as a model of the operation of collective ratemaking in the motor carrier industry. Price, not capacity, is the only subject of discussion for collective ratemaking, and the required mutual dependence of capacity decisions to support the conjectural-variation model is high in an industry with many firms. Each firm is assumed to join voluntarily in the output expansion to punish the firm that attempts to provide the competitive level of service but must believe that unilateral output expansions will otherwise be severely punished. This assumes a high degree of knowledge and coordination, so that each firm will be assured that its output expansion to punish a cheater will not itself be viewed as cheating, which in turn would invoke further output expansion in retaliation. Such coordinated capacity decisions for enforcing a price above competitive levels supported by output restrictions in the motor carrier industry cannot be made in rate bureaus.

In any event, the theory of noncooperative oligopoly invariably identifies the number of competitors as a key determinant of price levels.[161] The tendency of such outcomes to approach the competitive result as the number of competitors increases is a common feature of most of the models. If fear of oligopoly outcomes were a concern, the concern would also apply to a market structure without collective ratemaking. Indeed, the incentives toward increased market concentration arising from increased transactions costs among carriers with the loss of collective ratemaking (see below) could encourage noncooperative oligopoly outcomes. If noncooperative oligopoly is the concern, one answer is for public policy not to encourage increased concentration in the industry.

To the extent that they have thought at all about the problem, defenders of the *per se* doctrine have not advanced the theory that rate bureaus facilitate noncollusive oligopolistic output restrictions that sustain higher-than-competitive price levels. The fear is that collective ratemaking encourages a cooperative outcome—price fixing.

Brander and Spencer also characterize their model as possibly describing a collusive equilibrium in which firms voluntarily restrict output to raise prices and threaten to punish cheaters by simultaneously expanding output. If the model were to be applied to the case at hand, carriers would be hypothesized to set prices at noncompetitive levels, earn excess profits, and collude over market shares and capacity decisions. But as noted above, rate bureaus specify only the price, not capacity or entry decisions. Without the noncooperative enforcement mechanism of the conjectural variation to enforce output restrictions or enforceable[162] market-sharing agreements, each firm in Figure 7 will expand output to Q_3 at P_1. Each incumbent will also have an incentive to shave prices by discounting, and new entrants can profit by entering the industry. The theory fails to explain what keeps prices above competitive levels with free entry and what blunts incentives of each incumbent to expand service and attempt to increase market share. This, of course, is exactly what motor carriers did in response to regulatory reform—cut prices and expand their service territories.

This failure to provide an explicit, credible enforcement mechanism becomes even more problematic when the problem is viewed from the perspective of the entire industry. If existing firms have an incentive to expand service and new entrants are enticed into the industry as a result of excessive prices, the result is industrywide excess capacity at an excessive rate level. Owners of this excess capacity in turn have strong incentives to discount rates rather than leave capacity idle. Much of the excess capacity is owned by financially weak firms who are forced to slash rates merely to stave off bankruptcy. There is no way around the problem—by definition, a rate above competitive level implies excess supply. But if rates are set above collusive levels, there has to be an explicit permanent mechanism for keeping the excess capacity off the market, and none is offered.[163]

COLLECTIVE RATEMAKING AND ECONOMIC EFFICIENCY

In the final analysis, the *per se* theory simply asserts that collusion results in excessive price levels and economic inefficiency without offering a specific, credible explanation of how such a theory works to establish a noncompetitive industry equilibrium. This failure is troubling because there is a growing economic literature which has developed explicit models that show the contrary—collusion can best be explained as efficiency-seeking in a highly competitive industry.

This literature begins with a paradox in the *per se* theory of the incentives for collusion with free entry and exit. If any level of positive excess profits creates incentives for entry, what motivates cooperation among firms? With no mechanism to block entry and deter price cutting among incumbents, the benefits of collusion in raising prices are difficult to understand. And precisely because the higher prices are sustainable only as a result of voluntary cooperation,[164] the purported equilibrium is susceptible to being undercut by self-interested unilateral actions that are difficult to deter.[165] If collusion cannot achieve excess profits in a regime of free entry with no mechanism to punish incumbent firms that cut prices and expand output, the only rationale for collusion must then be efficiency gains.

The economics of a competitive equilibrium of collusive price setters enjoying efficiency gains from their cooperative efforts has been developed in a series of recent articles. Donald Dewey hypothesized a market where sellers were subject to uncertainty which would be reduced by agreements among competitors to share price and production data.[166] Because of free entry, collusion could not be used as permanent means to secure monopoly profits because these would only attract entry. Because firms are risk averse, the sharing of information reduces costs, and therefore price, and results in greater output and economic welfare than the case where interfirm cooperation was banned by the antitrust laws. Dewey thus characterized uncertainty as a market imperfection that could be reduced through cooperation among firms. So long as the benefits of cooperation are not restricted to incumbents, any attempt to create monopoly profits would provoke entry.

Lester G. Telser offers a similar model in which cooperation among competitors is required to achieve economic efficiency.[167] In Telser's model, uncertainty arises because sellers must sink costs prior to knowing what demand will be. Uncertainty can be reduced either by agreements on demand between suppliers and customers (e.g., long-term contracts) or coalitions among buyers and sellers that assign sales quotas to sellers in the presence of indivisibilities (e.g., start-up costs for a new entrant).

Dewey's theoretical construct was greeted with a number of criticisms in a series of reply articles.[168] The gist of the objections is not that inefficiently high prices can be sustained in the presence of free entry or that collusion cannot increase economic welfare. Rather the objection is that in practice, entry barriers are material, certainly in concentrated industries that have been the focus of antitrust enforcement. While the general application of specific assumptions employed by Dewey and Telser can be challenged, the principal thesis remains: unless entry barriers can be demonstrated,[169] collusion in unconcentrated industries is explainable more plausibly as an efficiency-enhancing exercise than as a search for monopoly profit.[170]

Interestingly, both Dewey and Telser's models assume low transactions costs to individual firms in cooperating (particularly no costs of antitrust litigation), and nonparticipants cannot appropriate for themselves the benefits of other firms' cooperation. If there is no "public good" to the cooperative behavior, each firm benefits only if it participates in the cooperative activity, thus moving toward an economically efficient level of cooperation. In practice in the trucking industry, individual transactions costs (including antitrust compliance and uncertainty) are high, and the benefits of cooperation are often appropriable by nonparticipants. This raises questions of the motivation for collusion even when the result is efficiency-enhancing (see further discussion in Chapter 4).

Another possibility is that motor carriers, like oil-exporting nations, will mistakenly believe that they have the power to set rates above competitive levels in a collusive manner. These high rates will cause excessive entry and capacity, a collapse of prices, and economic inefficiency arising from too much service, not too little.[171] While such an outcome cannot be ruled out, it is important to remember that the biggest losers from such an event will be the incumbent carriers themselves.

The Dilemma of Encouraging Cooperation among Horizontally and Vertically Related Rivals in the Motor Carrier Industry 4

An economist is a person who, when he finds something that works in practice, wonders if it will work in theory.
WALTER W. HELLER, in "A Fed Camp in the Rockies," *The New York Times*, 26 August 1985, p. D6.

THE TENSION BETWEEN COOPERATION AND COMPETITION

Collective ratemaking in the motor carrier industry raises difficult public policy issues regarding the application of the antitrust laws. In a nutshell, the fundamental antitrust dilemma is to develop strong incentives for unilateral competitive behavior while also simultaneously encouraging cooperation when the function is best provided by a joint venture. While this dilemma is found in most industries operating over a network, a number of factors make this balancing act uniquely difficult in the trucking industry.

The first is that a "joint venture" problem arises whenever service and pricing decisions must be coordinated by rivals to provide complementary services.[172] Motor carriers compete vigorously in providing single-line service. But they also join together to provide interline services according to prices and terms of service which must be determined in advance of the actual tender of freight. This complex web of interlocking pricing and service decisions for joint-line traffic operates in the context of a national transportation system. In an industry where costs are extremely complex and the definition of the product or service subject to variability, it is by no means obvious how the jointly provided product or service is to be defined and priced.

Jointly provided services therefore require a high level of multilateral cooperation in setting prices and terms of service.[173] Common agreement on classification and other dimensions of ratemaking, formatting of shipping documents, interline settlements, exchange of traffic data on interline shipments, tariff rules, packaging requirements, and other terms of service require close coordination by a carrier with its competitors.

The most difficult issues in antitrust law in transportation involve drawing a line between (1) legitimate efforts of carriers to use multilateral agreements to avoid a pointless and costly proliferation of bilateral agreements on rates and terms of service which would impose substantial transactions costs on joint-line service, and (2) collusion that suppresses economically justified rate/service options.

The second complicating factor in the trucking industry is that economically efficient communication of price and service information calls for broad applicability of motor carrier tariffs as to commodities, points, and carriers. Rate bureau tariffs are "open routed" in that they ordinarily apply both to single-line and joint-line service for numerous commodities and disparate shipping patterns over wide geographic areas. These broadly applicable collective tariffs apply to hundreds of participating carriers in the rate bureau unless a carrier has flagged out. But individual carriers also publish thousands of Individual Actions through the rate bureaus as well as thousands of tariff items in individual carrier tariffs outside of the collective ratemaking process. The second major antitrust problem is very simple: efficient construction of joint-line tariffs to aggregations of commodities, points, and carriers may not conform to a clean break between single-line and joint-line traffic so as to protect carriers from antitrust concerns of collusion.

In addition to the dimensions of required coordination among motor carriers to provide interline service and tariffs, there exists a third problem arising from the need for some degree of standardization of the mass of pricing data communicated by carriers to shippers. Customers find it useful to have a standard format by which the price and service offers of the carriers can be evaluated. Alternative procedures for organizing and communicating this information, however, have different significance for transactions and information costs. Even if motor carriers provided no interline service, the competitive consequences of alternative means of controlling the medium and establishing the format for setting prices and defining alternative standards of service must be considered. While the concerns of customers over compatibility of technology in other industries are obvious (e.g., Beta versus VHS formats for video cassette recorders), recent experience in the use of computer reservation systems in the airline industry has raised serious antitrust questions (including litigation) regarding the flow of price and service information when the medium is controlled by a carrier. The control over the flow of information to customers and the determination of these standards can be a substantial competitive advantage.

In practice, the same dimensions of price and service coordination are at issue for (1) joint venture, (2) joint tariff, and (3) carrier/shipper communication problems.[174] The joint-line service and tariff problem is deserving of separate and extensive treatment, however, because the high degree of required coordination to provide joint-line services in trucking raises the most obvious problems of applying antitrust laws. The next chapter therefore focuses primarily on the special antitrust problems that arise from attempting to apply the antitrust laws to single-line services while encouraging cooperation for joint-line services. Chapter 5 puts the pricing problem more generally into the context of the carrier/shipper communication problem.

BENEFITS OF A SYSTEM OF MULTILATERAL TRAFFIC INTERCHANGE IN THE TRUCKING INDUSTRY

The motor carrier industry has developed into a national system in which there is a relatively high level of cooperation among carriers in providing interline service via joint rates and through routes. Industry critics at one time alleged that the high level of traffic interchange was an undesirable consequence of regulatory restrictions on operating authority.[175] Interlining has indeed receded as a result of the elimination of meaningful operating authority restrictions by the ICC. In fact, use of interlining may be less than justified by efficiency considerations alone. Because of the antitrust concerns raised by providing joint-line service without immunity for single-line rates—addressed in detail below—carriers in today's regulatory environment have strong incentives to avoid interlining. However, it is also clear that economic efficiency will undoubtedly call for a residual amount of interlining unless deterred by antitrust concerns. Whatever interlining remains is undoubtedly the result of the economic efficiencies derived from joint-line service—what was called "convenience interlining" under the regime of strict regulation. The antitrust issue is to ensure that cooperation to achieve economically efficient interline service is not unnecessarily deterred by fear of antitrust prosecution and that the transactions cost of the necessary cooperation be minimized.

The magnitude of the present interlining problem may be grasped by reference to data on the volume of interlining in the motor carrier industry today. The Continuous Traffic Study (CTS) performed by each of the rate bureaus is a useful place to start identifying the amount of interlined traffic that would raise potential antitrust problems.

Tables 19 through 28 show CTS data on interline traffic from the major rate bureaus. Table 29 shows inclusive data of the 10 major rate bureaus, but is not as current. Overall, the data indicate that interline traffic is significant and is more prevalent among LTL than TL traffic. Class-rated traffic moves more often in interline service than commodity-rated traffic. Some traffic even moves over more than two carriers' systems.[176] The data indicate that interline traffic is declining, but it is not clear how much of this trend is explained by carriers' decisions that single-line

Table 19
Middle Atlantic Conference Interline Freight (Percentage)

Calendar Year	Total Traffic			Class Traffic			Commodity Traffic		
	Shipment	Billed Weight	Through Revenue	Shipment	Billed Weight	Through Revenue	Shipment	Billed Weight	Through Revenue
1978	21.1	14.9	19.3	22.4	17.8	21.2	9.9	11.2	13.0
1979	21.2	14.9	19.3	22.7	17.7	21.3	9.1	11.4	13.0
1980	18.0	13.4	17.2	19.0	15.8	18.8	9.1	10.1	11.7
1981	16.9	12.9	16.3	17.7	13.7	17.1	9.3	11.5	13.4
1982	17.1	12.8	16.4	18.2	14.0	17.6	8.4	10.7	11.5
1983	15.0	12.2	15.6	16.3	13.4	16.9	6.7	9.6	9.8
1984	13.6	10.6	14.0	14.6	11.6	15.0	5.3	7.1	7.9

Source: Middle Atlantic Conference.

Table 20
Eastern Central Motor Carriers Interline Freight

	YEAR	SHIPMENTS	BILLED WEIGHT	THROUGH REVENUE
TRAFFIC	1978	30.9	18.5	26.2
CLASS TRAFFIC	1978	31.3	24.4	23.8
COMMODITY TRAFFIC	1978	7.5	6.1	6.1
TRAFFIC	1979	29.2	16.7	18.9
CLASS TRAFFIC	1979	29.6	22.5	21.8
COMMODITY TRAFFIC	1979	6.9	4.6	4.8
TRAFFIC	1980	27.9	16.7	18.1
CLASS TRAFFIC	1980	28.4	22.2	20.7
COMMODITY TRAFFIC	1980	5.2	4.2	3.8
TRAFFIC	1981	25.5	15.3	16.9
CLASS TRAFFIC	1981	25.8	19.5	18.7
COMMODITY TRAFFIC	1981	6.8	2.5	2.8
TRAFFIC	1982	22.8	14.5	18.5
CLASS TRAFFIC	1982	23.0	17.4	16.8
COMMODITY TRAFFIC	1982	5.3	2.5	2.9
TRAFFIC	1983	18.5	12.3	13.5
CLASS TRAFFIC	1983	18.7	14.1	14.2
COMMODITY TRAFFIC	1983	4.4	1.9	2.9
TRAFFIC	1984	17.3	12.7	13.8
CLASS TRAFFIC	1984	17.3	13.7	14.2
COMMODITY TRAFFIC	1984	6.6	2.3	

Source: Eastern Central Motor Carriers Association.

Table 21
Eastern Central Traffic Distribution (Percentage of Shipments)

TYPE OF HANDLING	1969	1970	1971	1972	1973	1974	1975	1976
Single-Line	55.8	59.4	60.5	61.3	62.2	61.8	63.2	62.1
Joint-Line Originated	22.4	20.6	20.6	20.3	19.8	20.1	19.5	19.9
Joint-Line Terminated	18.3	17.8	17.2	16.9	16.6	16.8	16.0	16.3
Joint-Line Bridged	3.5	2.2	1.7	1.5	1.4	1.3	1.3	1.7
TOTAL	100.0	100.0	100.0	100.0	100.0	100.0	100.0	100.0

TYPE OF HANDLING	1977	1978	1979	1980	1981	1982	1983	1984
Single-Line	65.6	68.9	71.2	73.0	75.0	78.6	81.7	82.8
Joint-Lined Originated	18.3	16.3	15.0	13.4	12.5	11.7	10.1	9.0
Joint-Line Terminated	15.0	13.9	12.8	12.7	11.6	9.1	7.7	7.6
Joint-Line Bridged	1.1	.9	1.0	.9	.9	.6	.5	.6
TOTAL	100.0	100.0	100.0	100.0	100.0	100.0	100.0	100.0

Source: Eastern Central Motors Carriers Association.

Table 22
New England Motor Rate Bureau Traffic Distribution (Percentage of Shipments)

Type of Handling	1980	1981	1982	1983	1984
Single-Line	87.4	91.6	90.2	91.3	91.6
Joint-Line Originated	6.8	4.3	5.4	5.8	5.3
Joint-Line Terminated	5.7	4.0	4.3	2.8	2.9
Joint-Line Bridged	.1	.1	.1	.1	.2
TOTAL	100.0	100.0	100.0	100.0	100.0

Source: New England Motor Rate Bureau, Continuous Traffic Study: 1980 through 1984.

Table 23
Southern Motor Carriers Rate Conference Traffic Distribution (Percentage of Shipments)

TYPE OF HANDLING	1978	1979	1980	1981	1982	1983	1984
SINGLE-LINE	64.8	66.9	68.4	74.0	77.1	80.1	81.8
JOINT-LINE ORIGINATED	16.8	16.5	15.0	12.9	11.2	10.0	9.4
JOINT-LINE TERMINATED	17.1	15.4	15.4	12.1	11.0	9.3	8.2
JOINT-LINE BRIDGED	1.3	1.2	1.2	1.0	.7	.6	.6
TOTAL	100.0	100.0	100.0	100.0	100.0	100.0	100.0

Source: Motor Carriers Rate Conference, Inc., SMCRC Traffic Analysis Reports: 1984 Composite (Atlanta, Georgia: SMCRC, 12 September 1985).

Table 24
Rocky Mountain Tariff Distribution (Percentage of Shipments)

Type of Handling	1978	1979	1980	1981	1982	1983	1984
Single-Line	61.5	64.4	67.9	70.0	75.4	73.4	75.3
Joint-Line Originated	17.7	16.4	15.0	15.1	13.2	14.6	13.5
Joint-Line Terminated	17.8	16.5	14.9	12.9	10.1	10.7	10.0
Joint-Line Bridged	3.0	2.7	2.2	2.0	1.3	1.3	1.2
TOTAL	100.0	100.0	100.0	100.0	100.0	100.0	100.0

Source: Rocky Mountain Motor Tariff Bureau.

79

Table 25
Rocky Mountain Bureau Interline Freight (1984 Percentage)

	Shipment	Billed Weight	Revenue (Through)
Total RMB	24.7	20.3	23.7
Class Traffic	24.9	21.2	24.2
Commodity Traffic	15.5	10.0	12.6

Source: Rocky Mountain Motor Tariff Bureau.

Table 26
Niagara Frontier Tariff Bureau Percentage of Traffic Moving Joint-Line
(Revenue)

YEAR	CLASS	COMMODITY	TOTAL
1978	90	83	86
1979	90	81	85
1980	88	76	82
1981	88	76	82
1982	88	71	81
1983	78	63	71
1984	73	55	66
1985*	72	53	66

*Preliminary.
Source: Niagara Frontier Tariff Bureau.

service is more efficient and by the substantial increase in the geographic scope of carrier operations in response to regulatory reform. Some is undoubtedly explained by the fear of antitrust prosecution after the restrictions on single-line collective ratemaking and the uncertainty over the future of collective ratemaking itself. Carriers may simply be hedging their bets by deciding to pursue operating strategies that do not rely on joint-line service regardless of immediate effects on efficiency because of the uncertain legal future of interlining.

Table 27
Niagara Frontier Tariff Bureau Percentage of Traffic Moving Single-Line
(Shipments)

YEAR	LTL	TL	TOTAL
1978	91	71	85
1979	91	68	84
1980	87	63	83
1981	86	58	82
1982	87	54	81
1983	76	45	71
1984	71	40	65
1985*	70	37	65

*Preliminary.
Source: Niagara Frontier Tariff Bureau.

Economic efficiency is the sole rationale for the interlining that remains after carriers have rationalized their routes in response to their new freedoms under regulatory reform. Interlining permits a carrier to provide nationwide coverage of service without sacrificing the benefits of regional specialization. Even where the originating or terminating carrier could or does provide service in the geographic area of the connecting carrier, consolidation of pickup and delivery or "pooling" on an *ad hoc* basis can also be a benefit in reduced operating expenses.

The shipper also benefits from interlining because it increases shipper routing options. In addition, a shipper may prefer to concentrate dealings with only a few origin or destination carriers to minimize dock congestion and transactions costs or to maximize bargaining leverage. The same may be true in the case of receivers wanting a few delivering carriers.

Interlining and carrier specialization also substantially reduce the minimum scale for entry into the trucking industry. A regional carrier can succeed despite the incompleteness of service and the network advantages that would otherwise accrue to the large nationwide systems. Anything that raises the transactions costs of interlining (antitrust enforcement in particular) will be a serious competitive disadvantage to smaller, geographically specialized carriers.

Table 28
Central States Interline Freight (Percentage)

Calendar Year	Total Traffic			Class and Exception Traffic			Commodity Traffic		
	Shipment	Billed Weight	Through Revenue	Shipment	Billed Weight	Through Revenue	Shipment	Billed Weight	Through Revenue
1978	25.2	11.8	14.5	27.5	22.0	19.4	4.0	2.9	3.0
1979	22.7	10.4	13.0	24.6	19.5	17.1	3.7	2.2	2.3
1980	20.2	9.8	12.5	21.7	17.6	15.7	3.6	1.8	2.0
1981	16.8	7.4	10.9	18.5	14.7	14.2	2.6	1.4	1.8
1982	14.7	5.8	9.1	16.1	11.4	11.6	3.0	0.8	1.2
1983	10.9	5.1	7.5	11.8	9.3	9.4	1.4	0.6	0.8
1984	9.6	4.0	6.3	10.2	7.4	7.8	2.1	0.3	0.8

Source: Central States Motor Freight Bureau.

Table 29

Aggregate Traffic Distribution for Major Rate Bureaus (1976 and 1980)

Distribution of	Shipments		Actual Weight		Through Revenue		Through Mills	
	1976	1980	1976	1980	1976	1980	1976	1980
Single-Line	69.8	78.0	80.8	86.3	71.0	79.6	59.2	72.3
Joint-Line	30.2	22.0	19.2	13.7	29.0	20.4	40.8	27.7
Interstate	94.2	94.0	95.4	94.8	97.6	97.6	98.8	
Interstate	5.8	6.0	4.6	5.2	2.4	2.5	1.2	
LTL	96.4	96.9	40.6	47.1	69.6	73.1	97.2	
TL	3.6	3.1	59.4	52.9	30.4	26.9	2.8	

Data are from the 10 major tariff agencies plus independently filed tariffs appearing in the CTS.

Source: Russell C. Cherry and Leslie K. Meyer, "A Comparison of Descriptive Statistics for the 1976 and 1980 Continuous Traffic Study," presented to the Motor Carrier Ratemaking Study Commission (no date).

EFFECT OF THE LOSS OF COLLECTIVE RATEMAKING ON JOINT-LINE SERVICE: USE OF BILATERAL AGREEMENTS AND INCREASED TRANSACTIONS COSTS

For traffic to move in interline service, there must be an explicit agreement among the carriers, sometimes as many as three. Unlike an airline passenger, who can simply walk from one part of a terminal to another to become an interline passenger, joint-line traffic in the motor carrier industry requires a number of formal, prearranged agreements for traffic to move interline (as do joint ticketing and baggage interchange for airlines). Carriers must agree on a through route over a specified junction, or interchange point. These are specified in routing guides (i.e., tariffs that specify carrier interconnections). Ordinarily, the carriers must also specify tariff rules, packaging, and terms of contract—most importantly a joint rate, which is a single charge to be divided among the carriers according to a prespecified divisions agreement among the carriers.[177] Without such a joint-rate agreement, the charges would be determined by a combination of local rates. As a practical matter, absence of a joint rate often has the effect of "commercially closing" the junction because a single-line carrier's route in the tariff would thereby enjoy a lower rate.

It is sometimes said that the problem of interlining for motor carriers is just another example of joint ventures among competitors, some of which are fully integrated and some of which are not. This assertion ignores the fact that trucking is unique in the number of competitors who must join together on a day-to-day basis to offer an integrated nationwide service on a common carrier basis. Major transcontinental carriers have interline agreements with literally thousands of other carriers. Every shipper in the nation can tender traffic to any point in the United States on the basis of agreed-upon common tariff provisions applied to joint-line service.

If the ability to provide nationwide service is a desirable competitive advantage for local and short-haul carriers (and conversely if there is an efficiency advantage for long-haul carriers to tender the traffic to a short-haul or local carrier), and if a system of open interconnections among carriers is considered a desirable feature of the marketplace, then it becomes desirable to have a benchmark rate structure to tie the system together. Efficient provision of integrated nationwide service must start with a common set of price and service standards established by collective action by the carriers, which can be departed from in bilateral agreements as need dictates. It would be grossly inefficient to have a separate rate for every bilateral agreement applying to every origin and destination and every commodity. A great deal of averaging and simplification must be accomplished, and this is where the benchmark rate structure provides a useful purpose.

Collective ratemaking institutions have vastly simplified arrangements for negotiating interline agreements and facilitating interline shipments among motor carriers. Standardized procedures, rates and classification, equipment interchange and other terms of service, revenue divisions, and interline settlements reduce substantially the burden of negotiating interline agreements. Data provided by the Motor Carrier Ratemaking Study Commission showed that 94 percent of all joint-line traffic in 1980 moved under the collectively established class-rate system (subject now to possible discounts, of course).[178] Collective ratemaking provides a benchmark rate and tariff system which can be usefully employed as a fallback set of standards governing interline service on a multilateral basis. While certain elements of the interline arrangements are handled through multilateral tariffs established through rate bureaus, carriers are perfectly free to negotiate their own bilateral agreements on whatever terms are mutually agreeable.

Consider only the classification problem, and remember that the co-ordination problem actually involves thousands of carriers each inter-lining with one another. It is difficult to believe that with the loss of antitrust immunity for classification and joint-line rates, a list of carriers occupying 110 pages of fine print in the *National Motor Freight Classification* would act under the direction of an "Invisible Hand" to establish a consistent set of classifications, points, rates, and tariff rules for joint-line rates. Yet true diversity of joint-line classifications, rates, tariff rules, and so forth, resulting from bilateral negotiations, would result in a tariff structure for joint-line traffic of truly staggering complexity. Rates and classification would vary from one agreement to another in ways that would make rating a freight bill extremely difficult. But developing a benchmark rate structure might be construed in an antitrust proceeding as evidence of the very collusion and parallel behavior that prohibition of collective ratemaking for joint-line rates was designed to prevent.

To see why the loss of antitrust immunity would militate against a benchmark rate structure for interline traffic with a resulting adverse effect on transactions costs, we do not have to rely on the statements of concern by legal experts and trucking executives. We need go no further than the statements of opponents of collective ratemaking for predictions (or even yearnings) that joint-line ratemaking would and should be ended. For example, statements by the Department of Justice and the Federal Trade Commission give the carrier no comfort.[179] The FTC's statement on the issue[180] concedes that the result of the loss of immunity for single-line rates may well be the elimination of collective ratemaking of joint rates.

Critics consider the very existence of a nationwide integrated system for interline traffic as a sign of collusion and suppressed competition. They want "pricing diversity" and competition among carriers on the basis of their service offerings, including the particular advantages of a carrier's individualized classification system.[181] True diversity of this sort would substantially raise the transactions costs of negotiating joint-line rates and integration of service on through routes.[182]

The objective of ending antitrust immunity for collective ratemaking for interline traffic is to force bilateral agreements to assume the burden of negotiating the business arrangements now handled collectively.[183] The most immediate result would be a substantial increase in the transactions costs of such service.[184] If the result of these thousands of bilateral negotiations was the competitive diversity of pricing and service options desired by its proponents, the results on shippers and carriers can only be imagined. Carriers and shippers would constantly be disputing the inconsistencies among carriers in the tariff provisions, rules, classifications, and other aspects.

Depriving carriers of the availability of a collectively established standard as the basis for joint-line traffic is designed to force this traffic to move under a plethora of bilaterally negotiated tariffs. Negotiating these tariffs and establishing the appropriate rate would increase the transactions cost of interline service considerably—a consequence carriers would be highly motivated to avoid. Five means have been suggested to minimize the high transactions costs of bilateral agreements to establish joint rates and through routes: (1) publication of a benchmark rate structure without immunity, (2) use of combination or proportional rates, (3) ossification of the benchmark rate structure, (4) mergers and the domination of ratemaking by the large long-haul carriers, and (5) confining the antitrust immunity to joint-line rates only.

Each of these will be examined, but the results are readily summarized. If the data on rate competition in the previous chapter are found to be compelling, the answer is not to force the trucking industry to adopt one of these alternatives. As long as the industry is highly competitive, there is no benefit to be gained by imposing the tax of antitrust deterrent to collective ratemaking for joint-line traffic. Simply let the market decide.

PROPOSED SOLUTIONS TO THE PROBLEM

Publication of a benchmark rate structure without immunity

Critics sometimes argue that motor carrier rate bureaus or shipper associations could continue to publish standard or average rate tariffs based on average carrier costs without an explicit antitrust immunity.[185]

Other critics argue that, on the contrary, such activities are a *per se* antitrust offense and inhibit competition.

The overwhelming view of expert legal opinion[186] contradicts the assertion that "one national, or regional tariff may evolve"[187] for joint-line ratemaking without antitrust immunity. If it did, it would almost certainly result in investigations by the Department of Justice and possible prosecutions.[188] It would also defeat the whole purpose of opponents in advocating the abolition of collective ratemaking. If these "'standard' tariffs (or tariff, as one national, or regional, tariff may evolve) will form a ceiling to rates" and "*very* small shippers may pay these rates,"[189] how is that better than the present situation? The whole case for abolishing collective ratemaking was designed to put a stop to the establishment of a benchmark rate structure and to encourage ratemaking diversity. If nothing is really going to improve, it is unclear why collective ratemaking should be abolished. Proponents of this approach provide no estimates of benefits to the public and make no claims that are in any way an improvement over the present situation. This proposal is obviously the least credible solution to the problem.

The argument that carriers and others could continue to do what they are now doing in establishing a benchmark rate structure without antitrust immunity contradicts the clarity of the *per se* rule.[190] The proposals to have it both ways by allowing "reasonable" agreements on price, absent the antitrust immunity, simply fly in the face of a well-established *per se* doctrine on price fixing to the contrary. If price fixing is to be made a *per se* criminal offense, there should be a "bright line" between right and wrong.

Use of combination or proportional rates

Opponents of collective ratemaking for joint-line rates have often suggested that the joint-line pricing problem could be solved by abandoning joint rates and instead adopting a system of "combination" or "proportional" rates unilaterally established by each participating carrier.[191] These rates would apply only to each carrier's portion of the movement, and each would separately bill the customer. This assertion shows a lack of understanding of the competitive problem for joint-line traffic. To make the local rate or division competitive with a single-line movement, the carrier needs to know (1) the connecting carrier's unilaterally established proportional rate, and (2) the competing single-line rate. These vary from shipment to shipment, depending on the commodity and its origin. There is no one rate that works for every shipment.[192] Carriers must negotiate to establish the procedures by which the revenue "dilution" arising from the difference between the competitive joint-line rate and the sum of local rates will be absorbed. Of course, the present system solves these problems automatically by equating joint- and single-line rates, by applying a common set of tariff structures and rules, and by applying revenue division formulas agreed to in advance by the carriers.

A joint rate and through route by definition involve an explicit written agreement between the involved carriers on every element of the terms of service and price offered to the shipper; whereas a combination rate involves little agreement on anything. Under combination or proportional rates and routes, shippers would also have to deal with every carrier involved in the move and resolve any disputes and discrepancies among them.

The proposal to apply combination or proportional rates thus in reality amounts to a decision to make the joint-line service so unattractive to shippers and carriers that there will be substantially reduced interest in it. It is simply a means of imposing sufficient costs on joint-line traffic such that it is likely to be abandoned in favor of the remaining suggestions discussed below.

Ossification of the benchmark rate structure

Arguments supporting the end of collective ratemaking often forget that the law does not require that existing collective tariffs be expunged. The ban would apply only to new ratemaking initiatives, and all rates and tariff conditions already in effect would continue to exist. The effect would be to freeze the collective rate system in effect at the time of the proposed ban, and it could be changed only through individual action.

Under the proposed ossification solution, "many carriers will use the last collectively-set tariff as a benchmark adjusting their rates around an index of the collectively-set rates."[193] Since carriers are doing this anyway today, it is little wonder that supporters of this solution to the joint-line ratemaking problem conclude that "elimination of antitrust immunity for *all* collective ratemaking will probably have only a limited effect on the way in which rates are negotiated and published."[194] But proponents of the ossification solution make no effort to argue that the result is more efficient or more price competitive.

Virtually all tariff filings, to a greater or lesser degree, represent a supplement to the existing rate structure, leaving in place all other unchanged components. A new tariff usually references other tariffs and their future supplements rather than reproduces all unchanged provisions en masse. Consequently, ossification of the benchmark rate structure merely prohibits collectively changing the past results of collective ratemaking, but not continued use of the last collectively set tariff. The opponents who have criticized the present classification system, for example, would find it forever etched in stone, incapable of being changed because no carrier could act unilaterally without the concurrence of all connecting carriers for joint-line traffic, nationwide.

The obvious incentive in the face of the loss of antitrust immunity is for carriers to leave the existing tariffs in place rather than raise all the antitrust problems. In fact, we have a historical example of this. Obsolescence and ossification were the result in Arizona after collective ratemaking by motor carriers ended. The ban "effectively froze the previously ordered rate base system because the carriers could not collectively seek to alter the system."[195]

The down side to the ossification scenario is that the predictions from the original case for abolishing collective ratemaking are realized—an even greater Balkanization of the rate structure, tariff rules, classification, and so on, and the loss of a national system of interchangeable service under joint-line rates. The best that can happen is that everybody will be inundated with tariffs and the system will struggle along, albeit with an ossified tariff structure and much higher transactions costs on a bilateral basis rather than the present multilateral system.

Nobody would support such an outcome. It would be the worst of all possible worlds, since the opponents of collective ratemaking would have failed to destroy the present benchmark rate structure, and the ICC, carriers, shippers, and critics of the collective ratemaking system would be powerless to change it. The usefulness of the ossified collective rate structure as a benchmark would slowly degrade over time as it became more and more obsolete.

Carriers' antitrust problems are by no means solved under the ossification scenario. Suppose a carrier independently uses the last collectively set tariff as a benchmark for the bilateral negotiations. If it conforms to the industry pricing, tariff rules, and classification standards prior to the loss of collective ratemaking by using the last collectively set tariff as a benchmark, it exposes itself to indictment on an antitrust charge that the industry is sticking together to continue to fix prices and terms of service.[196] Indeed, in this scenario it is doing much the same as it is doing now, but without the immunity. But the result does not produce the diversity of competing rate structures desired by the opponents of collective ratemaking. Yet if every carrier truly goes its own way in setting rates, classifications, and tariff rules, carriers will watch the demise of the joint-rate system.

The ossification scenario presents a paradox for policy. The proposed ban on collective ratemaking only for single-line rates will turn out to be either

1. Pointless because it is redundant and ineffective in promoting more price competition because of continued effective use of the benchmark rate structure for joint-line rates; or

2. Destructive of the desired effective use of the ossified rate structure to minimize transaction costs of joint-line ratemaking, because it automatically exposes the carriers to unacceptable risks of antitrust enforcement.

Use of an ossified rate structure from a prior regulatory regime as the
benchmark for a competitive pricing system works best when the benchmark pricing structure is relatively simple. The inland barge industry is
a particularly interesting case in point. Offering prices are expressed in
reference to a standard rate level, in this case "Tariff No. 7," which had
been published by the water carrier rate bureau.[197] The loss of antitrust
immunity means that the benchmark rate level itself is "cast in stone,"[198]
preventing the reference point from responding to economic forces. This,
of course, eliminates any transactions cost savings by relying on a benchmark standard of price and service. The individual shipping contracts
traded on the floor of the exchange still require negotiation of 17 items.
Because there are strong incentives for many carriers not to participate,[199]
numerous concerns have been raised that the benchmark rate level as
reflected by reported discounts from the reference point price level was
not the product of an efficient market structure.[200] Nevertheless, in the
circumstances of the barge industry, it seems to work well enough.

If the evidence from Chapter 3 on regular bureau dockets is indicative,
the ossification of the collective rate structure has already begun in the
motor carrier industry. As opponents of the restrictions on single-line
collective ratemaking had predicted, use of the collective ratemaking
process has declined as carriers fear to use their residual rights and as
they take steps to minimize their dependence on the collective ratemaking process.

The transition period after regulatory reform is hardly a propitious
time for ossifying the collective rate structure. If the results of collective
ratemaking were distorted by regulation as critics claim, then the benchmark rate structure should be given the opportunity to respond to the
new competitive forces. Rate bureau meetings have been the scene of
numerous disputes over pricing philosophy by the carriers. It is difficult
to understand how an ossified benchmark rate structure is an improvement over one which is given the opportunity to evolve to meet
competition.

Industry consolidation and domination of the pricing function by the large carriers

If every carrier negotiated on a truly independent and bilateral basis
with every other carrier for the movement of joint-line traffic, the result
would be a stupendous number of contract terms under which freight

would move on a joint-line basis. The diversity that resulted would be intolerable, and the primary candidates to straighten out the problem would be the relatively few nationwide long-haul carriers. The coordinating function might move from the bureaus to the corporate headquarters of the nation's largest motor carriers. According to this scenario, these carriers would establish nationwide tariffs and industry standards, and the short-haul carriers would simply negotiate a share of the divisions. By the same token, incentives to merge to eliminate the need for joint-line service would be created by the advantages conferred on firms that could provide extensive single-line service without exposure to antitrust claims.[201]

This proposal is essentially to allow the standardization function to be performed by dominant carriers rather than rate bureaus. If carriers were required to continue to publish tariffs, the dominant carriers' rate structures would clearly become prime candidates for the benchmark as industry concentration progressed and the ossified collective rate structure became more and more obsolete. From a practical point of view, *a priori* concurrence in a competitor's pricing decisions has dubious legal standing, and exchange of price information among competitors is likewise doubtful in its legalities. Even apart from the dangers that this power will be abused is the likelihood that the end result will be an oligopoly of large nationwide carriers and their local agents who do not interchange traffic. Lost would be both the efficiencies of firm specialization and interlining as well as the vigorous competition of an unconcentrated market.

If there is a useful purpose to be served by a benchmark rate structure, clearly something will emerge to serve the function. The real policy question is which system will best promote competition on equal terms and efficiency—a multilateral one or one established by the largest carriers. But a decision need not be forced. If the larger carriers can more efficiently serve the coordination function of rate bureaus, they are certainly free to do so under a system which simply permits collective ratemaking as an option.

All available evidence suggests that the problem of increased transactions costs on joint-line traffic arising from the loss of antitrust immunity will be solved by a combined process of ossification, industry consolidation, and reliance on individual carrier tariffs. A few carriers who do not rely strongly on rate bureaus to minimize such costs are already questioning their usefulness. If present trends toward increased market concentration should continue, it is only a matter of time before the motor carrier industry develops into a more concentrated oligopoly of carriers, each of which engage in limited traffic interchange and only with its agents whose ability to interline with competitors is severely restricted. This threat to the highly competitive market structure of truck-ing means that the preservation of joint-line service depends on the success of the next and final solution which has been proposed.

Confine the immunity to joint-line rates only

Recognizing the desirability of establishing a multilateral system for traffic interchange on a nationwide basis, yet desiring to encourage in-novation and competition for single-line traffic where such coordination is presumed not to be needed, some critics of collective ratemaking frequently suggest that the answer is to prohibit collective ratemaking for single-line rates but allow it for joint-line rates. Proponents of the ban seem to agree that antitrust immunity is desirable for certain bureau activities, such as joint-line rates, general rate increases, and broad tariff changes but concluded that single-line ratemaking is properly the do-main of individual carrier judgments. Since the rates they charge for on-line traffic are their own business, why not ban any collective discussion of these rates?

Using this logic, the Motor Carrier Act of 1980 provided that collective ratemaking for single-line ratemaking would end in 1984, subject to certain significant exceptions.[202] While at first blush this appears to be a reasonable compromise, it immediately runs into substantial practical and legal difficulties.

The rationale for constructing a Chinese Wall between single-line and joint-line ratemaking is contained in the Senate commerce committee report:

The Committee has voted to implement a number of procedural reforms in the rate bureau process and, over a period of 3 years, phase out antitrust immunity for discussion or voting upon single-line rates. The Committee is aware of the fact that this will result in a significant change in the way that motor carriers price their services. It will mean that consideration of single-line and joint-line rates must be done separately. It will put a greater burden upon individual carriers to determine their own cost structures and the most optimum rates from their individual company point of view to offer the shipping public. But on balance, the Committee believes that there will be public benefits that greatly outweigh the burdens of changing to a new system—namely, more competitive pricing.[203]

Prior to the 30 June 1984 date for implementing the restrictions on single-line collective ratemaking, supporters of collective ratemaking predicted that the effect would be chilling on all collective ratemaking as well. Data on collective ratemaking activity since that date (see Chap-ter 3) confirm these predictions.

The chilling effect arises from the fact that neither motor carrier operations nor efficient construction of tariffs disaggregates into geographic and product markets that can be neatly labeled as characterized by cooperation and competition. Joint-line and single-line rates and service compete directly in the same marketplace. The fact that a carrier offers both services in a market could pose grave antitrust problems for that carrier should it use the benchmark rate structure for pricing joint-line traffic and there were no antitrust immunity for single-line ratemaking.[204] Statements by law enforcement officials either neglect this problem or propose that joint-line rates be offered only by carriers whose service territories connect on an end-to-end basis.

These suggestions are not very helpful because few pairs of carriers find themselves only offering end-to-end, complementary services. Where carriers also compete directly, the construction of bilateral joint-line tariffs that applied only to end-to-end movements would be an administrative nightmare and would probably not insulate them from antitrust exposure anyway. The end-to-end doctrine would mean the end of simplified broad tariffs and the construction of point-to-point atomized pricing for interline traffic. Because these issues illustrate so starkly the difficulty of compartmentalizing cooperative and competitive sectors and fashioning separate antitrust policies for each, they will be addressed in detail.

THE JOINT-VENTURE ANTITRUST PROBLEM IN THE MOTOR CARRIER INDUSTRY

Pricing of the joint-line service invariably requires coordinated decisions among the carriers. This required coordination has antitrust implications because of the way motor carriers structure both their operations and tariffs. From an operational point of view, one or both of the carriers may be providing single-line services in the same point-to-point markets covered by a broadly applicable tariff for joint rates. The joint-line rate agreement inherently raises questions of potential collusion in the price offers for the single-line service, since the former cannot be discussed and established without effectively setting a ceiling price for the latter.

Failing the construction of a Chinese Wall operationally, it is suggested that the same result be accomplished via narrowly constructed bilateral joint-line tariffs. Carriers would choose to offer either single-line or joint-line service in a particular market, and tariffs would be constructed so that they did not overlap both kinds of markets. If trucking tariffs could be highly disaggregated (i.e., published on a point-to-point, commodity-by-commodity basis), individual commodities and routes could be distinguished, and the problem could perhaps be solved by segregating tariffs in a way to solve the problem.

However, this proposed solution solves the antitrust problem only by eliminating the efficiencies of a multilaterally established, broadly applicable reference price system for joint-line traffic. The class-rate system is the fallback rate paid when a competitively established, specific rate does not exist. It applies to any traffic and is applicable to broad geographic regions. It simply is not efficient to sculpture tariffs for joint-line traffic on a bilateral basis to narrow point-to-point applications designed to minimize exposure to individual carriers' antitrust concerns.

Even if it were possible operationally to segregate single-line markets and joint-line markets for any two carriers, class rates simultaneously apply for literally hundreds of carriers participating in each rate bureau. The result is a standard multilateral agreement applying to hundreds of carriers involving thousands of bilateral traffic interchange possibilities over billions of combinations of origins and destinations with application to large geographic areas and comprehensive in its included traffic. For each of the pairs of carriers, offering joint-line services to craft special tariffs applying only to each particular bilateral agreement would destroy the simplicity of a common reference price for joint-line traffic. The difficulty of insulating the individual carrier's single-line price and service offerings from the influence of such a multilateral agreement—more precisely, insulating them from the appearance of an undue influence—should be obvious.

Antitrust problems arising from competition among single-line and joint-line rates

These problems can be illustrated by means of hypothetical examples. Assume carrier A has single-line authority between the two points where carriers A and B also provide interline service. Should antitrust immunity be removed for the single-line routing, carrier A would have a problem.

The problem arises in part because of the "distance taper" inherent in the costing determinants of most transportation rates. The rate (cost) per unit of weight declines as a function of distance: Thus two unrelated single-line rates combined for the connecting carriers will ordinarily be more than the comparable single-line rate. Open routing under the class-rate system is designed to keep the joint rates competitive with single-line rates by avoiding the use of combination rates.

One choice for A would be to continue the joint-line ratemaking relationship under the antitrust immunity for joint-line rates only via a bilateral agreement. Suppose A used this immunity to agree with B on a rate increase for the interline traffic. Although the single-line rate is never mentioned, it is clear to B that A intends to raise his single-line rate. Otherwise, B has been lured into an agreement to raise joint-line rates that will price it out of the market and will deprive it of the interline traffic. Has A violated the antitrust laws?

The other alternative for A is to simply cancel the interline agreement with B. After all, why bother to run the antitrust risk of interlining when A already has on-line service? Suppose A cancels the agreement and B goes bankrupt or suffers economic hardship because of the loss of traffic. Does B now have a claim for damages under the antitrust laws for predatory behavior in the form of a "vertical foreclosure" of a nonintegrated competitor?

In actual practice, the problem will become even more complex. We have assumed that the relevant market for antitrust purposes is service between the two points. Suppose interline service only is provided between the two points, but A and B also provide single-line service to other points that are competing sources of supply to the particular movement.

The antitrust paradox is the difficulty if not impossibility of granting full antitrust immunity to a competitor which offers joint-line service while applying the full force of the antitrust laws to that same competitor when offering a substitute service in the very same market.[205] This relationship of collective joint-line ratemaking to single-line ratemaking is undoubtedly the most difficult and least understood issue of applying the antitrust laws to transportation ratemaking. A classic Catch–22 problem faces carriers who attempt to negotiate interline agreements in an environment where there is no antitrust immunity for single-line ratemaking. A refusal to agree on a joint rate may be construed as a vertical foreclosure of competition by a nonintegrated producer designed to eliminate that competitor,[206] while an agreement to interline invariably involves price-sensitive discussions with an actual or potential competitor.

Position of law enforcement authorities: The end-to-end doctrine

Statements by antitrust enforcement agencies such as the Department of Justice and the Federal Trade Commission do not give the carriers much comfort. They only amount to a statement that there is no problem as long as you assume it away. Statements by the DOJ on the problem of the carriers' antitrust liability start out by seeking to trivialize the problem, but there is always a disturbing caveat at the end:

Nothing in the antitrust laws prohibits motor carriers from establishing joint-line rates *so long as such rates are devised in good faith and are not intended as a guise for colluding on rates for competing services* [footnote omitted]. Finally, the antitrust laws do not proscribe establishment of standard systems for classifying freight according to its transportation characteristics *so long as such systems are not used as facilitating devices to restrain competition* [footnote omitted].

While joint-line rates are important and even vital to the operations of the trucking industry, the establishment of such rates *does not ordinarily require antitrust immunity*. When two carriers that do not provide competing services, but *only connect end-to-end*, establish joint-line rates, there is no antitrust problem because there is no way in which such a joint rate could curtail competition between the participating carriers. Likewise, even when carriers that offer competing single-line services between the same two points also establish a joint-line rate for service between those same points, there is no antitrust violation *so long as the carriers do not use that joint rate as a means for collusion in the establishment of their separate single-line rates* [emphasis added].[207]

During the first hearing of the Motor Carrier Ratemaking Study Commission, William Baxter of the Department of Justice was asked if there would be any possible antitrust problems if two carriers setting joint-line rates were also single-line competitors for that same traffic, and Baxter answered with an uncategorical "no."[208] This, however, is not the Department of Justice's long-standing position:

There are situations where two or more carriers with competing single-line routes between two points may also offer interline service between such points through the interchange of freight at some intermediate point. Under such circumstances, joint rate or division of revenue negotiations between carriers that are also single-line competitors *would and should present antitrust problems* [emphasis added].[209]

Indeed, Baxter's testimony before the Study Commission points to the inherent contradiction involved. On the one hand, he sought to assuage "carriers that are party to a joint-line rate agreement for transportation between two points [that] also provide single-line services at the same rates between the same two points" by pointing out that "recent amendments to the Interstate Commerce Act, however, have substantially eliminated the danger that a jury might find that a violation had occurred solely on the basis of such evidence." However, he opposed antitrust exemptions for joint-line collective ratemaking because "they severely curtail the Act's more general prohibition against fixing single-line rates."[210] One simply cannot have it both ways.

Any attempt to reconcile all these statements can only lead to the conclusion that the Department of Justice's position is that interlining should take place only between end-to-end carriers, and that carriers with single-line authority should not be interlining under joint rates with their actual or potential competitors. Convenience interlining, or interlining with direct competitors at the request of a shipper or consignee, should be discouraged or even prohibited.

Carriers with nationwide operating authority are particularly exposed to the problems arising from the DOJ end-to-end doctrine. Many carriers received nationwide authority under the Commission's permissive policies, in many cases authority they did not even want.

The Motor Carrier Ratemaking Study Commission concluded that interlining carriers do not compete with one another as a matter of operating policy. Citing data that showed that most interlining is between large and small carriers for a combined long-haul (large carrier) and short-haul (small carrier) movement, the Study Commission concluded that the problem is *de minimis*[211] because long-haul carriers do not interline much with long-haul carriers, and short-haul carriers do not interline much with short-haul carriers.

Even apart from whether such aggregate data can be used to make inferences about individual markets, the Study Commission made the crucial assumption that long-haul carriers do not compete with short-haul carriers because the long-haul carrier chose not to provide single-line service for certain movements. This is, of course, exactly the type of joint-line movements expected on efficiency grounds. But this is also precisely the case where the single-line service does or could compete with the joint-line service. Furthermore, even if interlining could be confined to carriers with no overlapping service, a decision to sign an interline agreement would, according to the Study Commission's theory, require the carriers to agree in advance not to compete in the future. That agreement would amount to a territorial restriction that could in itself raise antitrust objections.

Attempts to solve the problem by tariff segregation

The Study Commission's contention that carriers rarely interline with their direct competitors misses the point. Even if one major transcontinental carrier has interline agreements with a hundred short-haul carriers with nonoverlapping service, each of them in turn undoubtedly has agreements with numerous other carriers, who in turn have agreements with many more carriers. Any efficient nationwide system of interconnected service needs a benchmark rate structure to facilitate interconnection, even if direct competitors do not interchange traffic.

Proponents of the Chinese Wall theory always use the misleading example of rates between two points, which suggests that there is a one-to-one relationship between the tariff in question and the type of service (single or joint) being provided. The attempt to apply antitrust only to single-line rates ignores the reality of efficient broad tariff construction, which often calls for rate structures that use weight, distance, and length of haul to rate millions or even billions of combinations of points using one simplified rate structure.[212]

The Department of Justice's opposition to collective ratemaking for joint-line rates suggests that segregation of carriers' operations alone would not be sufficient to solve the antitrust problem. Carriers' participation in broad multilateral joint-line tariffs with broad application and in competition with their single-line service would also raise difficulties. Suppose, for example, the carrier served some combinations of points covered by a particular tariff with joint-line service and some combinations of points with direct service. Is that carrier prohibited from collectively discussing and participating in the entire joint-line tariff in a rate bureau on the grounds that some portion of it competes with its single-line traffic? Does the fact that the tariff establishes other carriers' joint-line rates which compete with his single-line service "infect" the ability to set joint-line rates for that portion of the tariff where it clearly provides only interline service? Suppose a carrier could conceivably participate in the joint-line traffic but as a practical matter only serves the traffic with single-line service today. Is the carrier eligible to discuss and vote on the proposed tariff? Would every carrier possessing single-line authority for some portion of that traffic have to flag out of those points in the joint-line tariff or only on those points where the single-line authority is not dormant?

Even if the carrier managed to figure out the necessary restrictions in its service offerings to comply with the end-to-end antitrust doctrine, it is not clear how the Chinese Wall could be built in the collective tariff structure. Few broad tariffs could be constructed so that they apply only to every participating carrier's existing or potential joint-line traffic without also competing with single-line traffic.

The DOJ's proposal encounters enormous practical difficulties even in bilateral negotiations between carriers, much less in a multilateral process. Take the simplest case where a tariff is constructed between two states, and the traffic of two carriers, A and B, consists of the following sets of two-point combinations: (1) served by A only; (2) served by B only; (3) served by joint line only; (4) served by A on a single-line basis and also by joint line; (5) served by B on a single-line basis and also on a joint-line basis; (6) served by A and B on a single-line basis; and (7) served by neither A nor B. To meet the DOJ's objections, A would have to flag out of point combinations (1), (4), and (6), and B would have to flag out of (2), (5), and (6). One shudders to consider how a territorywide tariff for the Rocky Mountain Bureau would look after hundreds of carriers had completed this flagging-out process for all the countless point combinations.

In any event, simply flagging out of the tariff for points where the carrier has single-line service may not be enough. Carrier A has participated in discussions and voted on a collective joint-line tariff that determines rates in markets (1), (4), and (6). This tariff sets the joint-line rate against which it competes on a single-line basis even if it does not participate in that portion of the joint-line tariff. And what of the hundreds of smaller carriers who participate in bureau tariffs but do not attend General Rate Committee meetings? Are they supposed to review every docket and flag out of joint-line service where they are capable of serving the traffic via single-line service?

In short, the end-to-end doctrine for operations and the Chinese Wall for tariffs cannot absolve carriers of antitrust concerns without the loss of the efficiencies of constructing broad multilateral tariffs for joint-line traffic. The end-to-end doctrine really only amounts to yet another device to raise the transactions cost of joint-line service and its eventual demise in favor of industry concentration.

While the various theories of antitrust are being debated, the position of motor carrier rate bureaus, motor carrier executives, and their legal counsel is critical. The risks of antitrust litigation are so great that carrier participation in collective joint-line ratemaking is troublesome unless the immunity is clearcut. It is clear that their concerns are genuine and the problem real.

EFFECTS OF THE BAN ON COLLECTIVE RATEMAKING FOR SINGLE-LINE RATES ONLY

Based on the above analysis, one would conclude that a ban on collective ratemaking for single-line rates would have little effect on price competition while restricting the usefulness of the remaining antitrust immunity for joint-line traffic. And this is exactly what happened.

The MCA of 1980 appeared to recognize the need for antitrust immunity on joint-line ratemaking because the restrictions were confined to single-line ratemaking. To assess the impact on price competition, it is important to note that the restrictions on single-line ratemaking are totally negative. They do not open up new avenues for competitive rate-setting. As Figure 5 shows, the new law bans one competitive rate-making approach now in effect, regular docketing, in the hopes of encouraging another, Independent Action (IA).

To determine the effect on price competition, we must turn to the reasons why carriers docketed their proposals for collective action prior to the ban. Motor carrier pricing executives will tell you that time was one of the most important factors determining the choice of how a rate proposal would be implemented. Some carriers, for example, chose to publish many of their tariff changes outside the bureaus because they were exasperated with the amount of time needed in publishing tariffs in the bureaus. Others chose IA's, especially without notice, as a means of cutting down on the time required to implement the proposal.

The other aspect determining the choice of the tariff publishing method was the nature of the proposal. If a carrier believed a regular proposal would be appealed and rejected by the GRC, it might well use the IA alternative. As a result, there was a tendency for the least controversial proposals to be published through the regular approach and for many carriers to consider protests to the GRC to be a waste of their time in an atmosphere where anything goes. If the carrier is likely to resubmit a regular proposal as an IA, why bother to fight it? And why should a carrier waste time by submitting a controversial proposal through the regular procedure if he thinks it will have a good chance of being appealed to the GRC and rejected?

The tendency was for the regular process to incorporate proposals where other carriers' participation and advice was needed (e.g., proposals that cover both joint- and single-line rates), less controversial proposals, or proposals where the shipper preferred joint adoption by all bureau carriers rather than dependence on a single IA. IA's and private publication were used where the carrier desired quick action, was attempting to implement a controversial proposal, or hoped to gain a short-term competitive advantage.

The carrier always had the option of using the IA procedure at any time in the collective ratemaking process. If competitive pressures were present to cut rates, and the carrier intended to cut them, the availability of the regular procedure in no way reduced the competitive pressures to implement rate cuts. If shipper pressures were there for the carrier to cut rates, and to cut them in a hurry, it simply did not make sense for a proponent carrier to use the regular docketing procedure with the hopes that some other carrier would appeal the proposal and the GRC would vote it down and talk the proponent out of adopting the proposal. Indeed, one found that the agenda at the GRC meetings often moved quickly because many regular proposals had been withdrawn because the carrier had already used the IA procedure to implement an appealed docket.

But what of the shippers' point of view? Although the IA approach may be faster, there were often many circumstances where the shipper was better off using the regular procedure to implement a collectively set rate. To start with, it had a greater choice of carriers and did not depend on other carriers' individual decisions to join the IA. Furthermore, a rate published under the regular procedure usually had automatic application for both single-line and joint-line movements. If the IA procedure was used, the tariff applied only to the IA proponent and joiners. It applied to joint-line movements only when the traffic moved via joint-line routes that specifically concurred in the new tariff.

Equally important, shippers found that it was a lot easier for *them* to initiate changes to existing tariffs that initially went through a regular procedure. The reason is that there were severe restrictions on anyone but the docket proponent making changes to IA tariffs as a result of the MCA of 1980:

[T]he organization may not interfere with each carrier's right of independent action and may not change or cancel any rate established by independent action after the date of enactment of this subsection, other than a general increase or broad rate restructuring, except that changes in such rates may be effected, with the consent of the carrier or carriers that initiated the independent action, for the purpose of tariff simplification, removal of discrimination, or elimination of obsolete items.[213]

Because tariff proposals normally went into effect unless appealed to the General Rate Committee, a shipper could modify collective rates designed to serve its needs at its own initiative. Now the shipper is required to get every proponent and concurring carrier to take that action for tariffs that were originally proposed as IA's. This is hardly an appealing prospect to a major shipper wishing to redesign its distribution system.

These are only a few of the reasons why shippers often preferred regular proposals over IA's. Another reason was consistency and tariff simplification. Shippers often preferred to concentrate their clout on a few carriers and to incorporate concessions in simplified collective tariffs rather than to have a complex set of gimmicks in disparate IA's.

Carrier traffic executives will tell you that it was often the shipper that called the tune in deciding how rate proposals were handled at the bureau. In some cases, the shipper encouraged collective action to simplify the tariffs as they applied to its movements and to increase the carrier choices available. In other cases, the shipper preferred to concentrate its bargaining strength on a single or a few carriers and used the IA process to speed up the adoption of new tariffs. There was no one preferred approach from the shippers' point of view.

The continuing rate war suggests that the restrictions on single-line collective ratemaking in the MCA of 1980 have no meaningful direct effect on the level of price competition in the motor carrier industry. Any carrier that wished to gain a competitive advantage by initiating an IA without notice was perfectly free to do so prior to the restrictions, and such actions were so commonplace that they were at times overwhelming the bureaus' ability to publish them. It is difficult to see what additional stimulus will be provided by the restrictions on single-line collective ratemaking. If the motivation of the carrier was to gain an immediate competitive advantage by the rate change, he would have chosen not to take advantage of the collective ratemaking process anyway. Since the ban on collective ratemaking for single-line rates changes neither the motivation nor opportunities for individual carrier pricing initiatives, it is difficult to see how the intensity of price competition would be affected. The ban on collective single-line ratemaking will do nothing to encourage individual carrier rate initiatives, such as discounting, which are going on regardless.

Legal approaches to the problem

Opinions differ regarding the carriers' exposure to a charge of violating the antitrust laws where single-line and joint-line rates compete. It is extremely easy or extremely hard to prove collusion, depending on the burden of proof. On the one hand, it is fairly obvious that the two carriers acting jointly in the previous example could not be acting truly independently of the single-line carrier's intentions regarding the single-line rate. One could argue that any agreement on the joint-line rate is a *per se* violation of antitrust laws as applied to the single-line rate. On the other hand, is there an implied immunity for the carrier with the single-line rate on the grounds that the immunity for joint-line rate-making would otherwise be meaningless?

The Staggers Rail Act (SRA) and MCA have attempted to resolve the problem by muddling the burden of proof without extending the joint-line immunity explicitly to competing single-line rates. The MCA, for example, provides the following in Section 14 (b)(3)(E):

In any proceeding in which a party to such proceeding alleges that a carrier voted, discussed, or agreed on a rate or allowance in violation of this subsection, that party has the burden of showing that the vote, discussion, or agreement occurred. A showing of parallel behavior does not satisfy that burden by itself.

Section 219 of the Staggers Rail Act seems to provide additional protection to rail carriers:

(ii) In any proceeding in which it is alleged that a carrier was a party to an agreement, conspiracy, or combination in violation of a Federal law cited in subsection (a)(2)(A) of this section or of any similar State law, proof of an agreement, conspiracy, or combination may not be inferred from evidence that two or more carriers acted together with respect to an interline rate or related matter and that a party to such action took similar action with respect to a rate or related matter on another route or traffic. In any proceeding in which such a violation is alleged, evidence of a discussion or agreement between or among such carrier and one or more other carriers, or of any rate or other action resulting from such discussion or agreement, shall not be admissible if the discussion or agreement—

(I) was in accordance with an agreement approved under paragraph (2) of this subsection; or

(II) concerned an interline movement of the carrier, and the discussion or agreement would not, considered by itself, violate the laws referred to in the first sentence of this clause.

In any proceeding before a jury, the court shall determine whether the requirements of clause (I) or (II) are satisfied before allowing the introduction of any such evidence.[214]

Many antitrust attorneys are skeptical that the provisions on parallel behavior in the rail and motor carrier acts provide any meaningful protection to the carriers. The statutory provisions provide no basis for dismissal of an antitrust complaint and only amount to a rule of evidence.[215] Posner[216] reviews the literature and case law on "tacit collusion" and "conscious parallelism" and concludes that "the scope of the law is so vague and the criminal and civil penalties for liability are so severe that much efficient, and even procompetitive, joint action falling within the gray area of present law might be deterred for a considerable period of time before the issues of antitrust liability were definitively resolved." Although his comments were directed to the problem of rail carrier joint ratemaking (see the appendix to this chapter), they apply equally to motor carriers. This concern is also supported by the ICC's interpretation of the Staggers Rail Act which points out that the rail provisions on parallel pricing of joint- and single-line rates provide "only procedural protections, not complete immunity."[217]

What is a single-line rate?

A textual analysis of the prohibition on single-line ratemaking in the Motor Carrier Act serves principally to demonstrate the difficulties of isolating single-line ratemaking from the rest of rate bureau activities.[218] The difficulties of isolating and prohibiting single-line collective ratemaking are also revealed by examining the act itself:

1. Single-line rates as defined by the act are not discussed or voted on collectively, so the act bans something that does not exist.
2. The specific exceptions do not logically fall within the definition of single-line rates.
3. The exceptions to the exceptions do not fall within the definition of single-line rates and therefore introduce a logical fallacy and uncertainty in the law.
4. If the exceptions to the exceptions were not intended to add anything new to the proscription on single-line ratemaking, collective ratemaking could go on as usual after 1 January 1984.
5. If one makes the logical contortion that the exceptions to the exceptions define the only collective ratemaking that would be proscribed, only commodity rates and some class exception rates would appear to be banned, a rather silly outcome.

Consider the legislative definition of a single-line rate in Section 14 of the MCA:

(b)(1) In this subsection, "single-line rate" refers to a rate, charge, or allowance proposed by a single motor common carrier of property that is applicable only over its line and for which the transportation can be provided by that carrier.

In prohibiting "discussion of or voting upon single-line rates," 14(b)(3)(D) of the act provides for the following exceptions:

(i) general rate increases or decreases if the agreement gives shippers, under specified procedures, at least 15 days notice of the proposal and an opportunity to present comments on it before a tariff containing the increases or decreases is filed with the Commission and if discussion of such increases or decreases is limited to industry average carrier costs and, after the date of elimination of the antitrust immunity by this subparagraph, does not include discussion of individual markets or particular single-line rates;

(ii) changes in commodity classifications;

(iii) changes in tariff structures if discussion of such changes is limited to industry average carrier costs and, after the date of elimination of antitrust immunity by this subparagraph, does not include discussion of individual markets or particular single-line rates;

(iv) publishing of tariffs, filing of independent actions for individual members carriers, providing of support services for members, and changes in rules or regulations which are of at least substantially general application throughout the area in which such changes will apply.

These legislative provisions, taken together, permit a literal definition of the prohibition on single-line collective ratemaking that would make the statutory prohibition completely redundant. The statutory definition of a single-line rate conforms to what is now a single-line IA (i.e., a proposal that applies only to the proponent).[219] Taking the definition of single-line rate as stated in the act, then, one could conclude that the prohibition merely confirms existing practice—namely, IA's must be published without collective discussion or voting in the bureaus.

The ICC has taken a different view, which was recently upheld by an appeals court. Although it did not confront this issue when addressing the implementation of the prohibition of collective ratemaking for single-line rates, elsewhere the *Decision* states, "Until January (or July 1) 1984, rate bureaus may permit, but not require, single-line rates to be filed under collective procedures." This implies an interpretation of a single-line rate as any docket (even one proposed for regular collective procedure) applying in any way to single-line traffic.[220]

This interpretation is inconsistent with the definition in the Motor Carrier Act, which is far from a model of clarity on the subject. To begin with, the exceptions to the prohibition do not logically fall within the definition of single-line rates. The exceptions, moreover, appear to cover explicitly most of the existing rate bureau collective ratemaking activities: general rate increases or decreases, commodity classification, changes in tariff structure, and tariff publishing (including IA's), support services, and changes in rules and regulations.

In particular, it would appear that motor carrier rate bureaus collectively could continue to set class rates or commodity column rates since they are not "proposed by a single motor carrier [and are] applicable only over its line." Nor do they "include discussion of individual markets or particular single-line rates." Most actions on class rates would conform to "general rate increases and decreases" and "changes in tariff structures."

Another logical problem comes with the exceptions to the exceptions. These could be interpreted as either complementing and clarifying the definition of single-line rates or actually prohibiting something that was not otherwise defined as a single-line rate. If one takes the view that the exceptions complement the definition of single-line rate, then the exceptions to the exceptions take on the same character. In short, they do not disapprove anything in addition to what is defined as single-line rate.

One could take the somewhat strained view that the act is really only effectively prohibiting whatever falls within the exceptions to the exceptions. This interpretation would prohibit "discussion of individual markets or particular single-line rates." Under this construction, collective determination of commodity rates might be eliminated. Although they do not meet the legislative definition of a single-line rate if they are docketed under a regular procedure for collective ratemaking (they would not be "applicable only over its line"), nor do they conform exactly to the exceptions, they appear to be examples of exceptions to the exceptions.

If the law intended to restrict collective ratemaking to joint-line rates, it clearly has not done so. Joint-line rates are not explicitly mentioned as an exception to the prohibition,[221] and the exceptions explicitly include ratemaking activities that affect single-line traffic. Indeed, class rates generate the predominant share of revenues for tariffs set under collective procedures and would apparently continue to be set collectively under the act.

A literal reading of the act would appear to prohibit, at most, collective ratemaking for commodity rates and some exception class rates, not because they meet the legislative definition of a single-line rate but because they appear to fit the exception to the exception. Yet these commodity rates are widely recognized to apply to the most competitive sector of the trucking industry—large annual volumes moving in large lots, hardly lacking today in competitive stimulus. These shippers can usually take care of themselves, and, in any event, most of these collective rate adjustments have been downward in recent memory.

Shortly after the deadline for the ban on "single-line" collective ratemaking, the Niagara Frontier Tariff Bureau filed four collectively established tariffs that applied to single-line traffic, thus requesting a clarification of the definition of the term *single-line rate* in the act. These tariffs were rejected by the ICC,[222] and the decision was appealed and affirmed.[223]

APPENDIX: DEVELOPMENTS IN RAILROAD COLLECTIVE RATEMAKING

The extensive revision of railroad collective ratemaking policy instituted by the Staggers Rail Act of 1980[224] extended earlier changes in the 4R Act.[225] These changes in law were interpreted by the ICC "as narrowly as possible in favor of the benefits of competition."[226] The law as it is applied to rail rate bureaus, tariff practices, and regulatory practices of the ICC differs between the rail and motor carrier industry.[227] Nevertheless, it is useful to review the rail situation for parallels and differences that affect antitrust considerations for motor carriers.

At the outset, however, it is important to note substantial differences between railroads and motor carriers that preclude any direct translation from the rail experience with collective ratemaking to motor carriers.

First, most rail traffic moves on commodity rates which are especially constructed to meet the needs of individual shippers or groups of shippers, with the carrier routing specified; a substantial portion of motor carrier traffic moves under class rates with open routing that applies to all bureau carriers, for both single- and joint-line traffic.

Second, the motor carrier industry is substantially less concentrated than the rail industry and has lower barriers to entry. The transactions costs of bilateral negotiations between individual shippers and carriers for determining tariffs and classifications are much greater in the motor carrier industry relative to the freight bill.

Third, although generalizations can be highly misleading, there are differences in the traffic characteristics of railroads and motor carriers: motor carriers haul virtually every commodity consumed in America; whereas the rail industry is concentrating on shipping fewer types of commodities in larger quantities over greater distances.

Finally, regulation of rail rates by the Commission was limited by the Staggers Rail Act unless the shipper could show "market dominance" and the rate was above a jurisdictional threshold defined in terms of revenue/cost.

With these caveats in mind, the ICC's *Decision* on rail rate bureaus may be considered. The principal effects of these rulings were to

1. Require all single-line rate proposals to be processed separately from joint-line rate proposals;

2. Interpret the legislation with respect to handling single-line rates to prohibit changes on these rates in general rate increases and broad tariff changes;[228]

3. Interpret the "practicably participates" language of the act[229] as it applied to joint-line rates to grant antitrust immunity only to "direct connectors" in the movement; this required each "route set" to vote independently on a joint-line tariff, rather than to permit all carriers to adopt collectively a joint-line

tariff with open routing between the points (this part of the decision was not delayed by the Commission until the mandatory date of 1 January 1984, specified by the act).

These restrictions on rail collective ratemaking eviscerated collective ratemaking for single-line rail traffic and made joint-line collective ratemaking a bilateral process as well as a multilateral one. Combined with the abolition of some of the remaining collective ratemaking (even for joint-line rates) by the Staggers Rail Act on 1 January 1984, the result has been described as a chilling effect on collective ratemaking,[230] a large increase in IA's, and a substantial increase in tariff complexity.[231]

Although certainly not precedent, the ICC's narrow interpretation of the residual antitrust immunity granted by the Staggers Act to railroads must be considered in any evaluation of proposed changes in antitrust immunity for motor carriers. The Commission started with the provision that "since the general objective of the antitrust laws is the maintenance of competition, provisions concerning exemptions from these laws must be construed as narrowly as possible in favor of competition." Citing the act's statement of national transportation goals ("to require rail carriers, to the maximum extent practicable, to rely on individual rate increases and to limit the use of increases of general applicability"), the Commission ruled that "the use of general rate increases and broad tariff changes to set single-line rates is not approved."

The Commission required that the railroads "discontinue the inclusion of both single-line and joint-line movements in one proposal." Combined with a statutory prohibition on collective ratemaking on single-line rates and a prohibition on the inclusion of single-line rates in general rate increases, the result is to restrict antitrust immunity substantially in the rail industry.

This construction of the rail act is relevant to the motor carrier industry because the MCA of 1980 contained an explicit prohibition on collective ratemaking on single-line rates made effective during 1984. The ICC's construction, in effect, converts any rate proposal which applies to on-line rail traffic to the necessity for independent action. The definitions of single-line rate in the MCA of 1980 and the 4R Act (90 Stat. 44) are similar. However, the Motor Carrier Act differs from the Staggers Rail Act in that the Commission is not given the discretion to prohibit motor carriers from including single-line rates in general rate increases.[232]

The ICC's requirement to separate single-line and joint-line tariff proposals and the prohibition on collective discussion and voting on single-line rates in any manner (including general rate increases and broad tariff changes) will lead to a certain ossification of the rail tariff structure. The existing tariffs are "grandfathered." The incentive naturally is not to make changes rather than to restructure entirely the tariffs to conform to these rules. Carriers apparently can only act collectively to cancel extant collective tariffs which apply to single-line traffic and not amend them in any way.[233]

The ICC's interpretation of direct connectors for joint-line traffic incorporates the Department of Justice's theory of how joint-line ratemaking should function, and so it is interesting to contemplate how it might work for motor carriers. Under it, as many as 15 to 20 different combinations of lines vote separately on rates for an interline movement. The theory is that each of these route sets will compete for that particular movement. This, of course, greatly encumbers the collective ratemaking process, and it only works for point-to-point tariffs, rather than broad tariffs, such as class rates and mileage, scale and group rates which apply throughout an entire territory.

The ICC's extremely narrow definition of the antitrust immunity as it applies to joint-line rates (embodied in the direct connectors doctrine) also illustrates how an aggressive Interstate Commerce Commission could effectively scuttle collective ratemaking in trucking. If every motor carrier had to vote on a route-set basis on all joint-line tariffs, the motor carrier collective system for interline service would obviously break down. Many smaller carriers simply cannot afford to attend the rate bureau meetings today, much less the endless meetings required if every combination of two (and even three) carriers had to vote on every docket. This provision can only work when there are a small number of route sets and they all actively participate in voting on the dockets. Combined with an attempt to eliminate broad tariffs and encourage interlining only on an end-to-end basis, the result would be joint-line rates which apply only to major accounts and large-volume shipments over major routes.[234] One can only contemplate the mathematical possibilities when hundreds of members of a motor carrier rate bureau attempt to define all the possible route sets (including three-route movements) that could apply to all the particular shipments over all the combinations of points that are incorporated in territorywide tariffs today.

There is a lesson to be learned from the rail experience. Bifurcation of single- and joint-line rates in the rail industry is working, although far from ideally, because of special circumstances in that industry: the transition to minimal antitrust immunity and widespread deregulation of rail traffic; the grandfathering of existing tariffs; the fact that most rail traffic moves on commodity rates; and the substantially smaller number of direct competitors in the rail industry.

The Dilemma of Cooperation among Rivals: Communicating to Customers   5

> When one encounters a grandmother who has been sucking eggs for many decades with conspicuous success, one ought to hesitate before presuming to instruct her in the theory of egg-sucking. Instead one ought to try to find out how she does it, the presumption being that her departures from what theory prescribes may not be inefficiencies, but perhaps even the reverse.
> EDWARD C. BANFIELD, "The Economist's Public Library,"
> *The Public Interest* (Fall 1983): 141.

The results of the previous chapter may be briefly summarized. Price and service decisions among motor carriers must be coordinated to provide an interconnected system of nationwide interline service. Agreement on common terms of service—such as classification, formatting of shipping documents, interline settlements, exchange of traffic data on interline shipments, tariff rules and format, packaging requirements and other conditions of shipping, and point groupings for measuring distance—requires close coordination of a carrier with both its customers and its competitors. The most difficult issues in antitrust law in trucking involve drawing the line between (1) legitimate efforts of carriers to minimize the information demands and transactions costs in these agreements, and (2) collusion that suppresses economically justified rate/service options.

Two features of the motor carrier industry were found to contribute to the difficulty of constructing a Chinese Wall between single-line and joint-line services: the operational difficulties of segregating the two services into two noncompeting end-to-end markets on a bilateral basis and the impossibility of constructing information-efficient multilateral joint-line tariffs of broad applicability that do not compete with the single-line service offerings of all participating carriers. The cooperation required to establish such tariffs inherently raises antitrust concerns because it is inefficient to provide for individual bilateral interline agreements that are so idiosyncratic in their applicability that they do not also apply directly to markets where one or more of the carriers also serve single-line traffic.

The further one explores the difficulties of constructing bilateral joint-line tariffs designed to insulate the carriers from antitrust concerns, the clearer become the advantages of benchmark rate structures established by multilateral carrier participation. Transactions costs of providing traffic interchange can be reduced by permitting the construction of such tariffs without fear of antitrust prosecution, while encouraging bilateral negotiations when the negotiations costs are less than the benefits of departing from the multilateral benchmarks.

While not as clearly recognized, the collective rate structure also provides a comparable benefit in providing a benchmark rate structure for negotiations between carriers and shippers. The collective rate structure provides a convenient starting point for price negotiations for commodity rates, IA's, discounts, and so on. Use of bureau tariffs is entirely permissive, and departures from the benchmark are widespread.[235]

Confronted with this evidence of rate competition, cynics abandon their argument that rate bureaus should be abolished because they fix prices and embrace the novel idea that rate bureaus should be abolished because they do not fix prices. Price competition is taken as evidence that collective ratemaking serves no useful purpose.[236]

But this argument fails to consider the value of a benchmark rate structure as a point of departure against which individual carrier prices can be quoted. Critics never address the fundamental dilemma of their position: If collective ratemaking provides no useful purpose in a highly competitive market structure and indeed obstructs efficient pricing, why do carriers and shippers still place a value on using the collective rate structure?

Tables 30 and 31 demonstrate that the class-rate system was the backbone of the motor carrier pricing system during the period of rigid rate regulation. "For rate bureau member traffic in 1980, about 12 percent of all shipments moved under non-class rates such as commodity and exceptions rates, but these accounted for about 27 percent of revenues. . . . [M]ost LTL general freight moves under class rates, or discounted class rates."[237]

Critics argued that regulatory reform would change all that. Data, however, do not support the conclusion that the class-rate structure could disappear and never be missed. The use of discounting is up considerably, but the class-rate system is the glue that holds the individual pricing systems together.[238] The class-rate system has clearly survived the process of deregulation. The Rocky Mountain Bureau, which covers transcontinental (long-haul) traffic, reports that there has been a substantial increase in the percentage of its traffic moving over class rates and a virtual demise of the commodity-rate system (see Table 32).

Table 30
Percentage Distribution of Total Shipments, Ton-Miles, and Revenue for
Selected Rate Types (1976 and 1980)

	Shipments		Ton-Miles		Revenues	
	1976	1980	1976	1980	1976	1980
Class	90.1	89.5	55.0	60.8	75.0	72.3
Commodity	4.3	4.2	37.0	31.3	16.8	20.9
Com. Col.	2.0	2.4	5.0	4.8	4.0	3.9
Exception	1.7	2.0	1.7	2.0	2.1	1.5
Government	.4	.4	.9	.8	.5	.7
Nonreg.	1.5	1.6	.5	.7	.8	.7

Data are based on the freight of the 10 major tariff agencies, plus independently filed
tariffs appearing in the CTS.

Source: Cherry and Meyer, "A Comparison of Descriptive Statistics for 1976 and 1980
Continuous Traffic Study: A Report to the Motor Carrier Ratemaking Study Commission."
Arthur D. Little, Inc.

Most of the formerly commodity-rated traffic now moves under individual carrier tariffs or discounts off the class rate.

The explanation of the continued use of class rates as a benchmark is
a simple efficiency rationale: collective ratemaking reduces transactions
costs by providing a standard price and service (default values in computer terminology) that can always be used in all or in part in carrier/
shipper negotiations. When it is more efficient to negotiate departures
from the benchmark, buyers and sellers are choosing to do so. But when
the transactions costs are too high, when the benchmark rate or terms
of service are judged by buyers and sellers to be competitive, or when
there is a premium on the coordination of a large number of buyers and
sellers (joint-line rates or released rates, for example), the marketplace
has the collectively set tariff benchmark to fall back on. Carriers often
elect to express their individual prices as discounts off the bureau prices
rather than publish an entirely new innovative tariff. Abolition of collective ratemaking would arbitrarily abolish a system of ratemaking
which buyers and sellers are free to use when it suits their needs, but
it would not eliminate other avenues of unilateral pricing. It is difficult
to see how shippers and carriers could possibly benefit from this loss.

If anticompetitive pricing explained carriers' desire for collective

Table 31
Shipment Size and Rate Structure (1980 Percentage)

Weight	Number of Shipments				Revenues			
	Class Rates	Commodity Rates	Except. & C.C.*	Other Rates**	Class Rates	Commodity Rates	Except. & C.C.*	Other Rates
0–99 lbs.	94	2	2	2	95	1	2	2
100–499 lbs.	93	2	3	2	94	2	3	1
500–999 lbs.	86	5	6	3	88	5	5	2
1,000–4,999 lbs.	84	6	7	3	86	11	7	2
5,000–9,999 lbs.	77	12	8	3	80	11	7	2
10,000–19,999 lbs.	60	27	9	4	67	23	8	2
20,000 lbs. and up	23	63	9	5	32	56	8	4
TOTAL	88	5	4	3	73	19	6	2

Percentages may not total 100 due to rounding.

* Exceptions to class rates and commodity column rates.

**Other rates include freight-of-all-kinds rates, nonregulated rates, freight forwarder, linehaul assembly and distribution rates, and all other rates.

Source: Adapted from data from 1980 Continuous Traffic Study data by the MAC Group, "Statistical Overview of the Trucking Industry."

Table 32
Traffic Distribution for Rocky Mountain Motor Tariff Bureau (Percentage of Revenue)

Year	Minimum Charge	Class Rate	Commodity Rate	Released* Value
1979	7.40	66.03	26.57	
1980	7.45	69.85	22.70	
1981	8.26	72.39	19.35	
1982	8.91	77.85	13.22	0.11
1983	9.33	79.81	7.80	3.06
1984	9.03	82.84	4.44	3.68

*The bureau advises that this traffic was not separately accounted for prior to 1981 and has doubts as to the validity of the 1982 data, but has reported the numbers so that the totals will sum to 100 percent.
Source: Rocky Mountain Motor Tariff Bureau.

ratemaking, the practice would be widespread in all sectors of the trucking industry. After all, a desire to raise prices and increase profits can reasonably be assumed to be common to all market segments in the industry. But the monopoly pricing rationale fails to explain the differential reliance on collective ratemaking procedures within the industry. The practice is mainly confined to the less-than-truckload general commodity sector of the industry, where the efficiency rationale is most compelling.[239]

When it is considered that dozens of carriers participate in billions of point pairs involving millions of commodities, it is clear that economy of information necessitates a significant grouping of the information into a formal tariff structure.[240] The most efficient means of organizing this vast body of data[241] is not obvious, but it is clear that competition cannot work unless shippers have some method of summarizing and organizing price information so that they may compare price offers. The problem is magnified by the fact that numerous shipments among many points are involved for most shippers.

COLLECTIVE RATEMAKING AND TRANSACTIONS COSTS IN TRUCKING

When motor carriers cooperate among themselves to communicate their price and service offers efficiently to customers, this coordination function is referred to by various terms in the literature, such as providing a "clearinghouse," "forum," "benchmark rate structure," "list prices," and "consensual decision making." The obvious question is what distinguishes the trucking industry such that a collectively set benchmark is so useful? To answer the question, it is helpful to begin by addressing the need for a benchmark itself.

The establishment of a benchmark rate structure serves a number of functions which tend to reduce transactions costs in communicating price information and negotiating rates. First, in the absence of such a list price or data on prices of recent comparable transactions, the buyer must rely on knowledge of a vendor's costs to judge the reasonableness of a price offer. Given the complexity of the cost function in motor carrier operations (varying by location, time, and commodity characteristics), acquiring this cost information can itself be costly, especially when simply comparing price offers is the alternative.

Second, the service itself is heterogeneous and provided under widely differing circumstances as far as cost incurrence is concerned. The possibility for taking into account a variety of demand and cost differences in defining and pricing the product, and notifying buyers in advance of the price, suggests the possibility of many different price structures, all of them likely to be perceived in the aggregate as highly complex if each is expressed completely independently. Under such circumstances, some standardized system for defining the service attributes and organizing price information minimizes transactions and information costs, even in the absence of joint-line services.

Third, negotiating is costly, too. To the extent that the list price is a fallback price, or some simple adjustment of the list price serves that function, transactions are facilitated. Even more importantly, the larger the number of buyers[242] and sellers and the greater the service differentiation and cost variances involved, the greater the value of a benchmark rate structure to serve as a reference for judging price offers.[243] Furthermore, high transactions costs generally impose disproportionate costs on smaller carriers, particularly when they do not have detailed knowledge of their own cost structures.[244]

The complexity of the pricing data that must be organized in an efficient system for communicating price data may best be seen by reconstructing how rates are determined.[245] Motor carrier rates for common carriage may be broadly grouped as either (1) a class rate, which is a comprehensive system of ratemaking that establishes a rate for every conceivable movement, or (2) a commodity rate, which is far more limited in scope and generally tailored to meet some specific transportation demand.[246] Commodity rates are almost always below class rates, assuming an equal level of service. It is generally the class-rate system that is the benchmark rate structure in the trucking industry that serves as the reference point for bilateral negotiations.[247]

The elements of determining the price of a class-rated shipment[248] may be distinguished as follows:

1. *Classification*: Commodities with like transportation properties must be classified into similar groups. Furthermore, there must be a specified manner by which a particular shipment is "named" (i.e., how is one to translate a shipper's description of the commodity into a particular group of commodities as recognized by the rate structure)?

   Answer: Under the current class-rate system, the National Motor Freight Classification[249] publishes an elaborate and exhaustive list of every commodity that could conceivably move by motor carrier, together with an assignment of that commodity into one of 23 classes. See Figure 8 for an illustrative page.

Each class is in turn assigned a number, with 100 as a sort of base rate.

2. *Distance*: Given the origin and destination of the traffic, a means of specifying distance between any two out of billions of combinations of geographic points must be specified.

   Answer: Rate bureaus publish rate basis numbers reflecting distances between the most prominent origins and destinations and listed groups whereby other nearby points are included in the rates for the points for which rate basis numbers have been published. The tariff itself publishes the same rate for identical traffic with the same rate basis. More recently a similar method has been developed using postal zip codes.

3. *Weight*: "Breaks" must be established that determine weight differences to be recognized in the rate structure.

   Answer: The class-rate structure shows aggregations of weight responsive to cost differences for rating purposes.

4. *Rates*: Cost per unit for each of the pricing groups defined by the previous steps must be specified.

   Answer: Given the three previous ingredients, the publication of the rate ordinarily involves a statement of cents per hundredweight for different weight groups, distances, and commodity classes (see Figure 9). To these may be added additional fees such as accessorial charges (for special services) and "arbitraries" (for higher cost geographic locations).

5. *Carrier Concurrence*: Carriers (both single-line and joint-line) that concur in the rates must be identified.

   Answer: Carrier participation is listed in the bureau tariffs, and routing guides indicate which carriers participate in interline agreements.

6. *Tariff Rules*: Terms of service or limitations placed on the price offer must be specified.

Figure 8
Sample Page from the Freight Classification System: Class Assignment

Item	ARTICLES	CLASSES LTL	TL	MW
	MAGNESIUM METAL OR MAGNESIUM METAL ALLOYS: subject to item 133600			
	Blanks or Stampings (Unfinished Shapes), subject to item 133700			
133702	NOTE—(a) Applies only on articles consisting of one piece of metal, requiring additional forming or shaping operations to be performed on them to bring them to their final shape.			
	(b) Blanking, cutting, drawing, drilling other than drilling of holes for final fit or assembly, pressing, punching, spinning, stamping, or trimming other than trimming for fit at time of installation or assembly are considered to be additional forming or shaping operations.			
	(c) Chamfering, countersinking, drilling of holes for final fit or assembly, reaming, threading of holes, buffing, plating, polishing, finish painting or coating, or other surface finishing operations are not considered to be additional forming or shaping operations.			
	(d) Articles may be painted or otherwise coated for temporary preservation or protective purposes only.			
	(e) Articles not requiring additional forming or shaping operations named in (b) must be classed under the specific or "NOI" provision applicable thereto. In the absence of a specific or "NOI" provision, apply the provisions of "Magnesium Articles, or Forms or Shapes, NOI." When blanks or stampings constitute other articles for which a specific item is provided in an unfinished condition, such specific item must be used and the classes for blanks or stampings will not apply.			
133720	**Buffings or Grindings**	Not Taken		
133740	**Castings or Forgings,** NOI, see Note, item 133742, loose, LTL only if weighing each 15 pounds or over, or in packages	70	50	30
133742	NOTE—Applies only on articles consisting of one piece of metal, requiring work to be performed on them before being ready for assembly with other parts or articles or for use by themselves. Buffing, polishing, plating, painting, similar surface finishing operations, or heat treating are not considered to be such required work. Castings or forgings may have fins, sinkerheads, gates or other rough edges removed, they may be tumbled or cleaned and they may be painted or otherwise coated for preservation or protective purposes only. Articles not requiring work must be classed under the specific or general (NOI) description provided therefor; in the absence of such a specific or general (NOI) provision, the provisions for magnesium metal or magnesium metal alloy articles, NOI, are applicable.			
133760	**Channels;** LTL, in packages, or loose if weighing each 25 pounds or over; TL, loose or in packages	70	50	30
133770	**Dollies,** pallet, without standing ends, sides, stakes or standards, in packages	100	70	16
133780	**Forging Stock;** LTL, in packages, or loose if weighing each 25 pounds or over; TL, loose or in packages	65	45	30
133800	**Ingots, Pigs, Blooms, Billets, Slabs, Rods or Bars,** see Note, item 133802	60	40	36
133802	NOTE—Applies on materials, rough hot extruded, or cast, to be re-heated for purpose of re-rolling, re-extruding, forging or remelting.			
133830	**Plates, Sheets or Strips,** LTL in barrels, boxes or crates, or securely fastened to lift truck skids or pallets, or Plates ½ inch thick or over, loose or in packages; also TL, loose or in packages	65	45	30
133850	⊕**Powdered,** NOI, in steel barrels or in metal cans in boxes	100	70	30
133860	⊕**Powdered,** spherical, with or without salt coating, in steel drums	77½	50	30
133870	⊕**Scrap,** loose, LTL only if in pieces weighing each 25 pounds or over or in packages, or scrap turnings, sawings, scalpings, clippings or chips suitable for remelting only, in packages	60	40	30
133890	**Sticks,** suitable only for regrinding or remelting, in packages	65	45	30
133910	**Turnings,** NOI, in barrels or steel pails; also TL, in four-ply paper bags	70	50	30
133970	**Manikins or Lay Figures,** full formed or with flat backs:			
Sub 1	Papier-mache, in boxes	200	100	10
Sub 2	NOI, other than foam rubber or cellular or expanded plastic, in boxes	125	70	20
134010	**Manure,** animal, bird, dog, fowl or guano:			
Sub 1	In cans or cartons in barrels or boxes	60	35	36
Sub 2	In bulk in barrels or sift-proof boxes, or in bags; TL, in bulk or in packages	50	35	40
134040	**Marbles,** agate or cornelian, in barrels or boxes	100	70	20
134050	**Marbles,** clay, glass or porcelain, NOI, in bags, barrels or boxes	65	37½	36
134080	**Markers,** boundary, wrought iron pipe, galvanized, with bronze caps, with or without concrete filling, in packages	70	37½	40
134090	**Markers,** surveyors', or land marking, wire with plastic flag attached, in boxes	65	45	30
134100	**Markers,** talc, sawed or chipped, in barrels or boxes	65	37½	36
134120	**Marl,** LTL, in bags, barrels or boxes; TL, in bulk or in packages	50	35	40
134130	**Masks,** face, air filtering, paper or nonwoven textile fibre, with or without plastic or metal reinforcing strips, in boxes	125	92½	14
134140	**Masks,** NOI, in boxes:			
Sub 1	Other than folded flat or nested	200	100	10
Sub 2	Folded flat or nested	100	70	20
134160	**Mast Arms (Brackets),** with or without mast arm supports, street lighting, aluminum, in packages, or loose when weighing each 15 pounds or more	85	50	24
134180	**Masts,** radio broadcasting, tubular, steel, in sections	70	45	36
134200	⊕**Matches,** in boxes	77½	45	24
134205	**Material,** hogshead, wood and wire combined, NOI, not interwoven, in packages; also TL, loose	50	35	36
134210	**Material,** incendiary bomb extinguishing, dry, in boxes	50	35	40
134214	**Material,** shade, folding door or partition, consisting of wood slats, interwoven with tape, twine or yarn, in wrapped rolls or in boxes	70	45	30

For explanation of abbreviations and reference marks, see last pages of this tariff.

Source: National Motor Freight Traffic Association, Inc., *National Motor Freight Classification*. Washington, D.C.: NMFTA (3 April 1981): 555.

Figure 9
Sample of Published Rates for Different Weight Groups, Distances, and Commodity Classes

TARIFF ICC CSA 501-C
SECTION 3
RATE SECTION
FOR APPLICATION, SEE ITEM 3000

RATE BASIS	MIN CHG	WT GP	92.5	85	77.5	70	65	60	55	50	45	40	37.5	35
							CLASSES							
661 to 680	3255	L5C	1925	1783	1646	1513	1420	1329	1241	1154	...	...	...	...
		M5C	1600	1481	1372	1253	1180	1102	1029	955	...	...	...	...
		M1M	1318	1221	1129	1025	968	904	833	771	...	...	...	...
		M2M	1180	1080	991	895	834	775	709	646	...	...	...	...
		M5M	859	788	719	652	609	558	515	464	...	...	...	...
		M10M	791	727	664	605	558	515	474	432	...	...	...	...
		T	750	694	628	570	528	488	445	406	367	330	329	328
681 to 700	3261	L5C	1927	1795	1651	1516	1422	1330	1242	1155	...	...	...	...
		M5C	1620	1507	1383	1276	1191	1119	1037	972	...	...	...	...
		M1M	1341	1249	1147	1045	973	912	849	784	...	...	...	...
		M2M	1194	1103	1003	906	844	786	717	657	...	...	...	...
		M5M	872	803	730	664	615	565	521	474	...	...	...	...
		M10M	804	744	675	611	569	520	482	438	...	...	...	...
		T	766	706	643	579	538	497	459	414	374	334	332	331
701 to 720	3274	L5C	1952	1821	1672	1532	1448	1338	1254	1159	...	...	...	...
		M5C	1651	1542	1414	1295	1223	1135	1057	981	...	...	...	...
		M1M	1367	1271	1158	1064	1001	927	863	794	...	...	...	...
		M2M	1216	1124	1026	929	870	800	739	673	...	...	...	...
		M5M	895	822	752	671	624	582	531	483	...	...	...	...
		M10M	825	755	694	619	577	535	490	446	...	...	...	...
		T	784	718	661	595	550	509	469	420	384	339	337	335
721 to 740	3276	L5C	1968	1834	1690	1547	1449	1360	1258	1162	...	...	...	...
		M5C	1672	1561	1433	1313	1231	1158	1071	986	...	...	...	...
		M1M	1384	1292	1186	1077	1012	947	871	806	...	...	...	...
		M2M	1244	1136	1041	946	883	814	748	684	...	...	...	...
		M5M	910	831	763	690	634	588	540	492	...	...	...	...
		M10M	839	766	705	634	586	544	495	452	...	...	...	...
		T	797	729	669	603	561	518	475	432	389	341	340	339

Figure 9 (Continued)

RATE BASIS	MIN CHG	WT GP	CLASSES											
			92.5	85	77.5	70	65	60	55	50	45	40	37.5	35
741 to 760	3283	L5C	1990	1845	1703	1556	1457	1364	1275	1166	...	...	...	...
		M5C	1702	1569	1454	1320	1241	1167	1085	996	...	...	...	...
		M1M	1411	1302	1206	1097	1021	958	889	814	...	...	...	...
		M2M	1252	1158	1054	956	894	821	758	697	...	...	...	...
		M5M	924	843	773	699	644	601	548	505	...	...	...	...
		M10M	851	779	713	645	598	556	507	466	...	...	...	...
		T	807	743	676	609	568	523	480	436	395	347	345	342
761 to 780	3290	L5C	2016	1871	1725	1584	1487	1377	1288	1191	...	...	...	...
		M5C	1732	1604	1474	1356	1276	1185	1108	1024	...	...	...	...
		M1M	1432	1325	1218	1118	1045	970	906	827	...	...	...	...
		M2M	1280	1181	1074	980	902	841	775	706	...	...	...	...
		M5M	939	662	783	713	663	612	558	513	...	...	...	...
		M10M	863	792	720	657	610	564	515	473	...	...	...	...
		T	825	754	693	622	578	536	489	443	404	356	352	350
781 to 800	3297	L5C	2040	1888	1744	1596	1495	1396	1299	1194	...	...	...	...
		M5C	1758	1621	1498	1372	1287	1200	1119	1031	...	...	...	...
		M1M	1456	1347	1235	1134	1055	987	912	836	...	...	...	...
		M2M	1300	1197	1100	992	925	853	786	715	...	...	...	...
		M5M	955	880	802	723	668	619	565	520	...	...	...	...
		M10M	882	809	743	668	618	571	520	482	...	...	...	...
		T	836	766	701	630	590	540	497	457	409	365	361	357
801 to 825	3314	L5C	2049	1905	1756	1602	1507	1416	1312	1206	...	...	...	...
		M5C	1773	1650	1516	1383	1309	1223	1134	1047	...	...	...	...
		M1M	1470	1361	1258	1147	1074	1001	921	859	...	...	...	...
		M2M	1319	1212	1111	1003	934	870	796	725	...	...	...	...
		M5M	968	892	812	730	678	624	576	526	...	...	...	...
		M10M	892	820	748	675	623	577	534	484	...	...	...	...
		T	846	778	709	642	599	546	506	460	413	367	366	365

Source: S. E. Somers, Jr. *Statement before the Motor Carrier Ratemaking Study Commission*, 1 May 1982.

Answer: The class-rate system seems simple enough, but the need to apply it to every conceivable commodity from flagpoles to bowling balls has generated an elaborate need for tariff rules for applying the price system. An example is illustrated by Figure 10, which is a tariff rule that defines specifications for bags. While this rule seems routine, it must be remembered that the size, shape, and packaging of a commodity affects its handling costs, and motor carriers ship virtually everything. In addition to bags, the rules specify standards for bales, barrels, baskets, boxes, and so on down the alphabet. In all, the motor carrier classification manual alone contains 67 pages of rules.

**Figure 10
Sample Page from the Freight Classification System: Tariff Rules**

RULES

ITEM 202

DEFINITION AND SPECIFICATIONS FOR CROSS-LAMINATED
HIGH DENSITY POLYETHYLENE BAGS

Sec. 1. APPLICATION— Where 'bags,' 'multiple-wall bags' or 'paper bags' are provided for in separate descriptions of articles as outer shipping containers, bags meeting the requirements of this rule may be used for dry commodities only. Dry commodities are those which are not liquid or which do not contain any free liquid.

Sec. 2. CONSTRUCTION— Bags must be constucted of high density polyethylene film consisting of two plies of mono-axially oriented film cross-laminated so that the orientation of each ply is at an angle to the other so as to provide nominal thickness and minimum requirements as indicated in chart below:

	Net Weight of contents not exceeding 50 pounds	Net Weight of contents not exceeding 100 pounds
Nominal Thickness	2.5 mil	4 mil
Dart Drop Test (ASTM D1709-'B')	700 grams	1,085 grams
Tensile Properties Test (ASTM D882-'A')	5000 psi	5000 psi
Percent Elongation (ASTM D882-'A')	125 percent	125 percent
Puncture-Propagation of Tear (ASTM D2582)	2,000 grams	3,200 grams

ASTM refers to the American Society for Testing and Materials.

Sec. 3. CLOSURE— Bag closure must be siftproof and must be capable of withstanding loads of 1¼ pounds per mil per inch of seal.

Sec. 4. PERFORMANCE— Filled bags must be capable of withstanding 6 drops from a height of 4 feet onto a solid surface, one drop on each end, one on each face and one drop on each side without rupture or leakage.

Sec. 5. CERTIFICATION— Bags conforming with the foregoing specifications must bear certificate of bag maker stating that they do conform. The certificate may bear an identifying symbol or trademark of the bag maker in lieu of the bag maker's name and such symbol or trademark must be registered with the National Classification Board. Only one identifying symbol or trademark may be registered for each bag maker. The certificate must be of the following form, size (1¼ inches x 3 inches), type and wording, except that the size may be varied not to exceed ¼ inch in either or both directions:

> **FREIGHT SHIPPING BAG**
>
> Meeting Requirements of
>
> **APPLICABLE FREIGHT CLASSIFICATION**
>
> Guaranteed by
>
> _____

ITEM 203

DEFINITION AND SPECIFICATIONS FOR PLASTIC
SEMI-BULK BAGS

Sec. 1. Application— Where 'bags,' 'multiple-wall bags' or 'paper bags' are provided for in separate descriptions of articles as outer shipping containers, bags meeting the requirements of this rule may be used for dry commodities only. Dry commodities are those which are not liquid or which do not contain any free liquid.

Sec. 2. Construction— Bags may be constructed of polyethylene, polybutylene, polypropylene, polyvinyl chloride, polyester or neoprene, of sheet, film, woven or coated fabric construction, of a thickness or of a combination of laminates or liners or of a denier, with body heat sealed, sewn or adhered to meet the performance requirements specified within Section 3.

When bags are equipped with attached ropes, webbed straps, or sleeves to provide loops for use as sling lifting devices to facilitate handling by mechanical equipment, ropes, straps or sleeves used for lifting must harness, encircle or be attached to the bag body.

Bags may be constructed with spouts for discharging purposes with top and bottom filling or discharging openings secured with coated wire ties or other means which will provide a sift-proof closure.

Containers may be used again in transportation only when they are in such condition that they will protect contents as efficiently as new containers.

Bags meeting the provisions of this Item may be used as shipping containers for less-than-truckload (LTL) movement ONLY when tendered for transportation on pallets.

OR

Bags may be constructed without bottoms but must be attached to a rigid palletized floor with two metal clamping rings. Palletized floor must be constructed of molded high density polyethylene designed with 4 way fork lift entry. Bags with integral plastic pallet base may be shipped LTL when not over 35 cubic feet capacity and not over 54 inches in height.

Sec. 3. Performance— Container filled with product or other material to simulate actual net weight to be contained must be capable of withstanding without damage or loss of product a free drop of two feet onto a solid concrete surface.

Slings and method of harnessing or attachment to bag must be capable of providing a 2:1 safety factor tested by simulating a load of two times the actual weight apportioned each loop used for lifting purposes without failure. For example, if the total net weight of container is equal to 1,000 pounds and the container is outfitted with four loops for vertical lifting purposes, each loop must be capable of lifting a weight of 500 pounds. Testing may be accomplished by filling the container to a weight of 1,000 pounds and lifting by use of two opposing loops or by filling the container to a weight of 2,000 pounds and lifting by use of all four loops.

For explanation of abbreviations and reference marks, see last pages of this tariff.

Source: National Motor Freight Traffic Association, Inc. *National Motor Freight Classification*. Washington, D.C.: NMFTA (3 April 1981): 223.

In addition to the structure of prices, there are a large number of decisions which define exactly what transportation service will be provided. To those unfamiliar with the trucking industry, the service is assumed to be trivial—simply picking up freight in one place and putting it down someplace else. To those familiar with the industry, the varieties of service are as limitless as the various industries in the United States which represent the customers of the service.

In addition, it must be remembered that a bill of lading which a shipper fills out is a document binding the originating carrier (and for joint-line traffic, the connecting carrier) and shipper to certain contractual obligations, either explicitly or by reference to tariffs or other documents.[250] These are far more elaborate than would appear to the casual observer, because the terms must cover responsibilities of the parties for a wide variety of conceivable future eventualities.[251] Figure 11 illustrates a page from the classification manual showing the information required on various types of bills of lading.

Although standardized tariffs and classifications are the backbone of the class-rate system, commodity rates and exception ratings are usually framed as departures from this basic system. For example, a commodity tariff may refer specifically to the classification system and incorporate certain tariff rules by reference rather than enumeration. All such tariffs may be thought of as exceptions in the more general sense that they work as tariffs of limited scope by specifying what part of the benchmark rate structure does not apply. Thereby they still utilize the vast "machinery" which is incorporated into the agreement between shipper and carrier simply by reference (or by failure to specify an exception).

The question remains as to why the establishment of a benchmark requires antitrust immunity. Critics either (1) contend that the efficiency gains to carrier/shipper negotiations arising from the benchmark are *de minimis*, or (2) offer the same solutions for the carrier/shipper communication problem as were discussed above for joint-line rate negotiations. Publication of benchmark rates without immunity, ossification, and mergers apply at least in principle, but combination rates and immunity for joint line only would not apply to the shipper/carrier transaction costs problem. Suffice it to say that the proposed solutions have the same weaknesses in solving the carrier/shipper communication problem as discussed above in connection with joint-line service and need not be discussed further. Critics also propose third parties employing new computer technology as the solution to the shipper/carrier problem, and this is discussed in detail below.

EFFECTS OF THE LOSS OF COLLECTIVE RATEMAKING ON TRANSACTIONS COSTS AND INDUSTRY STRUCTURE

The multilateral system established under collective ratemaking provides for equal access by all carriers to a nondiscriminatory system for estab-

Figure 11
Sample Page from the Freight Classification System: Information Required for Bills of Lading

RULES

ITEM 360 — Concluded

Sec. 1 (f). When payor of freight or other lawful charges requires or requests, as a prerequisite to payment (see Notes 2 and 3):

(1) the return of any part of bill of lading sets or copies thereof, other than one shipper furnished copy (see Note 1), a charge of $1.00 for each such document or copy will be made; OR

(2) copies of freight bills or statements of transportation charges in excess of the number specified in **Sec. 1 (e)**, a charge of $1.00 for each such document or copy will be made; OR

(3) the preparation by the carrier of any forms requiring itemization, listing or description of single or multiple freight bills, for submittal with freight bills or statements of charges, a charge of 20 cents per line of itemization, listing or description (or portion thereof) subject to a minimum charge of $1.00 per page, per copy, will be made; OR

(4) any forms or copies of forms, other than those described in **Sec. 1 (f)(1)** or **Sec. 1 (f)(2)**, to be submitted with freight bills or statements of charges, a charge of $1.00 for each such form or copy will be made; OR

(5) that information not shown on the shipping order at time of shipment be shown on freight bills or statements of charges, a charge of $1.00 per shipment will be made.

(6) that proof of delivery be furnished in any form, a charge of $1.00 for each such document or copy will be made.

Sec. 1 (g). Carriers are not obligated to furnish bills of lading containing information beyond that shown in the examples set forth on pages 272 through 281, or as amended, of the classification.

Sec. 1 (h). Consignors may elect to have printed their own bills of lading, in which case, all requirements of **Sec. 1 (a) through 1 (d) and Sec. 2** of this item must be observed. These forms may also contain such information as: (1) identification or location of consignor or consignee, (2) commodity descriptions, (3) rates or classes, or (4) other information pertinent to the shipment.

Sec. 1 (i). On bills of lading furnished by carriers, freight bills and statements of charges issued by carriers, the Standard Carrier Alpha Code (SCAC) of the issuing carrier as shown in the Continental Directory NMF 101, ICC NMF 101 (or as amended), must be shown immediately adjacent to the carrier's name on the document heading. The SCAC designation must be printed in upper case boldface type.

Note 1— When as a prerequisite to payment, the shipper furnished copy of bill of lading is to be returned, it must be clearly and prominently marked by the shipper with specific instructions directing its return with freight bill.

Note 2— The charges set forth in **Sec. 1 (f)** will not apply to:

(a) Bank Payment Plans when documentation is limited to (1) deposit ticket(s) supplied by the bank, (2) supporting freight bills not in excess of the number set forth in **Sec. 1 (e)**, or (3) the return of a copy of the bill of lading furnished by shipper.

(b) Sight Draft Plans when documentation is limited to (1) sight drafts which do not require the carrier to provide information pertaining to the rating of the shipment(s) on the sight draft, (2) supporting freight bill(s) and statement(s) of charges not in excess of number set forth in **Sec. 1 (e)**, or (3) the return of a copy of the bill of lading furnished by shipper.

Note 3— The provisions set forth in **Sec. 1 (e)** and **1 (f)** will not apply to shipments moving on United States Government bills of lading.

Sec. 2. Information to be shown on a Bill of Lading.

Sec. 2 (a). The name and address of only one consignor and one consignee and only one destination shall appear on a bill of lading. When a shipment is consigned to a point of which there are two or more of the same name in the same state, the name of the county must be shown.

Sec. 2 (b). An 'Order' bill of lading will not be issued unless the name of the corporation, firm, institution or person to whose order the shipment is consigned is plainly shown thereon after the words 'Consigned to Order of.'

¶**Sec. 2 (c).** To insure the assessment of correct freight charges and avoid infractions of federal and state laws, shippers should acquaint themselves with the descriptions of articles in the tariff under which they ship. Commodity word descriptions must be used in bills of lading and shipping orders and must conform to those in the applicable tariff. Appropriate abbreviated descriptions are permitted provided the NMFC item number and appropriate Sub number thereof are shown. The kind of package used must be shown. Bills of lading and shipping orders must specify number of articles, packages, or pieces. Except as provided in Item 640, Sec. 3 (mixed packages), for each separate commodity description, the number and type of packages (bags, boxes, bundles, drums, etc.) and the gross weight must be shown.

‡**Sec. 2 (c).** To insure the assessment of correct freight charges and avoid infractions of federal and state laws, shippers should acquaint themselves with the descriptions of articles in the tariff under which they ship. Commodity word descriptions must be used in bills of lading and shipping orders and must conform to those in the applicable tariff. Appropriate abbreviated descriptions are permitted provided the NMFC item number and appropriate Sub number thereof are shown. The kind of package used must be shown. Bills of lading and shipping orders must specify number of articles, packages, or pieces. Except as provided in Item 640, Sec. 3 (mixed packages), for each separate commodity description, the number and type of packages (bags, boxes, bundles, drums, etc.) and the gross weight must be shown.

When freight is shipped in bundles or securely fastened to pallets, platforms or skids, the number of bundles, pallets, platforms or skids shall be shown on the bill of lading as the number of packages. Also, the number of packages or pieces in the bundles or on the pallets, platforms or skids may be shown in the description section of the bill of lading.

Sec. 2 (b). Articles indicated as explosives or as dangerous articles in Hazardous Materials Tariff (HMT) must be described on bills of lading and shipping orders as shown in that tariff. Abbreviations must not be used. When HMT descriptions differ from the tariff description in connection with which the applicable class or rate is published, the tariff description must also be shown on bills of lading and shipping orders.

Sec. 3. Inspection of Property. When carrier's agent believes it is necessary that the contents of packages be inspected, he shall make or cause such inspection to be made, or require other sufficient evidence to determine the actual character of the property. When found to be incorrectly described, freight charges must be collected according to proper description.

Sec. 4. Delivery of Shipments on Order Bills of Lading:

Sec. 4 (a). The surrender to the carrier of the original Order Bill of Lading, properly endorsed is required before the delivery of the property; but, if such bill of lading be lost or delayed, **Sec. 4(b)** will govern.

Sec. 4 (b). The property may be delivered in advance of the surrender of the bill of lading upon receipt of a certified check, money order or bank cashier's check (or cash at carrier's option) by the carrier's agent for an amount equal to one hundred and twenty-five percent of the invoice or value of the property, or at carrier's option, upon receipt of a bond, acceptable to the carrier, in an amount twice the invoice or value of the property, or a blanket bond may be accepted when satisfactory to the carrier as surety, amount and form. Amounts of money deposited by certified check, money order, bank cashier's check or in cash shall be refunded in full: Immediately upon surrender of bill of lading properly endorsed or when the carrier has received a bond, acceptable to the carrier, in an amount twice the invoice or value of the property.

Sec. 5. Insurance Against Marine Risk: The cost of insurance against marine risk will not be assumed by the carrier unless so provided specifically, in its tariffs.

For explanation of abbreviations and reference marks, see last pages of this tariff.

Source: National Motor Freight Traffic Association, Inc. *National Motor Freight Classification*. Washington, D.C.: NMFTA (3 April 1981): 251.

lishing the benchmark. Under such a system, smaller carriers compete effectively while being assured that no carrier controls the vital marketing channel for defining the benchmark and communicating service or price offerings.

Most of the proposed alternatives to collective ratemaking contemplate the replacement of this multilateral system with systems controlled by individual carriers or their agents. The risks that scale economies and barriers to entry in the channel of communication of prices could be used to reduce competition in the trucking industry itself are not insignificant.[252] The result of eliminating the multilateral system could be a substantial increase in industry concentration as carriers with control over the pricing channel use that power to foreclose competitive access by carriers lacking control over that marketing channel.

Many of the larger carriers have already moved toward the use of private tariffs outside of the bureau process. As long as the use of these tariffs does not threaten the competitive access of other carriers via the collective ratemaking process, these innovative systems should be welcomed as examples of the diversity which should be encouraged within the framework of collective ratemaking. So far these systems have not displaced rate bureaus, and there are no claims in the trucking industry that they have been used to deny competitive access. But complaints of the use of these systems to suppress competitive access for anticompetitive objectives in other transportation industries suggest vigilance.

These dangers also suggest that care should be taken not to handicap the ability of multilateral systems to compete with these individual carrier systems. Given the fact that rate bureau prices today serve as a list price for discounts, some carriers are questioning the benefits and costs of rate bureau membership. Carriers have always had an incentive to be "free riders" in the collective ratemaking system. Why not let others bear the cost of the rate bureau and target your marketing and service efforts on the most lucrative traffic resulting from this pricing system, perhaps by selective rate cuts and exemptions designed to cream off the most attractive traffic?

The issue today is how to motivate carrier support for the collective ratemaking process. For many carriers, the expense of rate bureau participation is considerable. If they are publishing their own discounts against the bureau tariffs, why not just withdraw?

There must be some benefit that a carrier can get from rate bureau membership that it cannot get someplace else. This is the essential principle of financing collective action.[253] For many carriers, this benefit is often in the area of setting joint-line rates and general rate increases. Management feels that it cannot operate effectively without antitrust immunity for joint rates, but this is the area that is now clouded by uncertainty over the scope of the immunity. Motor carriers and rate bureaus fear a step-by-step process whereby the collective ratemaking process would break down:

1. The loss of single-line ratemaking immunity causes carriers to withdraw from collective discussions on joint-line rates and from providing interline service with carriers that are also competitors.
2. Carriers would withdraw from bureaus while hoping their competitors would not, so that they could "free ride" by using the bureau prices as list prices.
3. Remaining carriers in the bureaus would find their costs of participation rising, thereby encouraging further withdrawals and causing a vicious circle that finally breaks the system down.

Two factors dominate motor carrier pricing executives' attitudes toward participation in bureau affairs. First, few executives are experts on the antitrust laws. Apprised of the confusion over exactly what would and would not be legal under the antitrust laws, most express grave reservations about active participation in joint-line ratemaking and other activities which would be at the fringes of legality. The benefits of bureau participation would simply not be worth it, if they had to get the advice of an attorney for every move they made. One simply cannot expect individuals to devote their careers to actions that are at the murky fringes of criminal antitrust violations. The second factor is cost. If the chilling effect on other bureau ratemaking activities is felt, carriers will be reexamining the cost of bureau participation. Large carriers especially may simply decide to pull out.

While the rate bureaus cost carriers a lot of money, the bureaus are nonprofit associations, and any substitute for the bureaus' activities will undoubtedly result in increased transactions costs. Carriers are supporting these organizations because they are meeting the test of economic efficiency as a clearinghouse for meeting multilateral problems in ratemaking, classification, and tariff rules. Antitrust concerns can easily tip this balance.

While rate bureau issues are predominantly focused on carrier concerns, it is also true that shippers have a vital interest both in rate bureau activities and in the consequences of changes in the ratemaking climate. Since shippers are often said to have "derived immunity" for ratemaking, and restrictions on carrier immunity would flow through to shippers,[254] significant issues of collective behavior by shippers would be raised by changes in antitrust immunity.[255] Although there seems to be widespread belief by shippers that such immunity exists, shippers can hardly be assured by statements of the recent assistant attorney general for antitrust:

In recent months a novel argument has surfaced from the proponents of collective ratemaking to the effect that shippers currently have some type of "derivative" immunity from the antitrust laws under the Reed-Bulwinkle Act [foot-note omitted]. Let me state in the most unequivocal terms: There is no respectable legal argument, based either on the statute itself, legislative history, or the relevant case law that would support in any way the proposition that shippers currently have derivative immunity from the antitrust laws through the Reed-Bulwinkle Act. . . . Therefore, the repeal of Reed-Bulwinkle will have no effect on the substantive rights of shippers under the antitrust laws in any way.[256]

The Motor Carrier Act of 1980 has had a substantial effect on the traffic management function. Rate negotiations, tariff proliferation, rating errors, audits and claims, computerization of rates and routes, and participation in rate bureau activities are all concerns of shippers in the new environment.

Shippers want price competition, and they want a variety of service offerings. But they also want a standard of price and service which can provide a starting point for negotiations with carriers.[257] The increased cost of negotiation and the loss of price data that would be the conse-quence of the loss of collective ratemaking represent a cost to the shipper.

A natural consequence of the breakdown of a multilateral system and the loss of a standardized system for comparing rates and services will be a decision by shippers to reduce these transactions costs by reducing the numbers of carriers with whom they do business.[258] This tendency would exacerbate the trends working on the supply side toward industry concentration.

THIRD-PARTY SYSTEMS

The Motor Carrier Ratemaking Study Commission offered the possibility that "third party" systems supplied by independent vendors could solve all the pricing communications problems without the antitrust immu-nity.[259] This conclusion relied on claims by suppliers of computerized tariff systems who asserted that they could supplant the role of rate bureaus and that the bureaus have obstructed the use of such systems.[260]

Some of these assertions must be taken as typical overpromising by computer vendors, endemic to the industry. And some of it is undoubt-edly motivated by potential new entrants hoping to gain a competitive advantage by encouraging the demise of the incumbents. Nevertheless, the possibility that the shipper/carrier communication problem could be solved without antitrust immunity through third parties must be given serious consideration.

At this point, the discussion ordinarily turns to an examination of the relative benefits of rate bureau services versus those of some of the emerging vendors of electronic tariff systems. The evidence is that com-puterized systems supply specialized services to certain segments of the market but by no means have the present capability of completely sub-stituting for hard-copy paper tariffs or becoming a complete bourse for communicating all motor carrier pricing or service information. The sheer mass of data in the motor carrier rate structure prevents computers from being used as a complete inventory of rates available to customers which is updated frequently by carriers, as is the case for the comput-erized reservations systems now being used by airlines.[261] What emerges from the debate is a lament by vendors that a substantial sim-plification of the price structure is needed to permit electronic tariffs to provide the complete market access function of a bourse.[262] While computer vendors blame vested interests for not making the needed changes in the tariff structure, skeptics call attention to the fact that computerized systems cannot provide all the capabilities of the pres-ent system. And rate bureaus point out that they have been in the forefront of computerized tariffs and have no vested interest in any particular technology.[263]

Once again, one must resist the temptation to try to resolve all these disputes and to recommend the best system. Such a determination is simply unnecessary and is certainly premature in light of lack of knowl-edge of emerging technologies.[264] Given the fact that such vendors are now meeting the needs of certain segments of the market and are per-fectly free to offer any additional innovative services to carriers and shippers they wish, the answer is simply to challenge these beliefs by inviting their proponents to prove them in the marketplace in compe-tition with the services of rate bureaus.

But there is a catch. Proposals to employ computerized tariff systems as a substitute for rate bureaus do not call for their owners to passively inventory carrier price offers. For such computerized systems to provide complete price and service information on terms of equal access requires coordinated and substantial changes by both buyers and sellers to achieve tariff simplification, as proponents readily admit.[265] But to ac-complish this coordination, vendors of computerized tariff information systems could run afoul of the same antitrust issues as rate bureaus without the antitrust immunity.[266] Rate comparisons on a computer screen require carriers to employ reasonably consistent parameters for ratemaking (such as distance, point groupings, weight, and classifica-tion). Presently these computerized tariff systems serve rate storage and retrieval functions but play no direct role in the ratemaking function. How independent vendors would cope in an environment in which each of thousands of carriers actually developed its own, say, independent freight classification system can only be imagined. Organizing the mass of data in some coherent fashion requires the imposition of some kind of class-rate structure so that data can be logically stored and retrieved.

Simply providing a jumble of rate quotes would prevent efficient retrieval of the data. But attempts by vendors to enforce standardization would potentially raise price-sensitive issues if vendors performed any coordination role to minimize transactions costs.

The problem with these proposals to replace rate bureaus with computers is that if computerized tariff systems offered by third parties provided the same services as the rate bureaus, then they would need the same immunity. If they provided inferior services, then this is simply an argument for preserving the status quo. But if they offer improved services without the antitrust immunity, then the answer is for the proponents to simply compete with the rate bureaus for the business.

Put another way, the attempt to put a distinction between (1) collusion to establish the level and structure of a set of reference prices (presumably a *per se* antitrust offense), and (2) providing an electronic bulletin board to provide for multilateral access of pricing and service information in the trucking industry is not easily done.[267] The present complexity of the motor carrier pricing function would require the third party wishing to design such an information system to perform many of the price-sensitive functions of rate bureaus.[268] And one person's idea of rate simplification can easily become the next person's idea of price fixing—as virtually every other attempt at tariff restructuring has learned.

These difficulties imply a charitable interpretation of the suggestions by vendors of private computer systems that the antitrust immunity of motor carrier rate bureaus be lifted. In a sense, these potential competitors of rate bureaus suffer a competitive handicap of not having ICC-approved antitrust immunity and therefore are unable to compete on even terms with rate bureaus. They have elected to belittle the need for the immunity of the bureaus without, however, offering any credible reason why they cannot prevail in competition with the rate bureaus, if indeed they have a better mousetrap and antitrust immunity is not needed.[269] Computer vendors should admit freely that the collective actions needed by carriers and shippers to implement their preferred solutions raise antitrust difficulties for both rate bureaus and third parties.

The ICC has been considering various ideas of introducing more competition into the collective ratemaking industry.[270] Some of the reasons given for such proposals—to reduce the potential for anticompetitive pricing by the carriers—make little sense. But one should not prejudge whether third-party systems could provide some services now provided better by existing rate bureaus by placing competitive disadvantages on the bureaus.

The proposals of third parties to use electronic tariffs and other innovative approaches should be logically separated from the question of the antitrust immunity. The radical restructuring of the pricing function envisioned by the proponents to implement their new marketing channel raises serious issues of the level of collusion required by the participants—witness the fact that these vendors have not prevailed in competition with a system they claim is inferior to the one they offer. Either their claims are invalid or the systems cannot be implemented effectively without the antitrust immunity. If the claimed benefits of the proponents of these third-party systems were valid, the answer is more, not less, antitrust immunity.

A CASE IN POINT: RELEASED RATES

The provision in the Motor Carrier Act of 1980 for eliminating the antitrust immunity for collective ratemaking for released rates is an example of how good intentions can run counter to the realities of motor carrier ratemaking. The MCA of 1980 required that released rates, in which the shipper was offered a lower rate in consideration for a limit on the carrier's liability for loss and damage, be initiated only through independent action.

For years the ICC's express consent was required for released rates, and critics charged that the Commission was too strict in discouraging this form of innovative ratemaking. Critics of collective ratemaking blamed the rate bureaus for blocking the use of released rates. They therefore reasoned: Why not deregulate the making of released rates, rid the system of footdragging by the rate bureaus[271] and the ICC, and encourage more competition among the carriers?[272] Yet the passage of the MCA created the spectacle of both carriers and shippers requesting the reinstitution of collective ratemaking for released rates.[273]

The prohibition of collective ratemaking for released rates is a microcosm of the issues arising from prohibiting single-line collective ratemaking. Proponents of the elimination of collective ratemaking for released rates presumably hoped to encourage the adoption of such rates because they offered shippers improved rate/service options. But the elimination of collective ratemaking simply eliminated an efficient means of implementing this ratemaking approach. The effect was an immediate decrease in released rate activity.

Released rates are a good example where collective ratemaking and individual carrier pricing actions are complementary, not in competition. If a ratemaking innovation is desirable, it should be encouraged by every means available, not by cutting off avenues of implementation. But that is exactly what has happened in the case of released rates.

Shippers complained that they would like to deal with released rates through classification changes and broad tariff changes, so that they do not have to negotiate separate arrangements with hundreds or even thousands of carriers. In setting up their insurance, claims, interlining and shipping practices, they often wanted to deal with carriers on a multilateral basis.[274]

More recently, shippers have focused their concern on the use of so-called automatic releases, whereby a carrier publishes a reduction in liability of which the shipper may be unaware. Since the reduced liability may not have been negotiated, the shipper may be unaware of the policy as it has emerged outside of the collective ratemaking process.

The released rates fiasco may be thought of as a good illustration of the dangers of ossifying the collective rate structure as it was under the regime of strict regulation, rather than giving it the opportunity to respond to competitive forces. There is a lesson here: many aspects of motor carrier transportation work best in a collective agreement among shippers and carriers. Rather than prejudging the issue on collective versus individual ratemaking, public policy should seek to implement whatever approach works best.[275]

A CASE IN POINT: ANTITRUST IMMUNITY FOR CLASSIFICATION

Critics of collective ratemaking deny that the antitrust immunity results in a simplified benchmark rate structure which provides an efficient reference point from joint-line ratemaking and minimizing transactions costs for carriers and shippers. Indeed, they claim that the present benchmark system, the class-rate structure, is unduly complex and that the commodity characteristics traditionally used in classification (see Table 33) incorporate too much value-of-service ratemaking and relied too little on cost-of-service attributes.[276] The classification system for establishing class rates is generally the target of these criticisms.[277] In the most extreme form, some claim that every carrier should compete with its own classification system.[278]

Freight classification is the construction of defining the pigeonholes to which services and rates are to be assigned. Every firm and industry must define exactly what the customer gets and exactly what is charged, and this process results in a process of standardization to a greater or lesser degree depending on consumers' needs for compatibility.

All outsiders to the process of motor commodity classification have no doubt at some point complained of its complexity and yearned for a simpler system. But attempts to change the system must confront the causes of the complexity in the present system. First, the present complexity serves the interests of many users. Implementation of any simpler system would undoubtedly create incentives for modifications, exceptions, and so on, that would only reintroduce the complexity. Attempts at simplification must overcome strong forces of entropy caused by competition itself. Second, much of the complexity results from the fact that motor carriers are regulated companies with a common carrier obliga-

Table 33
Transportation Characteristics Used to Establish Commodity Classification

1. Shipping weight per cubic foot

2. Liability to damage

3. Liability to damage other commodities with which it is transported

4. Perishability

5. Liability to spontaneous combustion or explosion

6. Susceptibility to theft

7. Value per pound in comparison with other articles

8. Ease or difficulty in loading or unloading

9. Stowability

10. Excessive weight

11. Excessive length

12. Care or attention necessary in loading and transporting

13. Trade conditions*

14. Value of service*

15. Competition with other commodities transported*

*The ICC, in *Investigation into Motor Carrier Classification, Ex Parte* No. MC–98 (Sub-No. 1), 367 ICC 243 (1981), eliminated these characteristics from consideration when making changes to the classification system.

tion. It is easy to have a simple pricing structure if you do not have to specify in advance the terms on which you are legally required to do business with any customer who demands service in an industry with a complex cost structure.

More competition in the motor carrier industry has certainly not contributed to tariff simplification as hoped for by its proponents. Indeed, the present spate of rate cutting has produced a substantial increase in the complexity of the ratemaking system.[279] The true sources of the complexity in ratemaking are not the class rates but rather the discounting, exception ratings, and commodity rates, among others, which are driven by competition.

The desirability of simplification of tariffs and the avoidance of cross-subsidy are not compatible goals in transportation pricing. Indeed, one could make the case that the class rates are too simple, giving rise to the complexity of all the exceptions and discounts. Very simple tariffs tend to incorporate cross-subsidy and generate distinctions between "good traffic" and "bad traffic" whenever there are significant within-class differences in the cost characteristics of the traffic. Carriers then practice "cream skimming" and shun the bad traffic. As good traffic starts eroding, more and more exceptions and discounts for good traffic start entering the rate structure, along with arbitraries and other surcharges for bad traffic. The greater the competitive forces, the greater the proliferation of rates to recognize major cost differences.

Deregulation-minded critics of classification are disingenuous on the complexity issue. Critics complain that the system does not account for attributes of the shipper (such as location and volume) but only the attributes of the commodity (such as density and packaging).[280] But expanding the range of what is considered would increase, not decrease, the complexity of the system. Most of the proposals for eliminating immunity would vastly increase the complexity if each carrier competed to offer the best classification, as proponents hope. Proposals to permit a national classification that merely provided multidimensional ratings of commodities on the basis of numerous attributes rather than a single rating would, of course, result in a great increase in complexity of both the classification and the ratemaking system.[281]

The need for a common classification system is strongly felt for interline freight and for the benchmark rate structure used by shippers.[282] Some might hope that with the loss of antitrust immunity for classification and joint-line rates, the carriers would somehow join together under the direction of the Invisible Hand to establish a consistent set of classifications, points, rates, and tariff rules for joint-line rates but go their own way in establishing entirely different tariff structures for single-line rates.

Under a system where each carrier developed its own classification and rate structure, each carrier might attempt to simplify its tariffs, but every system would be different (this is exactly what is contemplated by the proponents as each carrier competed to provide the best classification system). Even if every carrier offered a simpler classification, the shipper would be looking at a vast proliferation of new tariffs. Indeed, proponents of eliminating antitrust immunity would evaluate the success of their proposals on the degree of variety of the carrier offerings.

The Study Commission attempted to have it both ways by arguing that "all forms of collective ratemaking would be barred if antitrust immunity is eliminated" (p. xi), but that uniform classification could be retained if the "non-cost-related classification criteria" (see Table 33) were eliminated (p. xi).[283] No expert legal opinion sufficient to assuage those exposed to potential jail terms was cited in the commission's conclusion that a classification system purged of subjective noncost items would not violate the antitrust laws (pp. 503–505).[284] The report simply ignored the fact that carriers could be given no assurances that they would not be exposed to criminal prosecution. This is enough to create a chilling effect on collective classification.

If simplicity *per se* is the goal, hope for a simpler classification system lies entirely in a collective ratemaking system. The elimination of collective classification would simply ossify the existing classification system, making simplification impossible, since no individual carrier could unilaterally change the benchmark rate structure. One suspects that critics would be delighted with a far more complex rate structure with even more value-of-service pricing, if only it did not result from collective ratemaking. This suggests that simplification is not the real issue, but instead their objection to the use of a benchmark rate structure.

But establishing a common classification system poses the same antitrust dilemma outlined above for joint-line rates in general. If carriers engage in behavior that produces a simplified classification system on consistent terms, they are in danger of being accused of engaging in collusive behavior without antitrust immunity, since the resulting classification does not produce the diversity of competing classifications desired by the opponents of collective classification. To permit the legal establishment of the desired common system, one could extend antitrust immunity for classification to be applied only to joint-line rates, but the result is either (1) the widespread adoption of the same classification for single-line rates to meet shippers' desires for a common classification, or (2) the collapse of collective classification for interline traffic because carriers are intimidated from exercising it by antitrust enforcement designed to maintain the antitrust deterrent to collective action on single-line collective ratemaking.

But even if these arguments are wrong, there is a fundamental flaw in the assertion that the answer is to eliminate collective ratemaking for freight classification. If the present system is uneconomic and unresponsive to customer needs, there is nothing to stop individual carriers from today pursuing the alternative of independent action to establish improved classification. If the benefits of such alternatives are so great, carriers would be highly motivated to pursue them, and certainly they need not wait for Congress to abolish the collectively established alternative.

RATE SIMPLIFICATION AND COLLECTIVE RATEMAKING

The administrative costs of a complex rate structure can be large, and simple structures are preferred over more complex ones, other things being equal. A tribute to simplicity having been said, the tribute itself leads us nowhere. The proposed solutions to the complexity problem offered by critics primarily serve to show how many simple systems could be coexisting as unilateral offerings of the carriers. As an alternative to rate basis numbers and for zip codes considering distance in the rate schedule, highway mileage guides and other zone systems are offered. Some critics believe that freight classification should be abolished entirely in favor of "freight-all-kinds" (FAK) rates, while others propose abolishing the present classification scheme in favor of an entirely different one. The alternative proposals go on and on.

Appeals to abolish collective ratemaking to encourage allegedly more efficient rate simplification contain a fundamental flaw: Why would the abolition of collective ratemaking motivate the adoption of unilaterally adopted innovations when the threat of financial ruin during the post–1980 shakeout period was insufficient? If carriers were undercutting the collective rate level with independent actions, why were they not undercutting the artificial complexity allegedly induced by collective ratemaking with their own simplified tariffs? Critics would have us believe that the same carriers that were discounting the rate level clung stubbornly to an inefficient collective classification that each was nevertheless empowered to change unilaterally.

One strongly suspects that elimination of collective ratemaking would reverse the perspectives on complexity. Under today's system, many shippers often do not perceive undue complexity because only a small part of the vast tariff system applies to them. Carriers usually provide rate guides for particular shippers to simplify the problem. However, the carrier's rate clerk must be able to rate a variety of freight bills and must have knowledge of the entire system.

What it all boils down to is that critics of collective ratemaking probably do not object to complexity as such. Their concern is that the present complexity arises from a system that they do not like. But critics' proposals to simplify the benchmark rate structure would trade one kind of complexity for another—for example, the encouragement of more IA's, more backhaul rates, individual carrier classifications and rate structures, and more. The question of antitrust immunity thus does not turn on the complexity issue *per se*. The real question is whether there should be a benchmark rate system which by definition will be simple when compared to the sum of the results of bilateral negotiations. If the debate is over the process, not the outcome, simplicity is not the critical feature.

If one believes that the pressures for competition are sufficiently strong, the charge that motor carrier rate structures are too complex should not be subject to a definitive evaluation.[285] Such a determination is not necessary. The objective of public policy should be not to place artificial obstacles to the implementation of competing classification and pricing alternatives. If carriers under strong competitive pressures elect to keep the old system despite the fact that the critics do not like it, that decision should cause the critics to reexamine their presumption that they know more than buyers and sellers in the marketplace. Whether the result of more competitive pricing is more or less price discrimination will not affect the opinions of the parties, since whatever emerges under competition invariably becomes a standard for inferring the inefficiency of the prior regime.[286]

A CASE IN POINT: PUBLISHED PRICES

Most would agree that full disclosure of rates is a desirable goal if it can be achieved without a reduction in the level of competition. Buyers and sellers usually find price information on comparable transactions and the offers of other buyers and sellers in the marketplace very helpful in evaluating their options. The more sophisticated the product or service, the greater the usefulness of price data to evaluate the reasonableness of the alternatives faced by the buyer or seller. For example, information on the last trade and the bid/ask range is extremely helpful to securities buyers and sellers, and trading tends to slacken on the stock exchanges when the price data are delayed. Data on comparable sales are extremely valuable to real estate appraisers.

Buyers generally have two sources of data to evaluate the competitiveness of sellers' price offers. The most obvious source is the price offers of competing sellers and recently observed comparable transactions. This source works best for actively trading markets of reasonably standardized products or services and clearly has the lowest transactions and information costs. The other alternative is to acquire information about the sellers' costs. Cost information is itself costly to acquire and often easy to misinterpret, particularly in transportation networks supplying manifold services. Publishing price information normally is the preferred answer to increasing the efficiency of a transportation market.

While the benefits of full disclosure of prices from recent comparable transactions seem apparent, there are circumstances where economists believe secret rebates can lead to improvements in economic welfare. Under circumstances of a true cartel, secret rebates can help break the cartel by exploiting the fact that individual members have the incentive to depart from the cartel's pricing and output decisions. If the seller can gain anonymity and, thereby, avoid retribution from secret rebating, especially through complex pricing formulae for sophisticated products or services, the pricing power of the cartel is eroded. Opponents of collective ratemaking therefore feel that disclosure is a disadvantage because it purportedly discourages price competition.[287]

In the present circumstances of the motor carrier industry, however, the arguments for disclosure of price information through published prices seem compelling. There are many buyers of trucking services, and the cost of negotiating prices on a shipper-by-shipper basis could be quite high if carriers are not required to publish tariffs and abide by them. Shippers find that published bureau tariffs provide useful list prices, which are the starting point for negotiations, and feel a strong need for the protection of a published rate.[288] Existing rate cutting is evidence that secret rebating is not necessary to create an environment of rate competition.

A CASE IN POINT: GENERAL RATE INCREASES

The controversy over motor carrier rate levels suggests a closer look at the rationale for the antitrust immunity for establishing the level of the fallback rate, as opposed to the structure of the rates. The rationale for collective ratemaking expressed in terms of minimizing transactions costs would suggest little danger of anticompetitive price levels even in the absence of regulation. To minimize transactions costs, carriers would seek to make the reference tariff apply to as many transactions costs as possible. If the threat of independent action eliminated the threat of anticompetitive pricing, the goal of minimizing transactions cost could best be achieved by establishing a competitive rate level for the benchmark collective tariff.

Cutting against this incentive to minimize transactions costs, however, is the ceiling-price effect of the collective tariff. Price cutting will occur on the more profitable traffic moving under the collective tariff, but carriers have found that the existence of the collective tariff prevents unilateral rate increases on the less profitable traffic. This adverse selection process means that traffic moving under the collective tariff will become increasingly unattractive and require above-average rate increases despite what is happening to the overall average of rates.

The inflation of the benchmark rate structure, after regulatory reform encouraged selective rate cutting, can thus be explained by the ceiling-price effect. Rate bureau tariffs (the list prices) have been increasing faster than inflation while carrier discounts accelerated and carrier profitability declined.

If the process of rate increases and enhanced discounting were to continue unabated, the final result would be the elimination of the value of the class-rate structure as a posted price system and its use only as a list price. The only way to counter this tendency toward increased transactions costs is to make the benchmark tariff more cost-justified, but this leads to ever-increasing complexity to make the necessary cost distinctions, thereby reducing the benefits of a simplified benchmark as a standard for negotiating.

The complaint that the bureau sets cartel prices is curious in light of this ceiling-price effect. The present system of collective ratemaking, combined with vigorous use of independent action, is hardly an unalloyed benefit to the carrier. The shipper's hand in negotiations with carriers is obviously greatly strengthened by virtue of access to a stack of bureau tariffs being held out by dozens of competing carriers usually only too happy to get the business at the bureau tariff levels.

In the future, an exact opposite worry might be hypothesized: that there are some shippers for whom the transactions costs are so high and the costs of service so high that the collective tariff will almost always be the actual rate. If the efficiency gains for the traffic moving under the benchmark tariff are substantial enough, these transactions and information costs become a barrier to entry for pricing via independent action which can be used to set tariff levels that earn excessive profits. While the allocative efficiency losses are likely to be small (by dint of the same fact that the traffic would not be diverted), there is a question of equity resulting from the excessive costs imposed on shippers.

The present level of competition in the industry, however, precludes any excessive earnings. Nevertheless, these concerns over possible anticompetitive pricing of high transactions cost traffic—small shippers—suggest a reasonable compromise of continued regulatory oversight over rate levels through general rate increases established under antitrust immunity.

Conclusions and Recommendations 6

Without entry controls rate bureaus will either disappear because now there is no monopoly to implement, or, if they survive, it will be for reasons having nothing to do with "monopoly." They will survive because they serve to reduce uncertainty for carriers and shippers alike and/or because they make a contribution to cost reduction in the industry. I do see why motor carriers might wish to retain rate bureaus to keep these benefits even after the battle to retain entry controls was lost. But it is rather like Lee at Appomattox asking that his men be allowed to take their horses back home for spring plowing.

The hostility of deregulation advocates to rate bureaus is, I suspect, mainly a matter of unexamined ideology....To many supporters of antitrust, the exemption given to rate bureaus is very nearly a personal insult. This is especially true of rate bureaus in trucking because they view trucking as a naturally competitive industry.

DONALD DEWEY, "Neglected Issues in Collective
Ratemaking," Third Dana/ATA Foundation
Academic Symposium, Stanford University,
December 1981, p. 3.

EFFECTS OF COLLECTIVE RATEMAKING

The results of this study may be readily stated: there is no evidence to support the contention that motor carrier rate bureaus act as government-enforced cartels. The trucking industry has experienced the most brutal price war in modern history. Contrary to the criticism that rate bureaus enforce uniformity of prices, rate competition in the motor carrier industry over the last four years has been intense. Data on rate bureau activities show an avalanche of IA's in addition to the widespread rate cuts, particularly in the form of discounts off bureau tariffs. Far from suppressing rate competition, bureaus are establishing list prices which become reference points for individual carrier pricing and carrier/shipper negotiations.

ICC enforcement of rate regulation and entry controls, which adherents of the theory agree must be strict to enforce the alleged cartel, is in fact extremely permissive. Changes in entry policy, rate regulation, and rate bureau functions arising from the Motor Carrier Act of 1980 and administrative reform by the ICC effectively refute the cartel theory. Institution of no-notice Independent Actions by the ICC, combined with a glut of capacity in the industry, has greatly encouraged individual carrier price competition. Rate bureaus could not conspire to enforce a trucking cartel even if they wanted to.

Group ratemaking neither bails out the inefficient nor penalizes the efficient carrier. Because revenue needs are based on weighted average costs, every carrier has an incentive to beat the averages. And carriers of less-than-average efficiency will, by definition, be unable to earn money at rate levels based on the costs of the average carrier.

Today's collective ratemaking system has vastly simplified the arrangements for negotiating interline agreements and communicating price and service offers to shippers. Certain elements of the interline arrangements are handled through the bilateral agreement itself, and other elements are handled through the tariffs. Standardized procedures for terms of service, revenue divisions, and interline settlements minimize substantially the transactions costs burden.

EFFECTS OF ABOLISHING COLLECTIVE RATEMAKING

The elimination of antitrust immunity for single-line rates only, while attempting to preserve the immunity for joint-line rates, broad tariff changes, general rate increases, and classification, is not working in the way intended by its supporters. There is no principle of antitrust economics or law that permits the full force of the antitrust laws to be applied to one part of a market while granting meaningful antitrust immunity for the same competitors in the remainder.

There is no evidence that the restrictions on single-line collective ratemaking in the MCA of 1980 are encouraging more competitive pricing. These restrictions actually eliminate existing avenues for rate cutting. Some shippers may actually find that their position has worsened because they previously preferred to have a tariff item adopted collectively by the bureau rather than haphazardly by individual carriers. Because existing tariffs are grandfathered, the result is the beginning of the ossification of the existing tariff structure.

Joint-line and single-line rates and service compete directly in the same marketplace. The fact that a carrier offers both services in the same city pair would pose grave antitrust problems for that carrier with antitrust immunity removed for single-line ratemaking. Statements by law enforcement officials either assume this problem away or propose that joint-line rates be offered only on an end-to-end basis. Their suggestions are not very helpful because few pairs of carriers find themselves only offering end-to-end, complementary services. Where carriers also compete directly, the construction of tariffs that applied only to end-to-end movements would be a nightmare and would probably not insulate carriers from antitrust exposure anyway. The end-to-end doctrine would mean the end of simplified broad tariffs and the construction of point-to-point atomized pricing for interline traffic.

If collective ratemaking for interline traffic was threatened by the loss of antitrust immunity, bilateral agreements would have to assume the burden of handling the business arrangements now handled collectively. The result would be a substantial increase in the transactions costs of such service. It would definitely discourage joint-line service, a price which proponents usually acknowledge, and sometimes even welcome. If the result of these thousands of bilateral negotiations was the competitive diversity of pricing and service options desired by its proponents, the bewildering results for shippers and carriers can only be imagined. Carriers and shippers would constantly be disputing the inconsistencies among carriers in the tariff provisions, rules, and classifications, among others.

EVALUATION OF THE COORDINATION/COMPETITION TRADEOFF

When it is all said and done, the choice is between (1) the effects of increased transactions costs of bilateral arrangements on efficiency and industry concentration, and (2) the potential high prices from collusion fostered by collective ratemaking. The paradox is that the tariff conformity that reduces transactions costs would also facilitate anticompetitive price fixing in a market susceptible to cartelization. If the anticompetitive dangers were realistic, the tradeoff would be difficult indeed and in all likelihood point to a fallback to the usual presumption of a *per se* opposition to any arrangement that facilitates price fixing.

Evidence of vigorous price competition in the trucking industry, however, suggests that the dangers from price fixing are likely to be *de minimis*. The simple truth of the matter today is that rate bureaus cannot oppose competitive pricing in the motor carrier industry. Most carriers certainly wish that somebody would stop the rate cutting, but the rate bureaus simply do not have the power to do so today. Both carriers and bureaus have resigned themselves to the fact that the task is to compete. Without the government-enforced cartel policed by tight ICC constraints on rates and entry, the difficulties of enforcing noncompetitive prices on a sustained basis would seem to be insurmountable. And there are indeed substantial benefits of collective ratemaking in reduced transactions and information costs.

A system of competition, collective ratemaking, and residual regulation in the motor carrier industry offers a sound basis for resolving the tension between the need for coordination and competition. Carriers would have the opportunity to integrate their ratemaking procedures and services to meet a legitimate need. Carriers would be highly motivated to use the collective process to reduce transactions costs in the pricing function and would be constrained by competition from using it to advance anticompetitive interests. Carriers and rate bureaus would be motivated to make the resulting rates as competitive as possible to reduce transactions costs (i.e., bilateral negotiations among carriers and shippers). When particular circumstances create a situation where the private costs of negotiations justify the private benefits of specialized services and prices, carriers and shippers would be encouraged to engage in Independent Actions. And where the private costs exceed the private benefits, a circumstance likely to be frequent in light of the large number of buyers and sellers and disparate transactions, the parties would always have a fallback reference point established by the collective ratemaking process.

Granting multilateral collective ratemaking organizations the ability to compete on equal terms against bilateral negotiations is also likely to have major benefits in terms of promoting an industry structure conducive to competition in the trucking industry. Preserving the alternative of the multilateral system would increase the difficulties of a large motor carrier seeking to control this vital marketing channel in order to gain a competitive advantage. It would ensure the continued existence of relatively low barriers to entry in the industry because any newcomer would have access to the collective system on equal terms with incumbents. Furthermore, it will reduce the incentives to merge as a means of overcoming the antitrust concerns arising from joint-line ratemaking and the perceived need to offer a full complement of services without need for coordination with rivals—an understandable but regrettable incentive which would be created by eliminating the antitrust immunity for such cooperation.

These trends are troubling because the demise of collective ratemaking is likely to be irreversible. The real danger at present is that ill-advised efforts to suppress collective ratemaking will place such a competitive disadvantage on smaller firms that industry concentration will increase to the point that critics of collective ratemaking will be right—with collective ratemaking in the hands of a few carriers with the power to collude to set noncompetitive rates, we will have lost the policy option of allowing collective ratemaking constrained only by a permissive system of regulation. Antitrust immunity simply preserves collective ratemaking as an option. If alternative mechanisms prove to be more responsive to the needs of carriers and shippers, they will have met the test of competition.

The principal argument in opposition to antitrust immunity for col-

lective ratemaking is that cooperation among competitors facilitates collusive price fixing. As yet there is no evidence to support these claims
in the post–1980 environment. As long as entry is free and entry barriers
are low, as long as rate bureaus and carriers individually are unable to
restrict supply, and as long as evidence of unrestrained price competition
is available, the dangers of abuse of collective ratemaking are likely to
be *de minimis*.

What if the above analysis is wrong and collective ratemaking does
not enhance efficiency? Even if one believed that bilateral negotiations
between buyers and sellers and between carriers offering joint-line services were always inherently more efficient, or if one simply were not
sure of the facts one way or the other, or believed they might change
in the future, these beliefs would not support the call for the end to
collective ratemaking.

As long as competitive forces in the motor carrier industry are vigorous, the market should decide which system of tariffs is the most
efficient. Transportation policy on collective ratemaking in trucking
should "let a thousand flowers bloom." We have everything to gain and
very little at risk by letting the bureaus compete freely against bilateral
and unilateral ratemaking deals. But Congress should not prejudge the
matter by arbitrarily prohibiting multilateral tariffs under collective
ratemaking. Instead of forcing all negotiations into a bilateral mode, the
availability of collective ratemaking would permit bilateral negotiations
to be freely pursued when the benefits exceed the costs. With carriers
free to negotiate whatever they want to with individual shippers today
and doing so at a stupendous rate, and with only minimal constraints
on entry, the danger of abuse of collective ratemaking is insignificant.
If the critics are right and individual carrier tariffs and bilateral joint-line
rates are more responsive to the marketplace, then the bureaus will fall
of their own weight. But if transactions costs can be saved and the
bureaus are providing a service that meets the needs of carriers and
shippers, collective ratemaking can continue to survive in competition
with unilateral or bilateral tariffs. Let the market, not unexamined ideology, decide which system of tariffs is the most efficient and for what
services.

Notes

1. INTRODUCTION

1. Reed-Bulwinkle Act, 62 Stat. 472 (1948) (codified as amended at 49 U.S.C. 10706). See Eliott Bunce, "A History of the Reed-Bulwinkle Act," presented before the Motor Carrier Ratemaking Study Commission, February 1982, and David H. Coburn, "A Review of the Reed-Bulwinkle Act in the Context of Other Antitrust Exemptions," presented before the Motor Carrier Ratemaking Study Commission, March 1982.

2. See Stephen J. Thompson, "Trucking Rate Bureaus" (Washington, D.C.: Congressional Research Service, Library of Congress, 26 February 1979), Report No. 79–57 E.

3. For a history of the origins of the antitrust immunity and the functioning of the rate bureaus, see Motor Carrier Ratemaking Study Commission, *Collective Ratemaking in the Trucking Industry: A Report to the President and the Congress of the United States* (Washington, D.C.: U.S. Government Printing Office, 1 June 1983), Chapter 4, especially pages 146–91, hereafter cited as Study Commission *Report*.

4. See Annette M. LaMond, *Competition in the General Freight Motor Carrier Industry* (Lexington, Mass.: Lexington Books, 1980), for a survey of the economics of the industry.

5. For a sampling of the literature supporting deregulation, see Paul W. MacAvoy and John W. Snow, ed., *Regulation of Entry and Pricing in Truck Transportation* (Washington, D.C.: American Enterprise Institute for Public Policy Research, 1977); Thomas Gale Moore, "Deregulating Surface Freight Transportation," in *Promoting Competition in Regulated Markets*, Almarin Phillips, ed. (Washington, D.C.: Brookings Institution, 1975); James R. Frew, "The Existence of Monopoly Profits in the Motor Carrier Industry," *Journal of Law and Economics* 24, no. 2 (1981): 289–315; and National Academy of Sciences, *Motor Carrier Economic Regulation* (Washington, D.C.: NAS, 1978).

6. Pub. Law No. 96–296, 94 Stat. 793 (codified in various sections of 49 U.S.C.). For a survey of the provisions of the MCA, see Donald V. Harper, "The Federal Motor Carrier Act of 1980: Review and Analysis," *Transportation Journal* 20, no. 2 (Winter 1980): 5–33.

7. See Grant M. Davis, "The Collective Ratemaking Issue: Circa 1984," *Transportation Practitioners Journal* 52, no. 1 (Fall 1984): 60–68.

8. 49 U.S.C. 10 706(b)(3)(D).

9. See testimonies of Professors George Hilton, George Wilson, Thomas Gale Moore, and Alfred Kahn before the Study Commission, for example.

10. See Dwight Dively, "Applications of Regulatory Theory to the Trucking Industry," *Research in Law and Economics* 6 (1984): 211–26.

11. See William B. Tye, "Status Review on Regulation of Trucking and Collective Ratemaking," in *Boundaries between Competition and Economic Regulation*, J. Rhoads Foster et al., eds. (Washington, D.C.: Institute for the Study of Regulation, 1983); "Collective Ratemaking Backers Far Outnumber 'Antis' in MCRSC Record," *Traffic World* (20 December 1982): 22–23; and Grant M. Davis, "Educator Sees Flaws in Report of Ratemaking Study Commission," *Traffic World* (9 May 1983): 35–40, for a review of shipper positions. See Management Analysis Center, "Developments Expected by Participants," report prepared for the Motor Carrier Ratemaking Study Commission, Washington, D.C., July 1982, p. 10, for a contrary view that "individual shipper positions on collective ratemaking and continued immunity were decidely [*sic*] mixed."

12. An Independent Action is a tariff item proposed and implemented by an individual carrier through a rate bureau solely for its own account and not a collective carrier action, although the tariff item is published by the rate bureau, and other carriers may subsequently adopt the tariff item for their account.

13. See, for example, Tr. p. 24, lines 10–11, and Tr. pp. 123–28, in the first Washington hearing of the Ratemaking Study Commission, 18 November 1981.

14. For a more complete review of the facts that come to light during this period, see Robert E. Mabley and Walter D. Strack, "Deregulation—A Green Light for Trucking Efficiency," *Regulation* (July/August 1982): 36–42, 56; *Prepared Statement of William B. Tye*, before the Motor Carrier Ratemaking Study Commission, 19 March 1982; Tye, "Pricing Under the Motor Carrier Act of 1980," *Proceedings: Seminar on Transport Pricing, Costing, and User Charges* (Washington, D.C.: Transportation Research Forum, Washington Chapter, 6–7 April 1982); Tye, "Motor Carrier Act of 1980 Requires New Marketing Strategy in Trucking," *Traffic World* (16 March 1981): 32–33; and Tye, "Implications of Motor Carrier Regulatory Reform for Carrier Planning and Marketing," *Transportation Research Record 804: Surface Regulatory Reform: Rail, Truck, and Intermodal* (Washington, D.C.: National Academy of Sciences, 1981). For further data on the effects of the rate war, see Jerry A. Hausman, "Information Costs, Competition, and Collective Ratemaking in the Motor Carrier Industry," *The American University Law Review* 32, no. 2 (Winter 1983): 377–92.

15. Thomas L. Friedman, "The Rocky Road for Truckers," *The New York Times* (24 January 1982).

16. "What the ICC did do was to allow virtually any independently announced rate to go into effect without examination...the number of independent actions and discount rates has taken something of a quantum leap. Independently announced rates by carriers in the ten major bureaus increased from 28,207 in 1979, to 60,600 in 1980, a 115 percent increase." Joseph M. Clapp, Senior Vice President, Roadway Express, "Impact of the Motor Carrier Act of 1980—A Motor Carrier Perspective," presented at the Transportation Research Board Annual Meeting, Washington, D.C., 19 January 1982.

17. Statement of Denis A. Breen, before the Motor Carrier Ratemaking Study

Commission, 18 November 1981. See also James C. Miller III, "First Report Card on Trucking Deregulation," *The Wall Street Journal* (8 March 1982).

18. Denis A. Breen, Bureau of Economics, Federal Trade Commission, "Regulatory Reform and the Trucking Industry: An Evaluation of the Motor Carrier Act of 1980." Bureau of Economics, Federal Trade Commission. Submitted to the MCRSC, March 1982.

19. See Denis A. Breen, "Antitrust and Price Competition in the Trucking Industry," *The Antitrust Bulletin* 28, no. 1 (Spring 1983): 201–25.

20. *Testimony of Gary Broemser*, U.S. Department of Transportation, before the Motor Carrier Ratemaking Study Commission, 18 November 1981. See also statements before the Study Commission by Thomas A. Trantum, Thomas Gale Moore, and James M. Voytko on 19 March 1982 in Boston.

21. The apotheosis of the theory that the elimination of collective ratemaking would have no meaningful effect on the economic performance of the trucking industry was found in contract research by Management Analysis Center (MAC) sponsored by the Study Commission, "The Motor Carrier Market Place Without Collective Ratemaking," September 1982. This report concluded (p. 52) that "with the exception of this possible negative outcome for some sections of the rate auditing industry the elimination of antitrust immunity for *all* collective ratemaking will probably have limited effect on the way in which rates are negotiated and published." In contrast to the prior arguments against collective ratemaking, MAC stressed how little traffic is moving under bureau tariffs, how unconcentrated the market is, how competitive are carrier pricing strategies, and how insignificant the protection of antitrust immunity really is.

22. In contrast to previous assertions that nothing good could ever come from a rate bureau, opponents of the antitrust immunity began to suggest that the efficiency gains of collective ratemaking were so compelling that carriers would find a way around a partial or even a total loss of antitrust immunity. The theory is that the efficiency gains could be the basis for urging the courts to accept a rule-of-reason test for price fixing in the motor carrier industry rather than the usual *per se* standard. See, for example, Statement of Elliott Seiden and Eugene C. Crew before the Study Commission on 19 March 1982; and "DOJ Official Says Antitrust Immunity 'Much Ado About Nothing,'" *Transportation Antitrust Report* (November 1984): 8. One attorney who had previously spoken out against collective ratemaking at the hearings of the Study Commission, Eugene Crew, in "Rate Bureaus and the Rule of Reason," *Traffic World* (12 December 1983): 64–67, later noted that "[i]f competition is the flywheel of our economy, information is the grease which makes that flywheel turn." Since "[w]ithout this co-operation among competitors, the nation's transportation system would be severely impaired," the efficiency gains from collective ratemaking would "probably be held lawful" under the rule of reason. Missing from this rule of reason approach was any explanation of why motor carrier executives should be threatened with jail terms if indeed there were efficiency gains from collective ratemaking that they should preserve via the rule of reason rather than via a clearly articulated immunity.

23. See William B. Tye, "Scenarios of the Motor Carrier Industry without Collective Ratemaking," *Transportation Practitioners Journal* 52, no. 4 (Summer 1985): 493–511.

24. See Garland Chow, "An Economic Inquiry into the Options and Impacts of Rate Regulation on Motor Transportation Markets," paper presented at Third Dana/ ATA Foundation Academic Symposium, Stanford University, 8–9 December 1981.

25. The commission was initially deadlocked five to five on the issues in late 1982, but the defeat of one of the congressional members (Senator Howard W. Cannon) permitted his removal as a member of the Study Commission and the appointment of an opponent of collective ratemaking in early 1983. As a result of the delay, the restrictions on collective ratemaking for single-line rates were postponed from 1 January 1984 to 1 July 1984. A minority of Study Commission members issued a spirited rebuttal of the majority report (pp. 27–61) and Senator Cannon also issued a statement (pp. 63–72). The minority in effect questioned whether the chairman had "packed" the commission after the initial tie vote by not replacing another member (voting with the chairman) whose qualifications to serve had also become suspect and complained that the *Report* did not reflect substantial disagreement among the members.

26. The Study Commission's *Report* focused on issues where it apparently believed that the case against collective ratemaking was the easiest to make in an era of permissive regulation and widespread rate competition: effects on discrimination, uniformity of rates, cross-subsidies to small communities, and rate stability. The transactions costs issues discussed below were either ignored or assumed to be solved by bilateral negotiations between carriers or even multilateral agreements in the absence of antitrust immunity. The commission's unwillingness to examine the transactions costs issues discussed below produced a number of logical inconsistencies as the majority hoped to retain the benefits of collective ratemaking without the immunity. For example, the *Report* concluded that if "non-cost related classification criteria" were eliminated from "uniform classification," antitrust immunity would not be needed. This view has been denied by many antitrust experts (see discussion to follow). Indeed, the Study Commission chairman's cover letter to the *Report* itself inconsistently states that without the immunity, "the current pricing practices of the industry would very likely be *per se* violations of current antitrust standards." See also *Report* at p. 513, where it is stated that "[t]he net effect is that *all forms* of collective ratemaking would be barred if antitrust immunity is eliminated."

27. See, for example, the statement of John K. Maser III on behalf of the National Industrial Traffic League (NITL) and Richard G. Velten on behalf of the National Small Shipments Traffic Conference (NASSTRAC) and the Drug and Toilet Preparation Traffic Conference (D&TPTC) on 18 November 1981 at the Washington Hearing of the Study Commission.

28. Proponents of eliminating antitrust immunity for collective ratemaking have always been puzzled by the overwhelming support by shippers for the system before the recent change in ICC policy. Former ICC Chairman Darius Gaskins in his remarks before the National Industrial Traffic League, 19 November 1980, p. 10, colorfully compared shippers' support for collective ratemaking to "a turkey's support for Thanksgiving."

29. Although no hard data are available, reports indicate that large shippers are negotiating discounts of 30 to 50 percent off published tariff rates, or even higher in some cases, while smaller shippers are more likely to pay the published rate. See *Testimony of Paul O. Roberts* before the Surface Transportation Subcom-

mittee, U.S. Senate, September 1985. While seemingly blessing trucking deregulation as an unmitigated success, the Study Commission *Report* (p. 245) found that general freight rates increased less than inflation before deregulation and greater than inflation in 1980–1981. The motor carrier industry seems to agree that this trend has continued. See *Statement of Thomas J. Donahue* before the Senate Committee on Commerce, Science, and Transportation, 9 September 1985. The combination of these trends suggests a decided shift in the rate structure to the disadvantage of small volume shippers, just as the opponents of deregulation had feared, although the effect has not been carefully quantified.

30. See Bill Paul, "Trucks' Rates on Small Loads Stir Big Fight," *The Wall Street Journal* (28 July 1983): 21.

31. As one shipper representative put it, "[T]he practical result, due to Commission inaction, has been the worst of all worlds for the LTL shippers: the carriers can collectively set rate increases and the Commission disclaims responsibility for examining their reasonableness."

See "Senate MC [Motor Carrier] Act Oversight Hearing is Rerun of Last Year's Review," *Traffic World* (26 September 1983): 115. Shippers also complained that they were caught between an ICC that refused to do its duty and the Keogh Doctrine, which said that shippers had no recourse for antitrust damages against a rate lawfully filed with the ICC, even in the absence of antitrust immunity and even if the rate were the product of an antitrust offense.

32. The executive director of NASSTRAC complained that

> What happened in about an 18-month period was rates on LTL traffic increased at a rate . . . that was three to five times the rate of inflation. Meanwhile truckload rates, because of competition, barely kept pace with the rate of inflation. . . . [W]e finally came to the conclusion that antitrust immunity or collective ratemaking on LTL rates without a referee, the ICC, actively engaged in reviewing that process, was a one-sided process. In effect, it was a license to accomplish what we considered to be unreasonably high rate increases. . . .
>
> This changed a group that was basically conservative, 100 per cent behind the system, and had supported the system for 40 years to one that filed a petition with the ICC suggesting that antitrust immunity be eliminated for collective ratemaking as it affects shipments under 1,000 pounds.

See "NASSTRAC Executive Backs Packwood Bill but Urges More Shipper Protection," *Traffic World* (9 April 1984): 38.

33. "Shipper Group Alters Ratemaking Stand: Supports Abolition," *Transport Topics* (16 May 1983): 1. The NASSTRAC proposal would have permitted collectively determined general rate increases for two years, made the setting of joint-line rates and divisions not a *per se* antitrust offense, and provided for a collectively established freight classification system to be supervised by shippers and carriers.

34. *Ex Parte* No. MC–172, "Withdrawal of Antitrust Immunity for Collective Ratemaking on Shipments Weighing 1,000 Pounds or Less," 46 Fed. Reg. 48,399, 12 October 1983.

35. "Shippers End Support for Collective Rates," *Transport Topics* (28 November 1983): 1.

36. The ICC voted four to zero on 9 August 1984 to discontinue the proceeding. The Commission may have been influenced by an ICC staff report by C.C. Barnekov, "Analysis of Evidence in *Ex Parte* No. MC–172, 'Withdrawal of Antitrust Immunity,'" 6 August 1984. The Barnekov study concluded, among other things, that rate bureaus "may reduce the cost of price making for small and medium sized carriers" and "facilitates price comparisons and reduces transactions costs for customers." "Industry concentration could be increased by elimination of rate bureau immunity." The relative increase in small shipment prices were found to be "market-based" and reflect the correction of a previous "regulatory distortion" which systematically underpriced small shipments. Elimination of such cross-subsidies was judged to be one of the benefits expected from deregulation. The ICC staff study also faulted the findings of the MCRSC on the grounds that the system it condemned was the one prior to the Motor Carrier Act of 1980, not the one that emerged as a consequence of those reforms or the one expected to develop in the future.

37. The bases for these fears are discussed in depth later in the text.

38. Daniel Machalaba, "Trucking Association, Powerful for Decades, Has a Load of Trouble," *The Wall Street Journal* (24 February 1984): 1.

39. The president of the American Trucking Associations (ATA) said that "the ATA would seriously consider endorsing the sunsetting of the ICC" if collective ratemaking was discontinued and "the ICC continues to ignore the Motor Carrier Act provisions on entry and rates." See "D&TPTC Urged to Back Truck Industry Moves to Maintain Stability," *Traffic World* (8 November 1982): 50–51.

40. "Pricing Executive Sees End of Motor Carrier Collective Ratemaking," *Traffic World* (11 February 1985): 34.

41. See Thomas Gale Moore, "It's a Success, but Truck Deregulation Remains a Long Haul," *The Wall Street Journal* (26 July 1983), and Moore, "Keep on Deregulating Trucking," *The Wall Street Journal* (12 July 1985).

2. OVERVIEW OF ISSUES

42. See Nicholas A. Glaskowsky, Jr., Brian F. O'Neil, and Donald R. Hudson, *Motor Carrier Regulation: A Review and Evaluation of Three Major Current Regulatory Issues Relating to the Interstate Common Carrier Trucking Industry* (Washington, D.C.: ATA Foundation, 1976); Jessie J. Friedman, "Collective Ratemaking in Trucking: The Public-Interest Rationale" (Washington, D.C.: October 1977); "Collective Ratemaking by Motor Common Carriers: Economic and Public Policy Considerations," *Transportation Law Journal* 70 (October 1978): 33–53; and "What's Wrong with the Case Against Collective Ratemaking: Rejoinder to James C. Miller III," *Transportation Law Journal* 11, no. 2 (December 1980): 301–22. These articles are reprinted in Regular Common Carrier Conference, American Trucking Associations, *Issues in American Trucking* (Washington, D.C.: 1981).

43. James C. Miller III, "Collective Ratemaking Reconsidered: A Rebuttal," *Transportation Law Journal* 11, no. 2 (December 1980): 291–99, and *Report to the President of the National Commission for the Review of Antitrust Laws and Procedures* (Washington, D.C.: U.S. Government Printing Office, 1979), Chapter 4.

44. See Donald L. Flexner, "The Scope of Antitrust Immunity and of Per-

missible Collective Activity in the Motor Carrier Industry," in *Competition in Transportation Sector* (Washington, D.C.: The Federal Bar Association, 1984), and Parker Folse, "Antitrust and Regulated Industries: A Critique and Proposal for Reform of the Implied Immunity Doctrine," *Texas Law Review* 57 (May 1979): 751–828. Exceptions to the doctrine that antitrust laws will apply are often found in the cases of political action (the Noerr-Pennington exemption) and state action (the *Parker* v. *Brown* case). Until recently, there has been a decided trend toward tightening these exemptions and expanding the scope of the antitrust laws in the regulated industries. But see "Administration Moving Antitrust Policy in New Directions," *The New York Times* (20 January 1985): 25. Anticipating a reversal of this trend, Lester M. Bridgeman, "Antitrust Impact on Motor Carriers of the Proposed 'Kennedy Bill' Repeal of the Reed-Bulwinkle Act," *Transportation Journal* 19, no. 1 (Fall 1979): 19–39, contended that a strong case could be made that "mere collusive making of tariff rates by competing carriers" (e.g., collective rate setting, not involving coercion, discrimination, or predatory intent) would not constitute a *per se* violation of the antitrust laws if those rates were subject to ICC jurisdiction. In *U.S.* v. *Southern Motor Carriers Rate Conference, Inc., et al.*, 1979–1 CCH Trade Cases, § 62,552 (N.D. Georgia, 1979), 467 F. Supp. 471 (1979), the trial court found collective ratemaking for intrastate traffic by motor carriers without express immunity to be a *per se* antitrust offense. The court rejected both the state action immunity and Noerr-Pennington defenses by the rate bureau. That decision was affirmed by the Appeals Court (702 F.2d 532 (1983)), but this decision was overturned by the Supreme Court in *Southern Motor Carriers Rate Conference, Inc.* v. *United States*, 53 U.S.L.W. 4422 (1985). The Supreme Court ruled that although collective ratemaking for intrastate traffic was not "compelled," it was nevertheless pursuant to a "clearly articulated state policy" and could not be judged a *per se* offense as long as the carriers were "actively supervised." As the Court noted, if the antitrust immunity required the states to "compel" collective ratemaking, it would infringe on the right of independent action that is the safety valve in disciplining the competitive process and would result in even greater restraints on trade. As Eugene C. Crew stated in his testimony before the Study Commission on 19 March 1982, "while Congress has been legislatively repealing many immunity statutes, the courts have been judicially repealing many of the *per se* rules." This would appear to leave matters up to an unclear rule-of-reason standard to judge the legality of collective ratemaking in a regulated trucking industry in the absence of antitrust immunity.

45. For a review of the issues raised by the coexistence of the two forms of social control of business, see Walter Adams, "Business Exemptions from the Antitrust Laws: Their Extent and Rationale," in *Perspectives on Antitrust Policy*, Almarin Phillips, ed. (New Jersey: Princeton University Press, 1965); Phillip E. Areeda, "Antitrust Laws and Public Utility Regulation," *Bell Journal of Economics and Management Science* 3, no. 1 (Spring 1972): 42–57; Andrew F. Popper, "Collective Ratemaking: A Case Analysis of the Eastern Central Region and an Hypothesis for Analyzing Competitive Structure," *Transportation Law Journal* 10 (1978): 365–88; Popper, "Did the Motor Carrier Act Alter Antitrust Immunity for Collective Ratemaking," *Your Letter of the Law* 26, no. 6 (March 1981): 25–39; Popper, "The Antitrust System: An Impediment to the Development of Negotiation Models," *The American University Law Review* 32, no. 2 (Winter 1983): 283–

334; Paul Stephen Dempsey, "Rate Regulation and Antitrust Immunity in Transportation: The Genesis and Evolution of this Endangered Species," *The American University Law Review* 32, no. 2 (Winter 1983): 353–76; and Cornelius M. Kerwin, "Assessing the Effects of Consensual Processes in Regulatory Programs," *The American University Law Review* 32, no. 2 (Winter 1983): 401–23.

46. These concerns over the net benefits of antitrust enforcement are being raised in markets where benefits from collusion are not even alleged. See William J. Baumol, "Use of Antitrust to Subvert Competition," *The Journal of Law and Economics* 28, no. 2 (May 1985): 247–65, and Lester C. Thurow, "Let's Abolish the Antitrust Laws," *The New York Times* (19 October 1980).

47. A widely cited article by Peter Asch and J.J. Seneca, "Is Collusion Profitable?" *Review of Economics and Statistics* 58, no. 1 (February 1976): 1–12, found a negative relationship between collusive behavior and firm profitability while noting that the results were subject to a variety of explanations.

48. See, for example, John C. Spychalski, "Antitrust Standards and Railway Freight Pricing: New Round in an Old Debate," *American Economic Review* 71, no. 2 (May 1981): 104–109, and Grant M. Davis, "Collective Ratemaking and Societal Benefits," Third Dana/ATA Foundation Academic Symposium, Stanford University, 8–9 December 1981.

49. Donald Dewey, in "Information, Entry, and Welfare: The Case for Collusion," *American Economic Review* 69, no. 4 (September 1979): 587–94; and Lester G. Telser, "Cooperation, Competition, and Efficiency," *Journal of Law and Economics* 28, no. 2 (May 1985): 271–95; and Barry S. Eisenberg, "Information Exchange among Competitors: The Issue of Relative Value Scales for Physicians' Services," *Journal of Law and Economics* 23, no. 2 (October 1980): 441–60.

50. See Crew, "Rate Bureaus and the Rule of Reason." As one court noted, "In an industry which necessarily requires some interdependence and cooperation, the *per se* rule should not be applied so indiscriminately." See *Hatley* v. *American Quarter Horse Association*, 522 F.2d 646 (5th Circuit, 1977). For the lead case in which efficiency gains were cited as a reason for modifying the *per se* rule against price fixing, see *Broadcast Music, Inc.* v. *CBS*, 441 U.S. 1 (1979). In this case, the Supreme Court raised issues of direct relevance to the motor carrier industry in evaluating the reasonableness of a collective licensing agreement: whether the arrangement increased economic efficiency and provided economic benefits, whether there was a legal and practical right of direct dealing, the uniqueness of the market conditions and the practical requirements of buyers and sellers, the costs of individual sales transaction, and the complexities of the required schedule of prices under direct negotiations. All these would have to be considered in establishing whether a particular collective licensing scheme was a *per se* offense. For an economic defense of the practice of a form of collective ratemaking in music publishing, see William M. Landes, "Harm to Competition: Cartels, Mergers, and Joint Ventures," in *Antitrust Policy in Transition: The Convergence of Law and Economics*, Eleanor M. Fox and James T. Halverson, eds. (Washington, American Bar Association, 1984): 73–82.

51. "Commerce Secretary Baldridge Wants Elimination of Major Antitrust Law," *Traffic World* (18 March 1985): 75–76. See *National Cooperative Research Act of 1984*, Public Law 98–462, 98 Stat. 1815, 15 U.S.C. 4301, for an example of recent efforts to promote cooperation among competitors to encourage joint

research and development activities because of a belief in the inefficiency of independently funded efforts in world competitive markets.

52. Joseph F. Brodley, "Joint Ventures and Antitrust Policy," *Harvard Law Review* 95 (May 1982): 1521–88.

53. Eugene Crew and Joel Lintzner, "Joint Rates between Competitors—A True Antitrust Dilemma," *Traffic World* (2 May 1983): 77–82.

54. List prices tend to be used in markets where products are differentiated and costs of negotiation are considered low relative to product value (handicraft markets in less developed countries and specialized consumer durables such as homes). Posted prices are more likely to be used where standardized products are sold with standardized costs of production (most consumer markets in developed countries).

55. The analogy is to a competition-reducing merger that promised efficiency gains. See H. Michael Mann, "Collective Ratemaking: A Victim of Traditional Antitrust Doctrine?" *The American University Law Review* 32, no. 2 (Winter 1983): 393–99, for a discussion of the economic issues in assessing the tradeoff between potential anticompetitive consequences and efficiency gains. For an analysis of the dangers of the welfare tradeoff approach to evaluating such reductions in competition, see William B. Tye, "On the Application of the 'Williamsonian Welfare Tradeoff' to Rail Mergers," *Logistics and Transportation Review* 21, no. 3 (September 1985): 239–48.

56. As Roger Noll put it:

> Evaluation of antitrust exemptions . . . cannot be separated from an evaluation of regulation itself, which in turn requires evaluating the rationale for abandoning the competitive model in favor of economic regulation. . . . [S]ome exemption from antitrust is necessary if regulators are to be allowed to regulate. . . . Indeed, antitrust exemptions were often enacted because successful antitrust actions undid a major part of the effects of regulation, an example being the enactment of the Reed-Bulwinkle Act in response to a successful antitrust action against railroad rate bureaus.

See "Antitrust Exemptions: An Economic Overview," in *Report to the President and the Attorney General of the National Commission for the Review of the Antitrust Laws and Procedures*, Vol. 2 (Washington, D.C.: U.S. Government Printing Office, 1979): 170, 175.

57. Much of the writing in opposition to collective ratemaking is by persons schooled in economic theory but without practical knowledge of the trucking industry. Focusing the discussion on industry structure rather than on practice encourages them to do what they do best. The same is true for regulators:

> Above all, appropriate public policy during the transition [to deregulation] should avoid trying to outguess the market by imposing regulatory actions designed to achieve preconceived visions of the long-run industry equilibrium. (In a world of rapid technological, demographic, and other changes, forecasting the eventual equilibrium is likely to be beyond anybody's vision, including that of the most enlightened regulator.)

See John R. Meyer and William B. Tye, "The Regulatory Transition," *American Economic Review* 75, no. 2 (May 1985): 50.

58. Transactions costs are the administrative and legal costs of negotiating and policing sales agreements. See Armen A. Alchian and William R. Allen, *University Economics* (Belmont, Calif.: Wadsworth Publishing Company, 1968): 469–72.

59. Even if they were not, a case could be made that regulatory restraint should be applied to prevent the abuse of collective ratemaking while achieving the efficiency gains, if they were sufficiently large. Even if anticompetitive concerns were negligible, there is a reasonable case for permissively regulating collective ratemaking in order to answer the concerns of shippers over the possible abuse of an unregulated antitrust immunity.

60. As Senator Cannon put it in the Study Commission *Report*, p. 67:

> Ironically, the strongest arguments in favor of entry deregulation are the strongest arguments as to why collective ratemaking is simply not a grave threat to the public. Those of us who have promoted entry freedom have argued for years that the structure of the trucking industry is inherently competitive. That is, capital barriers to entry are sufficiently low that entry by new firms is relatively easy.

61. The free rider problem also exists if the carrier's objectives are noncompetitive prices—in fact, this is the usual mechanism that causes price-fixing conspiracies among numerous sellers to collapse.

62. In-depth, personal interviews were conducted with ratemaking executives of the following carriers: Consolidated Freightways, P.I.E., Transcon, AAA Cooper, Georgia Highway Express, Spector Red Ball, Hemingway, Jones Motor, Silver Eagle, Overnite Transportation, Roadway Express, Interstate, Sanborn's Motor Express, and Holmes Transportation. The carriers were selected to represent different sizes and regions. Although the study reflects the results of these interviews, it does not necessarily represent the views of the carriers. Indeed, some are already defunct as a result of the trends discussed in the following chapter.

63. *Report*, pp. ii, iii.

64. *Report*, p. iv, Chapter 5.

65. *Report*, p. vi.

66. *Report*, p. xii.

67. *Report*, p. xii.

68. The Study Commission stated that "historical rationales have very limited value in determining the current need for collective ratemaking" (p. i), and that "historic data simply cannot capture the true breadth, depth, and diversity of recent changes on both sides of the market" (p. 52), but proceeded to evaluate the institution using historical objectives and often studies done prior to regulatory reform to make conclusions on the current operating environment.

69. *Report*, p. xiii, Chapter 8.

70. Other goals as far-reaching as fairness equity, full employment, inflation, and economic growth, for example, were considered by the commission but not addressed in any detail in the *Report*. See "Rate Commission's Darby Says Study is on Schedule," *Transport Topics* (9 August 1982): 3.

3. THE STRUCTURE AND PERFORMANCE OF THE TRUCKING INDUSTRY

71. See Thomas Gale Moore, "The Beneficiaries of Trucking Regulation," *Journal of Law and Economics* 21, no. 2 (October 1978): 327–43; Moore, "Deregulating Surface Freight Transportation," in *Promoting Competition in Regulated Markets*, Almarin Phillips, ed. (Washington, D.C.: Brookings Institution, 1975); George W. Hilton, "Experience under the Reed-Bulwinkle Act," *ICC Practitioners Journal* 28, no. 10 (September 1961): 1207–19; "The Basic Behavior of Regulatory Commissions," *American Economic Review* 62, no. 2 (May 1972): 47–54; Kenneth D. Boyer, "Equalizing Discrimination and Cartel Pricing in Transport Rate Regulation," *Journal of Political Economy* 89, no. 2 (April 1981): 270–86; and *Statement of George Hilton*, before the Motor Carrier Ratemaking Study Commission, Phoenix, Arizona, 10 December 1981, for a history of the government-enforced cartel theory of rate regulation in transportation. See also *Testimony of Denis A. Breen*, Senior Transportation Economist, Bureau of Economics, Federal Trade Commission, before the Motor Carrier Ratemaking Study Commission, 18 November 1981; and *Testimony of W. Bruce Allen*, before the Ratemaking Study Commission, Orlando, Florida, 2 April 1982.

72. *Testimony of George W. Wilson*, before the Study Commission, Boston, Massachusetts, 19 March 1982, pp. 1, 2.

73. *Testimony of Thomas Gale Moore*, before the Study Commission, Boston, Massachusetts, 19 March 1982, pp. 1, 6.

74. See F.M. Scherer, *Industrial Market Structure and Economic Performance* (Chicago: Rand McNally & Company, 1973), Chapter 1.

75. Management Analysis Center, "Statistical Overview of the Trucking Industry," presented to the Motor Carrier Ratemaking Study Commission, August 1982, p. 43.

76. Transportation Policy Associates, *Transportation in America* (Washington, D.C., November 1985): 5.

77. Transportation Policy Associates, pp. 49, 56.

78. U.S. Department of Justice (DOJ), *Merger Guidelines* (14 June 1984), reprinted in *Antitrust and Trade Regulation* (14 June 1984): Special Supplement, p. S–5. 49 Federal Register 26,823 (29 June 1984). The DOJ expresses the index by moving the decimal point four places to the right as compared with the data in Table 3.

79. The data are maintained by the rate bureaus with the assistance of Arthur Andersen & Co. For a detailed discussion of this data base, including the criteria for inclusion of carriers, see "Report of Arthur Andersen & Co.," in Volume 1, *Reports and Studies on Behalf of Motor Carrier Rate Bureaus, I.C.C. Ex Parte No. MC–128, Revenue Need Standards in Motor Carrier Increase Proceedings*, 4 January 1980.

80. Irwin H. Silberman, Statement before the Surface Transportation Subcommittee, U.S. House of Representatives, 6 November 1985, p. 10, reports that one-third of the carriers in the LTL study group went out of business or substantially reduced general commodity (LTL) operations since 1976. For a review of the evidence immediately after regulatory reform, see Irwin H. Silberman, *Analysis of the Financial Performance of the General Freight Motor Common Carrier*

Industry, submitted to the Motor Carrier Ratemaking Study Commission, July 1982. See also William Legg, *1985 Analysis of the Motor Carrier Industry* (Washington, D.C., American Trucking Associations, 1985).

81. Silberman, p. 11.

82. James C. Harkins, *Statement before the U.S. Senate Committee on Commerce, Science and Transportation*, 9 September 1985.

83. The operating ratio is the ratio of operating expenses (not including interest, profit, and income taxes) to revenue.

84. In the second quarter of 1985, revenues, expenses, and tonnage all declined sharply against the same period of the year earlier in the sample of 144 common carriers of general freight. Tonnage fell to the lowest level since 1967. See Regular Common Carrier Conference, *Quarterly Operating Results of the Motor Common Carriers of General Freight: Second Quarter 1985* (Alexandria, Va.: Regular Common Carrier Conference, 1985).

85. Garland Chow and Richard Gritta, "Motor Carrier Bankruptcy: An Industry Assessment of Financial Condition," *Proceedings of the Transportation Research Forum* 26, no. 1 (1985): 434–40. More recent data presented by Harkins (1985) show 31 percent of the larger general commodity carriers with operating ratios exceeding 100 and more than half exceeding 97.5—a level where revenues are not usually sufficient to meet expenses including interest and taxes.

86. Empirical results suggest that price-fixing conspiracies are most likely to result when "numbers are small, concentration is high, and the product is homogeneous." See George A. Hay and Daniel Kelly, "An Empirical Survey of Price-Fixing Conspiracies," *Journal of Law and Economics* 17, no. 1 (April 1974): 27. Richard A. Posner, "A Program for the Antitrust Division," *University of Chicago Law Review* 38 (1971): 516–19, identifies the following characteristics:

> few firms accounting for most sales, inelastic demand at the competitive price, slow entry, standard product, many customers, "the members of the cartel sell at the same level in the chain of distribution," price competition appears more important than other forms of competition, there is a high ratio of fixed to variable costs, demand is static or declining over time, and finally, sealed bidding.

87. See James E. Meeks, "Legal Issues and Consequences of Changes in Motor Carrier Ratemaking Regulations," Third Dana/ATA Foundation Academic Symposium, Stanford University, 9 December 1981, p. 33. See also Donald Dewey, "Neglected Economic Issues in Collective Ratemaking"; and Garland Chow, "An Economic Inquiry into the Options and Impacts of Rate Regulation on Motor Transportation Markets" (both papers presented at the Third Dana/ATA Foundation Academic Symposium, Stanford, December 1981) for similar conclusions. See also Richard A. Posner, "Effects of Railroad Rate Bureaus on Economic Efficiency," Verified Statement before the ICC, *Ex Parte* No. 290 (Sub-No. 2), *Railroad Cost Recovery Procedures*, 16 July 1980.

88. Meeks.

89. Noll, p. 174.

90. Denis A. Breen, *Testimony before the Motor Carrier Ratemaking Study Commission*, 18 November 1981.

91. A number of studies have documented the effects of the MCA of 1980.

For a survey of recent studies, see James C. Nelson, "The Emerging Effects of Deregulation of Surface Freight Transport in the United States," *International Journal of Transport Economics* 10, no. 1–2 (April/August 1983): 219–36. For an excellent review of the MCA, *Ex Parte* 297 (Sub-No. 5), and the antitrust immunity issues raised by it, see Meeks. Dean Meeks arrives at essentially the same conclusions as herein, albeit from a legal rather than an economic point of view.

92. Motor Carrier Act of 1980, P.L. 96–296 §4(3) 1980, 49 U.S.C. §10101(a)(7) (1980).

93. A number of other changes were made, such as the prohibition of the Standing Rate Committee, addition of sunshine requirements, and changes in qualifications for voting and other bureau by-laws which have a lesser impact on the role of rate bureaus in rate setting. See *Ex Parte* No. 297 (Sub-No. 5), *Motor Carrier Rate Bureaus—Implementation of P.L. 96–296.*

94. *Statement of Marcus Alexis*, Acting Chairman, Interstate Commerce Commission, before the Subcommittee on Surface Transportation of the House Committee on Public Works and Transportation, on the Motor Carrier Act of 1980 (10 June 1981), pp. 2, 23.

95. See Interstate Commerce Commission, *Ex Parte* 297, *Motor Carrier Rate Bureaus—Implementation of P.L. 96–296*, served 30 December 1980. See also *Statement of Robert Shepard, Jr.*, Interstate Commerce Commission, before the Motor Carrier Ratemaking Study Commission, 18 November 1981.

96. In an *Ex Parte* MC–122 (Sub-No. 2) *Decision* dated 17 February 1982, the ICC approved 30-day leases from owner-operators to private carriers and instituted a proceeding to permit regulated carriers to do the same.

97. See Donald V. Harper, "Entry Control and the Federal Motor Carrier Act of 1980," *Transportation Law Journal* 21, no. 4 (1980): 56; *Testimony of Alison B. Swan*, before the Motor Carrier Ratemaking Study Commission, 10 December 1981, p. 18, and Tr. p. 50, lines 21–24; and *Testimony of John Semmens, Semantic Confusion in Economic Regulation* (no pagination) and Tr. pp. 225, lines 10–14.

98. See *Testimony of Lawrence M. Hecker* at Tr. p. 9, lines 15–24, Phoenix hearing.

99. Docketing is the procedure by which a proposed tariff change is entered by the bureau in its files, and interested parties are notified of the proposed action (either for a regular proposal collective action or for an IA).

100. "We will not permit use of special permission authority to circumvent another carrier's competitive initiative in this situation." *Decision*, p. 33.

101. See *Statement of Marcus Alexis*, pp. 29–30: "Since passage of the Act, carriers have used the traditional independent filing procedure extensively. The number of such filings at major rate bureaus in 1980 doubled from 1979; the increases for the eight major general commodity bureaus for which data were available ranged from 44 percent to 347 percent."

102. The Emergency Procedure was omitted from Figure 5 because it has been replaced with the no-notice IA for carriers seeking a speedy implementation of a new tariff. The Emergency Procedure previously provided for a bypass of the public hearing which was otherwise mandatory.

103. The difference between an IA and a private tariff is the fact that no other carrier can join a private tariff without the approval of the publishing carrier,

and it is not buried with voluminous other tariff matter applying to other carriers. The choice depends on the convenience of the carrier and the type of proposal. Most discounts from bureau tariffs appear in private tariffs, for example.

104. "Rate bureau officials contend that the right of independent action has been free and unrestrained, but historically rate bureaus have protested their own members' IA's and there is evidence that rate bureaus have even cancelled or modified their own members' IA's. [footnote omitted] . . . Given the variety of methods by which significant independent action can be thwarted many have concluded that the 'right of independent action' is really an illusory right" [footnote omitted]. *Breen Statement* of 18 November 1981 before the Study Commission (first Breen statement).

105. "There has been greater pricing innovation and more independent ratemaking since the Act. The number of independent rate filings has approximately doubled from 1979 to 1980. The vast majority of these are rate reductions and many apply to LTL as well as TL traffic." *Statement of Marcus Alexis*, p. 3. See also Office of Transportation Analysis, Interstate Commerce Commission, "Staff Report No. 10: Highlights of Activity in the Property Motor Carrier Industry," March 1986.

106. The Eastern Central Motor Carriers Association reported an increase in the total number of tariff pages from 42,038 in 1980 to 65,982 in 1981. The Southern Motor Carriers Rate Conference reported an increase from 50,547 to 60,745 for the same period. The 1981 *Annual Report* of the Middle Atlantic Conference reported that "[w]ith the sharp downturn in tonnage and the excessive amount of competition in the field, the pressure for reductions in LTL and TL rates has been unreal. Frankly, it has been almost impossible for us to cope with the numerous requests we have received for changes in our tariffs and carrier individual tariffs."

107. Carriers often found that the GRC meetings were moving quickly because of a reduction in the number of appealed regular dockets and the fact that carriers have frequently elected not to wait for the next meeting but rather have instructed the bureau to publish the appealed regular docket proposal as an IA.

108. The Eastern Central Motor Carriers Association reported that 99.8 percent of the 1,603 IA's during November/December 1981 were rate cuts. During the comparable period in 1980, the figure was 99.3 percent of the 595 IA's. At MAC, 88 percent of regular proposals were for rate cuts in 1981, as were 94.8 percent of IA's.

109. See Harwood Hoover, Jr., "Pricing Behavior of Deregulated Motor Common Carriers," *Transportation Journal* 25, no. 2 (Winter 1985): 55–61. See also *Statement of Marcus Alexis*, p. 11:

> Most rate reductions are initiated by individual carriers through independent filings or independent actions. Major rate bureaus report sharply increased filings of independent rate actions, the vast majority of which are rate reductions. In two large general commodity bureaus that were recently sampled, over 95 percent of independent actions were rate reductions. Furthermore, these reductions are being offered to both LTL and TL shippers. In our two sample bureaus, 34 percent and 44 percent of independent actions were for LTL rates. The growth in the number of

independent filings in the eight major general commodity bureaus for which data were available has ranged from 44 percent to 347 percent. Other evidence of innovative rate decreases exist as well. One major LTL carrier, Overnite Transportation Co., offers a 10 percent across-the-board reduction in all class-rated shipments, with an additional 5 percent reduction for shipments delivered to their terminals. These rate reductions were matched by 50 other carriers. Commercial Lovelace, Roadway Express, Transcon, and Yellow Freight are further examples of large carriers offering their own innovative LTL rate programs.

110. As one Wall Street industry analyst put it:

The principal concern in the investment community with respect to motor carrier equities in the LTL sector is price discounting. At this time, the industry is experiencing the strongest volume growth that I have seen in my fifteen years of covering the industry. Yet, price discounting is the most severe it has been since discounting began in mid–1980. Investors have to ask the question, "If discounting is this bad now, what will it be like when we go into a recession?" That is a frightening thought for investors. It appears that the industry is going through a second shakeout. This is evidenced now by at least four carriers being in bankruptcy, near bankruptcy, or in the state of liquidation at this time. Consequently, I'm not very optimistic about the price performance over the near-term for LTL motor carriers which are those carriers that comprise the large majority of motor carrier equity holdings in the public market.

Wall Street Transcript, 4 June 1982, p. 2.

111. Hausman, "Information Costs."

112. In the *Statement of Martin E. Foley*, Director, Bureau of Traffic, Interstate Commerce Commission, before the Motor Carrier Ratemaking Study Commission, 29 January 1982, p. 11, the ICC notes the data in the first quarter of fiscal year 1982. Motor carriers filed 134,145 tariff publications and only 11 were suspended and one was investigated.

113. Nancy L. Rose, "The Incidence of Regulatory Rents in the Motor Carrier Industry," *Rand Journal of Economics* 16, no. 3 (Autumn 1985): 299–318, found that the ICC's deregulation campaign caused a loss of 31 percent of motor carrier equity values. See also Michael W. Pustay, "Regulatory Reform of Motor Freight Carriage in the United States," *International Journal of Transport Economics* 10, no. 1–2 (April/August 1983): 259–80; and Thomas Gale Moore, "Rail and Truck Reform—The Record So Far," *Regulation* (November/December 1983): 33–41. Moore found that deregulation caused real truckload rates to fall by 25 percent from 1977 to 1982 and real less-than-truckload rates to fall about 12 percent. Moore's survey, however, included only the largest shippers who have benefitted most by the rate war. Nevertheless, the results clearly support the conclusion of substantial rate cuts.

114. So many carriers are offering so many discount programs and special pricing incentives and changing them so fast in light of competitive conditions that it is difficult to keep track of them all. Most of the bureaus publish data on these programs so that motor carriers can keep up with the discounts. For an

illustration of the variety of discounts, see Middle Atlantic Conference, *Individual Carrier Discount: Tariff Index and Profile*, 29 September 1981. Carriers are substantially increasing the time spent monitoring the pricing actions of their competitors. Rate bureaus and other agencies are increasing their tariff-watching services which competitors are reviewing daily to take necessary competitive responses. See, for example, Middle Atlantic Conference, *Nationwide Watching Service Bulletin: Individual Tariffs Containing Threshold, Volume and Aggregate Tender Discount Rates or Charges.*

115. See Ray Bohman, Jr., *Guide to Cutting Your Freight Transportation Costs under Trucking Regulation* (Gardner, Mass.: Bohman Industrial Traffic Consultants, 1981).

116. Grant M. Davis and Charles S. Sherwood, *Rate Bureaus and Antitrust Conflicts in Transportation: Public Policy Issues* (New York: Praeger, 1975); Charles S. Sherwood, "The Operational Reality of Independent Rate Making: Some Empirical Findings," *Transportation Journal* 15, no. 2 (Winter 1975): 5–12.

117. The major rate bureaus report a substantial increase in publishing individual carrier tariffs after 1980. Eastern Central, for example, published 168 individual carrier tariffs in 1981. A survey of 20 General Rate Committee members at ECMCA showed 312 new individual carrier tariffs or supplements with effective dates from October 1981 to January 1982. The Southern Motor Carrier Rate Conference reports that its watching service reported 214,503 pages of tariffs applicable to SMCRC territory in 1979, 256,849 in 1980, and 445,919 in 1981. The conference believes that these figures reflect the large amount of individual carrier tariff publications. Roadway Express, in testimony before the Study Commission, indicated that it filed 1,504 IA's through the bureaus but published substantially more private tariff items (3,185). See *Statement of Joseph M. Clapp*, Akron hearing.

118. See Joseph M. Clapp, "Deregulation—Revolution? Evolution? Clearing Up Some Existing Confusion," *Traffic World* (1 July 1985): 28–33; and Gene T. West, "The Challenge of the Eighties! What a Major Carrier is Doing," *Traffic World* (1 July 1985): 48–55, for a discussion of some of the simplified private tariffs being offered.

119. F.S. Thompson, "How to Improve Profits with an Innovative Pricing System," *Transport Topics* (28 June 1982): 7.

120. The new rate proposals combine elements of independent and collective ratemaking. See "Collective Ratemaking is Still Favored by Roadway with 'E-Z Rate' System," *Traffic World* (12 September 1983): 30. Early after the passage of the MCA, Georgia Highway Express (now Transus) and AAA Cooper introduced a new rate scale for shipments of less than 5,000 pounds that uses the classification system, the bureau rate basis numbers, and bureau shipping rules. But they have a fixed charge per shipment (depending on the number of shipments), an excess pieces charge, and low rates per hundredweight, which encourage multiple tenders. See "AAA Cooper Transportation 'Explains' Filing of Independent Action Rates," *Traffic World* (10 November 1980): 49–50. Georgia Highway Express was long a critic of the class-rate system. See H.D. Winship, Jr., "New Procedures in Motor Carrier Restructuring Proceedings: Initial Statement on Behalf of Georgia Highway Express, Inc.," before the ICC, *Ex Parte* MC–98, 8 March 1976, filed 24 March 1976.

121. See Leslie M. Goldner, "LTL-Carrier Pricing Practices for Individual Shippers: The Aftermath of Deregulation," *Traffic World* (11 February 1985): 83–88; and Frank Wilner, "Creating a Linkage between Rate and Costs: A Survival Tactic for Small Carriers under Deregulation," *ICC Practitioners Journal* 48 (November/December 1980): 65–81.

122. For a review, see William B. Tye, "Implications of Motor Carrier Regulatory Reform for Carrier Planning and Marketing," *Transportation Research Record 804: Surface Regulatory Reform: Rail, Truck, and Intermodal* (Washington, D.C.: Transportation Research Board, National Academy of Sciences, 1981), pp. 17–23. See also Michael L. King, "Transportation Official at GE Finds His Role Rises with Fuel Prices," *The Wall Street Journal* (31 December 1981): 1; Albert R. Karr, "Iowa Trucker Prospers after Deregulation Eases Rules on Routes," *The Wall Street Journal* (13 February 1984): 1; and Daniel Machalaba, "More Companies Push Freight Haulers to Get Better Rates, Service," *The Wall Street Journal* (18 December 1985): 1.

123. *Broemser Testimony* before Study Commission, p. 7.

124. See *Breen Statement* of 18 November 1981.

125. The requirement to publish and file rates is ancillary to entry and pricing. Most critics would agree that publishing rates is not harmful unless it is used along with other devices to deter competitive pricing. Unless one is attempting to undermine a true cartel, public information on pricing is essential to helping competition work. Since there never have been output or capacity controls (by either the bureaus or the ICC), we are left only with entry controls and rate regulation.

126. The motor carrier industry has in fact changed from one with barriers to entry to one with barriers to exit. The ICC's permissive entry policy stands in sharp contrast to the impediments to leaving the industry imposed by the Employment Retirement Income Security Act (ERISA). See "Law to Protect Multi-Employer Pensions is Causing Hardship for Many Businesses," *The Wall Street Journal*, 5 March 1985.

127. Numerous critics have also charged that regulation by the ICC, particularly in the form of using the operating ratio as a standard of revenue adequacy, led to excessive rate levels and profitability. The present analysis addresses the effect of collective ratemaking on rate levels, as opposed to regulation itself. For an analysis of issues raised by motor carrier revenue adequacy, see William B. Tye, A. Lawrence Kolbe, and Miriam Alexander Baker, "The Economics of Revenue Need Standards in Motor Carrier General Increase Proceedings," *Transportation Journal* 20, no. 4 (Summer 1981): 1–25.

128. For a development of this theory, see Merton J. Peck, "Competitive Policy for Transportation," in *Perspectives on Antitrust Policy*, Almarin Phillips, ed. (Princeton, N.J.: Princeton University Press, 1965).

129. See Tr. pp. 6–7, Washington hearing. See also *Allen Testimony* before the Study Commission.

130. See also *Statement of William F. Baxter*, before the Motor Carrier Ratemaking Study Commission, 18 November 1981, p. 6, and Tr. pp. 40–41, first Washington hearing.

131. James C. Miller III, "Economic Regulation of Trucking," *Report to the President and the Attorney General*, ed. by the National Commission for the Review of Antitrust Laws and Procedures, Vol. 2 (Washington, D.C.: U.S. Government Printing Office, 22 January 1979): 193.

132. See Ann F. Friedlaender and Richard H. Spady, *Freight Transport Regulation* (Cambridge, Mass.: The MIT Press, 1981), pp. 201–202. One of the opponents of collective ratemaking, Professor George Hilton, testified that there is virtually no cross-subsidy in trucking. See Tr. pp. 220–21, Phoenix hearing. As Hilton (Tr. 243–45) testified at the hearing:

> It was thought, as of about 10 years ago, that there was very serious misallocation of freight by the distance between rail and truck, that the regulation tended to make freight move by truck to long distances relative to rail, simply because rail could act freely in an unregulated environment. . . . Estimates are as high as 2.9 billion dollars a year for the cost of that. It is now known that such estimates are incorrect. . . . Subsequently the estimates of the misallocation between mode, as a result of the ICC, have been greatly reduced. There is a further problem, anybody who habitually ships by rail has to keep bigger inventories than somebody who ships by truck, only because of uncertainty in arrival time. . . . So at present it looks as if misallocation is not very great.

More recently, Ronald R. Braeutigam and Roger G. Noll, "The Regulation of Surface Freight Transportation: The Welfare Effects Revisited," *Review of Economics and Statistics* 66 (February 1984): 80–87, have quarreled with the estimating techniques and conclude that earlier studies had underestimated the welfare effects.

133. See Study Commission, *Report*, pp. 242–43, 257–58.

134. See Study Commission, *Report*, pp. 238–40, 257–58; and Thomas Gale Moore, "The Beneficiaries of Trucking Regulation," *Journal of Law and Economics* 21, no. 2 (1978): 327–43; and Moshe Kim, "The Beneficiaries of Trucking Regulation, Revisited," *Journal of Law and Economics* 28, no. 1 (April 1984): 227–41.

135. W. Bruce Allen, "The Impact of Collective Ratemaking on Motor Carrier Rates: A Test," *International Journal of Transport Economics* 10, no. 1–2 (April/August 1983): 281–310. Interestingly, the Study Commission did not allege that collective ratemaking created the possibility of higher profits but rather concluded that rate levels were dependent, "dollar for dollar," on costs. See *Report*, p. 230. "The Rate level changes in response to changes in underlying cost conditions," and collective ratemaking has no direct effects on the rate level via higher profits. See *Report*, p. xiii.

136. Senate Commerce Committee, Motor Carrier Reform Act of 1980, p. 13. See also Denis Breen, Federal Trade Commission, "Regulatory Reform and the Trucking Industry: An Evaluation of the Motor Carrier Act of 1980," submitted to the Motor Carrier Ratemaking Study Commission, March 1982, p. 50. Although the main text of the Study Commission *Report* evaluated the somewhat more subtle forms of the argument discussed below, the Summary at p. v embraced the most extreme form of the theory, that collective ratemaking protects the least efficient carrier.

137. See data above on concentration of industry profits in a relatively few carriers.

138. Dabney J. Waring, "No Protection for the Inefficient Carrier in Collective Ratemaking," paper presented before the Motor Carrier Ratemaking Study Commission, Kansas City, Mo., 5 March 1982.

139. See *Study*, p. 244.

140. As is widely recognized, it is regulatory ratemaking at the level of the firm, not the industry, that incorporates the potential for discouraging efficiency of individual carrier management. See Russell C. Cherry, "The Operating Ratio Effect and Regulated Motor Carriers," *Proceedings of a Workshop on Motor Carrier Economic Regulation* (Washington, D.C.: National Academy of Sciences, 1978): 269–88. For this reason, critics such as Moore, in "The Beneficiaries of Trucking Regulation," acknowledge that each trucking firm has an incentive to reduce costs given the collective rate level, contrary to the findings of the Study Commission. Moore argues that operating ratio regulation plus constraints on entry under regulation create incentives to inflate labor costs. Given permissive rate regulation and free entry, this argument clearly is not presently valid. See Andrew F. Daughety, "Regulation and Industrial Organization," *Journal of Political Economy* 92, no. 5 (October 1984): 932–53.

141. *Report*, pp. 242–43.

142. The proposition that competitive markets establish prices on the basis of the most efficient supplier, a pillar of the commission's finding that collective ratemaking must be abolished, is simply not an accurate characterization of the authority it cites. Compare F. M. Scherer, *Industrial Market Structure and Economic Performance* (Boston: Houghton Mifflin, 1980): 12–14, with *Report* at pp. 242–43.

143. Daniel H. Buchanan, "The Historical Approach to Rent and Price Theory," *Economica* (June 1929): 123–55, reprinted in *Readings in the Theory of Income Distribution* (Homewood, Ill.: Richard D. Irwin, 1951); and C.E. Ferguson, *Microeconomic Theory* (Homewood, Ill.: Richard D. Irwin, 1969), Chapters 13 and 14.

144. See any economics text on the subjects of competitive supply and economic rent (e.g., James M. Henderson and Richard E. Quandt, *Microeconomic Theory* (New York: McGraw-Hill, 1958): 120–21). Walter Nicholson, *Microeconomic Theory—Basic Principles and Extensions* (Hinsdale, Ill.: Dryden Press, 1978): 406–408, is particularly clear in showing how economists since the days of David Ricardo have realized that the prices of agricultural commodities, for example, are determined by the productivity of the least fertile land under cultivation, not the most fertile. This increasing cost phenomenon is the basis for the typical upward sloping supply curve in a competitive industry.

145. See Allan M. Cartter, *Theory of Wages and Employment* (Homewood, Ill.: Richard D. Irwin, 1959), Chapter 2, for a discussion of Henry George's proposed tax on economic rent.

146. George J. Stigler, *The Theory of Price* (New York: Macmillan, 1966): 268.

147. *Report*, p. 230.

148. Steptoe and Johnson, "Overview of the Case for Collective Ratemaking in the Post 1980 Competitive Environment," presented to the Motor Carrier Ratemaking Study Commission, 8 December 1982.

149. James Amnable, "The ICC, the IBT, and the Cartelization of the American Trucking Industry," *Quarterly Review of Economics and Business* 13 (1973): 36–43.

150. *Report*, p. 240.

151. George W. Bohlander and Martin T. Farris, "Collective Bargaining in Trucking—the Effects of Deregulation," *Logistics and Transportation Review* 20, no. 3 (1984): 223–38. Moore, "Rail and Truck Reform," cites data that show a

16 percent decline in real per-hour labor costs for all trucking labor and a 19 percent decline in real wages for drivers and helpers. What is included in these figures is not clear. The U.S. General Accounting Office, *Effects of Regulatory Reform on Unemployment in the Trucking Industry* (Gaithersville, Md.: GAO, 1982), concluded that the substantial decline in total trucking employment after passage of the act was attributable to the recession, but that Teamster employment declined as a result of regulatory reform.

152. See *Thomas G. Moore Testimony* before the Study Commission on 19 March 1982; and W. Bruce Allen, "The Impact of Collective Ratemaking on Motor Carrier Rates: A Test," *International Journal of Transport Economics* 10, no. 1–2 (April/August 1983): 281–310.

153. See *Allen Testimony* before the Study Commission of 2 April 1982, pp. 9, 11, for a statement of the unsolved problem: "Cartel behavior parallels that of a monopolist. . . . Society would prefer another unit of motor carrier service over a different use of the resources, but the service would not be produced by a monopolist. *Restricted output is the key to his inflated price*" (emphasis added).

154. Andrew Mas-Collel, "Noncooperative Approaches to the Theory of Perfect Competition: Presentation," in *Noncooperative Approaches to the Theory of Perfect Competition*, Andrew Mas-Collel, ed. (New York: Academic Press, 1982): 2. See also P.A. Geroski, L. Philips, and A. Ulpa, eds., "A Symposium on Oligopoly, Competition, and Welfare," *Journal of Industrial Economics* 33, no. 4 (June 1985): 369–552.

155. Such a noncooperative equilibrium is called a Cournot/Nash equilibrium because each competitor chooses a quantity as the decision variable and sells at the market price. The Bertrand model of oligopoly makes price the strategic choice variable and therefore does not appear to be appropriate for assessing the effects of collective ratemaking in the motor carrier industry.

156. James Friedman, *Oligopoly Theory* (Cambridge, England: Cambridge University Press, 1983).

157. James A. Brander and Barbara J. Spencer, "Tacit Collusion, Free Entry and Welfare," *The Journal of Industrial Economics* 33, no. 3 (March 1985): 227–94. The authors describe their results as applying to tacit collusion, but the mechanism is decidedly noncooperative.

158. More generally, where entry is not free, the noncooperative equilibrium could result in output levels generating prices in excess of average costs and thus excess profits.

159. Two critics of collective ratemaking, Russell C. Cherry and Carl Buckman, "Market Structure and Concentration in the Regulated Trucking Industry," *American Economic Review* 71, no. 2 (May 1981): 385–88, state that a positive conjectural variation "implies a degree of sophistication about competitors' behavior that is alien to the trucking industry. The industry is far from having the degree of sophistication that one might associate with many oligopolies." See also Russell C. Cherry, "Rate Effects of Collective Ratemaking and the Meaning of Concentration in Regulated Motor Carriage," prepared for Transportation Systems Center, U.S. Department of Transportation, July 1982.

160. As a practical matter, a carrier does not start a truck from point A to point B and hope that someone puts freight on it. Output decisions designed to conform to strategic interaction requirements may be impossible to implement

simply because dispatchers are delegated the responsibility of scheduling service to meet demand. These decisions cannot be made at the highest levels of management with a view toward their effect on competitors' service decisions, much less at a rate bureau.

161. See Mas-Collel, "Noncooperative Approaches," p. 3; and Richard C. Levin, in "Railroad Rates, Profitability and Welfare under Deregulation," *Bell Journal of Economics and Management Science* 12, no. 1 (Spring 1981): 1–26; and "Railroad Regulation, Deregulation, and Workable Competition," *American Economic Review* 71, no. 2 (May 1981): 394–98, which posited a model of noncooperative oligopoly for the rail industry in which the number of competitors was the critical determinant of price levels.

162. Even with a collusive agreement, there is a difficulty of enforcing the cartel agreement. It can be shown that with perfect information, the cartel can be enforced by a strategy where each firm charges the cartel price and produces the cartel-dictated output as long as all others also do the same. If any firm cheats, then a self-enforcing strategy is for all firms to switch to the noncollusive equilibrium. This strategy mutually creates an incentive for each firm to ostensibly adhere to the collusive agreement and not be the first to depart—while secretly cheating on both price and output, as the recent oil pricing experience shows. The only real way around the problem in the presence of high enforcement costs is a pooling agreement.

163. Although various definitions have been offered for the terms *market power* and *monopoly power*, they usually involve power to raise prices by restricting output. See, for example, Phillip Areeda and Donald F. Turner, "Predatory Pricing and Related Prices under Section 2 of the Sherman Act," 88 *Harvard Law Review* (1975): 697–733. Indeed, the "Chicago School" alleges that antitrust policy should focus only on reducing the "burden of monopoly" created by output restrictions designed to increase price. See William M. Landes, "Harm to Competition: Cartels, Mergers and Joint Ventures," in *Antitrust Policy in Transition: The Convergence of Law and Economics*, Eleanor M. Fox and James T. Halverson, eds. (ABA Press, 1984). While one need not go this far in defining an antitrust offense, by definition there will be excessive quantity supplied at a noncompetitive high price, resulting from the anticompetitive practice of price fixing, and there must be some control mechanism to restrict output.

164. Note that Brander and Spencer's model achieved an inefficient equilibrium with an assumption of a noncooperative "conjectural variation." In equilibrium, their firms do not benefit from the higher prices because of free entry but cannot take advantage of the inefficiency to earn extra profits precisely because the equilibrium is noncooperative.

165. Any efficiency is the source of additional profit to any incumbent firm that eliminates the inefficiency. Inefficient market structures must be supported by some market imperfection, such as imperfect information or transactions costs that eliminate the profit potential. Collusion would of course serve to enforce an anticompetitive result, but there must be a credible deterrence to cheating. Otherwise, each firm has an incentive to stay outside the collusive agreement or, once inside it, to undercut the agreement.

166. Donald Dewey, "Information, Entry, and Welfare: The Case for Collusion," *American Economic Review* 69, no. 4 (September 1979): 587–94.

167. Lester G. Telser, "Cooperation, Competition, and Efficiency," *Journal of Law and Economics* 28, no. 2 (May 1985): 271–95.

168. See Kari Bullock and Sumner J. LaCroix, "Welfare and Collusion: Comment," *American Economic Review* 72, no. 1 (March 1982): 256–58, and following pages by other commenters.

169. Or more generally, some market imperfection that can be enhanced to the benefit of incumbents must be demonstrated.

170. See Donald Dewey, "Welfare and Collusion: Reply," *American Economic Review* 72, no. 1 (March 1982): 276–81. Eisenberg, "Information Exchange among Competitors," found that relative value scales for physicians' services (a function similar to freight classification) improved pricing efficiency without leading to higher rates.

171. This is the objection to collusion, even in the absence of market power and the presence of short-run efficiency gains, offered by Roland H. Keller II, "Welfare and Collusion: Comment," *American Economic Review* 72, no. 1 (March 1982): 256–67.

4. ENCOURAGING COOPERATION AMONG RELATED RIVALS

172. In the terminology of the antitrust law, the same two carriers are vertically related (end-to-end service) in some markets and horizontally related (parallel service) in others.

173. See *Testimony of Tim Ravey* and *Testimony of David R. Free*, before the Motor Carrier Ratemaking Study Commission, Phoenix, Arizona, 10 December 1981; and *Statement of H.L. Cook*, Akron hearing, 29 January 1982, for a description of the ratemaking and service aspects of interline freight.

174. See C.C. Barnekov, "Analysis of Evidence in *Ex Parte* No. MC–172, Withdrawal of Antitrust Immunity," ICC Staff Report, 6 August 1984.

175. Prior to regulatory reform, the arguments against collective ratemaking were that operating authority restrictions imposed on the carriers by the ICC encouraged excessive interlining and that the problem of joint-line ratemaking would go away with deregulation because carriers would not need to interline if they had all the operating authority they needed. See *Seiden Testimony* of 19 March 1982. Now that this argument no longer applies, opponents reverse their argument and state that interlining is such a critical part of the business that carriers will do whatever is necessary to establish joint-line rates, despite the loss of collective ratemaking. The revisionist position is that "by 1982 there are signs that this decline [in percentage of traffic that is interlined] has slowed down and is reaching its limits, as it will never be economical for all shipments to be single-lined" (footnote omitted). See MAC, "The Motor Carrier Market Place," p. 40. See also Study Commission *Report* at pp. ix, xi.

176. The Study Commission's data showed that 23.6 percent of LTL shipments were interlined in 1980, but the figure ranged from 14 percent for the largest cities to 59 percent (originating traffic) to 61 percent (terminating traffic) for small towns and rural communities (*Report*, pp. 401, 402, 417). The Study Commission found that interline service was more likely to involve small communities than larger ones. See *Report*, pp. 323, 336. See also Russell Cherry, "Rate Effects of Collective Ratemaking," pp. 1–7.

177. Technically, there is a distinction between the joint rate and the through route. A joint rate applies to a total movement and requires the concurrence of the two carriers and a separate divisions agreement over the split of revenue. The through route is contained in a routing guide tariff that identifies carriers and gateways where traffic is interchanged, usually subject to joint concurrence in the joint rate.

178. *Report*, p. 344.

179. See also *Testimony of Alison Swan* at the Phoenix hearing, Tr. p. 57, lines 1–13, for another frank acknowledgment of what is likely to happen.

180. *Statement of Denis Breen*, Washington hearing, Tr. p. 60, line 16.

181. *Broemser Testimony* before the Study Commission on behalf of the DOT, 18 November 1981, pp. 2–3.

182. Indeed, the situation has almost gotten out of hand already as a result of individual carrier pricing initiatives. As one motor carrier executive related to me:

> The best quantitative measure of tariff proliferation is the Watching Service Bulletins provided by the Bureaus. There have been so many tariffs published we have stopped counting. Add to this the great number of additional items published in agency tariffs and the total amount is staggering.
>
> As a result of this proliferation, our rate and audit production has suffered noticeably. There are too many exceptions, allowances, and discounts to check before arriving at a proper rate and charge. The traditional rating check of commodity, exceptions, and class-rate tariffs has been made much more difficult by the addition of column commodity, special commodity, and aggregate tender tariffs. Rating errors have increased to the point where our overcharge claims and payment exceptions are a major part of our daily work. Customer irritation has increased as well.

183. Study Commission *Report*, pp. 505–509. While denying that the carriers needed antitrust immunity for an interline agreement, the ICC nevertheless recently refused to grant approval of such immunity on the grounds that carriers have operated under such agreements for years without explicit immunity. See Docket No. 38,991; 367 ICC 939 (1984).

184. See also Posner and Hausman for a description of the role of rate bureaus as efficient means of providing joint services by competitors by reducing transactions costs of interfirm agreements.

185. See MAC, "The Motor Carrier Market Place," p. 48.

186. The consensus is that collective ratemaking cannot exist in any form without explicit antitrust immunity for interstate movements. See William E. Kenworthy, "Antitrust Considerations in Motor Carrier Ratemaking—Rate Bureau Operations and Alternatives," *Transportation Law Journal* 11 (1979): 65–89.

187. MAC, "The Motor Carrier Market Place," p. 49.

188. Six companies were indicted in 1982 for violation of Section 1 of the Sherman Act. The gravamen of the complaint was that these six truck brokers used common rate sheets to determine rates for hauling tomatoes. *Food Transport Week* 11, no. 8 (22 February 1982): 1. See also testimony of attorney witnesses at the Boston hearing before the Study Commission. The "Minority Views" and "Additional Views" in the Study Commission *Report* noted that case law sup-

ports an inference that "information exchanges, even absent an agreement on prices" are "criminally suspect" citing a Supreme Court decision that neither specific intent to violate the antitrust laws nor an agreement on prices is required (pp. 11–12, 40–41, 52). For a review of the economic issues raised by information exchanges on prices by competitors, see Richard A. Posner, "Information and Antitrust: Reflections on the *Gypsum* and *Engineers* Decisions," *Georgetown Law Journal* 67, no. 3 (February 1979): 1187–1203.

189. MAC, "The Motor Carrier Market Place," p. 49.

190. Critics' claims that the benefits of the pricing benchmark could be achieved without the immunity fly in the face of advice of counsel to their clients. James R. McGibbon and Douglas E. Rosenthal, *Antitrust Primer for Motor Carrier Executives* (Washington, D.C.: American Trucking Associations, 1982:) 23–24, state:

> Exchanges of price information between competitors involve so serious an antitrust risk, even when there is no specific agreement to fix prices, that they should never be undertaken unless counsel has confirmed that an antitrust exemption or other specific exception to the general rule is applicable. Indeed, the Justice Department has brought at least one criminal indictment with respect to systematic exchanges of information on the current prices being charged by particular sellers to particular customers.

See also Kevin M. Williams, *Antitrust Compliance Manual for Motor Carriers* (Washington, D.C.: Regular Common Carrier Conference, American Trucking Associations, no date).

191. See *Statement of the Assistant Attorney General in Charge of the Antitrust Division and Acting Associate Attorney General* (former Assistant Attorney General Shenefield), before the Committee on Commerce, Science, and Transportation, U.S. Senate, 3 December 1979, pp. 10–11:

> However, the inability to negotiate joint rates or the division of revenues does not mean even in these circumstances that interline service would have to be discontinued. Such service *could* continue, without fear of antitrust exposure even when there were competing single services operated by both connecting carriers. In such instances, carriers could unilaterally either publish proportional rates, or simply apply local rates.

192. For examples, see Dabney T. Waring, Jr., "No Protection for the Inefficient Carrier in Collective Ratemaking," before the Motor Carrier Ratemaking Study Commission, Kansas City, Missouri, 5 March 1982. William J. Baumol, in "Some Subtle Pricing Issues in Railroad Regulation," *International Journal of Transport Economics* 10, no. 1–2 (April/August 1983): 341–55, went so far as to argue that antitrust immunity to encourage collusion to set joint-line rates would cause rates in general to be lower, regardless of demand conditions. For doubt of this position as it applies to a competitive industry such as trucking, see William B. Tye, "Some Subtle Pricing Issues in Railroad Regulation: Comment" and "Rejoinder," *International Journal of Transport Economics* 11, no. 2–3 (August/December 1984): 207–16, 219–20.

193. MAC, "The Motor Carrier Market Place," p. 48.

194. MAC, p. 52.

195. *Testimony of Ronald V. Meeks* before the Motor Carrier Ratemaking Study Commission, 10 December 1981, pp. 3–4, and Tr. pp. 185–86.

196. Referring to a different proposal but one that raises similar antitrust concerns, Elliott M. Seiden, Chief of the Transportation Section of the Antitrust Division of DOJ, stated,

> Such an underlying agreement to adhere to a specific set of factors in classification or to the information provided on these factors might expose carriers to antitrust liability after the withdrawal of immunity for single-line rates. Such an agreement, given the industry's long history of collective classification and ratemaking, may facilitate illegal single-line rate agreements.

See Testimony before the Study Commission at the Cambridge Hearing, 19 March 1982, p. 17. He further noted (p. 15),

> There is no question that the freight classification, as presently administered and used, is anticompetitive and would be, absent immunity, highly vulnerable to antitrust attack. . . . [M]any aspects of the current system inhibit competitive, cost-based pricing and are therefore inconsistent with the goals of the Motor Carrier Act of 1980.

197. Daniel M. Gladwell, "The Barge Freight Call Session of the Merchants Exchange of St. Louis: An Innovation in Transportation Pricing," *Transportation Journal* 20, no. 1 (Fall 1980): 5–18.

198. Gladwell, p. 7.

199. Gladwell states that many barge companies prefer to keep their prices secret while taking advantage of the information about price levels from the public trades on the floor of the exchange. This has raised concerns about the representativeness of the trades which become the reference price for unpublished trades.

200. Robert J. Hauser and Steven A. Neff, "The Pricing Efficiency of the Barge Freight Call Session," *Proceedings of the Transportation Research Forum* 25, no. 1 (1984): 331–36.

201. Posner, pp. 17, 20, notes that the elimination of antitrust immunity raises the transactions costs of interfirm service agreements and exposes rail carriers to the risk of antitrust prosecution. One attractive way of reducing these costs and risks is through mergers designed to eliminate the need for interfirm cooperation. Shippers can be expected to make their way through this confusion by concentrating their volume more and more among a few large carriers, a process that is already under way. The vast proliferation of tariffs today and the discount structure (which raises the discount percentage as the volume of business increases) have also contributed to this tendency toward concentration of freight.

202. Senate Commerce Committee, Motor Carrier Reform Act of 1980, p. 14. See also *House Report*, for similar language.

203. Motor Carrier Reform Act of 1980, p. 13. See also House Public Works and Transportation Committee, p. 28, for similar language.

204. Management Analysis Center, Inc., "Ratemaking Analogies," report prepared for the Motor Carrier Ratemaking Study Commission, Washington, D.C.,

August 1982, cited railroad perishable traffic as an analogy where antitrust immunity is not available. They note, however, that "fear of anti-trust action has precluded interline arrangements with primary competitor railroads" (p. 14).

205. Eugene Crew and Joel Linzner, "Joint Rates between Competitors—A True Antitrust Dilemma," *Traffic World* (2 May 1983): 77–82.

206. In the most recent case on the subject, *Aspen Skiing Co.* v. *Aspen Highlands Skiing Corp.* 105 S. Ct. 2847 (1985), 53 U.S.L.W. 4818 (1985), the Supreme Court ruled that "valid business reasons" may be offered to justify a refusal to deal, although there is no "unqualified duty to cooperate." Since the defendant offered no reasons according to the decision, the standard for "validity" was left in doubt.

207. *Statement of William F. Baxter*, before the Motor Carrier Ratemaking Study Commission, 18 November 1981, pp. 9, 13.

208. Washington hearing, Tr. p. 60, line 16.

209. *Statement of the Assistant Attorney General in Charge of the Antitrust Division and Acting Associate Attorney General* (former Assistant Attorney General Shenefield), before the Committee on Commerce, Science, and Transportation, U.S. Senate, 3 December 1979.

210. *Statement*, pp. 9, 12. See also Tr. pp. 30–31.

211. *Report*, pp. 338–39, 341–42.

212. Eastern Central Motor Carriers Association publishes tariffs covering service at 23,000 points in the East and 41,000 points in the West, producing 1.9 billion point-to-point pairwise markets. See *Statement of James T. Henry*, Akron hearing, 29 January 1982, p. 10.

213. Section 14 (b)(3)(B)(ii).

214. 49 U.S.C. 10706 (a)(3)B.

215. See Kenworthy, p. 85.

216. Posner, pp. 28–33.

217. *Section 5b Application No. 2: Western Railroads—Agreement*, p. 38.

218. The ICC purportedly implemented the prohibition on single-line rates in *Ex Parte* No. 297 (Sub-No. 5), *Motor Carrier Rate Bureaus—Implementation of P.L. 96–296*, 19 December 1980. The ICC *Decision* merely suggests that bureaus implement the MCA of 1980 by an amendment to their by-laws: "After January 1, 1984 (or July 1, 1984), all single-line rate proposals will be treated as independent actions. After this date, there shall be no discussion or voting on single-line rates by bureau members or committees." Other than to prohibit the inclusion of single-line and joint-line rates in one proposal, the *Decision* did nothing to clarify the confusion arising from the distinction between single-line traffic (which can move under a collectively set tariff) and a single-line tariff (an IA). The ICC's prohibition on combining single- and joint-line proposals, incidentally, limits a right of independent action had under the old law (IA's could apply for both single- and joint-line traffic for concurring carriers).

219. Of course, the definition is not identical to an IA because joint-line rate proposals can also be docketed as IA's.

220. See also Study Commission *Report*, pp. 498–501, which cites the legislative history to support this interpretation.

221. The MCA of 1980, unlike the Staggers Rail Act, makes no explicit mention of joint-line rates in the legislative scope for antitrust immunity. The lack of an

explicit immunity certainly cannot be encouraging to those who feel threatened by antitrust immunity for collective ratemaking on joint-line rates. Curiously, Section 22(b)(1) of the MCA extended the ICC's authority to establish through routes and rates for the first time to trucking:

> The Interstate Commerce Commission may, and shall when it considers it desirable in the public interest, prescribe through routes, joint classifications, joint rates (including maximum or minimum rates or both), the division of joint rates, and the conditions under which those routes must be operated, for a motor common carrier of property providing transportation subject to the jurisdiction of the Commission under subchapter 11 of chapter 105 of this title with another such carrier or with a water common carrier of property.

222. "Justice Department, Shippers Convince ICC to Reject NFTB Single-Line Rates," *Traffic World* (17 September 1984).

223. The court, in *Niagara Frontier Tariff Bureau, Inc.* v. *United States*, Docket No. 84–1548, (D.C. Circuit, 1986) resolved the ambiguity in the statute itself in favor of what it deemed Congress had intended to do.

Appendix: Developments in Railroad Collective Ratemaking

224. P.L. 96–448, 94 Stat. 1895.

225. Railroad Revitalization and Regulatory Reform Act of 1976, P.L. 94–210, 90 Stat.

226. Interstate Commerce Commission, "Section 5b Application No. 2: Western Railroads—Agreement," served 21 January 1981. See Section 219 of the Staggers Rail Act of 1980. For a discussion of the act and the ICC *Decision* from the rail rate bureau point of view, see *Remarks of J.D. Feeney*, Western Railroad Association, to the 4th AICCP Western Transportation Law Seminar, 3 March 1981, and *Remarks of J.D. Feeney* to the National Conference of State Rail Officials, 9 July 1981.

227. See also Richard Lande, "How Collective Ratemaking Improves the Canadian Economy," *Transportation Practitioners Journal* 52, no. 2 (Winter 1985): 198–220, for a review of issues in rail collective ratemaking in Canada.

228. This option was granted by the act to the Commission, according to the Commission's interpretation. The ICC had already proposed this prohibition prior to the Staggers Act as well as the direct connectors definition of permissible collective ratemaking for joint-line rail rates in a 13 August 1980 notice.

229. The bureau is not allowed to "discuss, to participate in agreements related to, or to vote on rates related to a particular interline movement unless that rail carrier practicably participates in that movement" (Section 219(a)).

230. See "Conrail Plans to Resign from Rail Rate Bureau Due to Changes in the Law," *Traffic World* (16 November 1981): 26: "Conrail has not been fully participating in rate bureau activities for about a year, *due to uncertainty over the antitrust laws*" (emphasis added).

231. See speech given by James N. Baker, Chairman, Western Railroad Traffic Association, 3 November 1981, meeting of American Short Line Railroad Association, Rancho Mirage, California. Mr. Baker notes that "[m]eeting consid-

eration under the direct connector procedures has proved to be extremely time consuming and cumbersome . . . carriers generally are opting in the alternative to obtain advance concurrence from connections to through routes and to take joint independent action as the means of accomplishing an adjustment . . . the rate bureaus no longer are the principal instrumentality for accomplishing rail pricing objectives."

232. A similar prohibition in the 4R Act did not deter the ICC from proposing to exclude single-line rates from general rail rate increases and broad tariff changes in the 13 August 1980 decision (364 I.C.C.1, Section 5b Application No. 2, *Western Railroads Agreement*). See Railroad Revitalization and Regulatory Reform Act of 1976 [49 U.S.C. 10706(a)]. However, the SRA has an explicit goal "to require rail carriers, to the maximum extent practicable, to rely on individual rate increases and to limit the use of increases of general applicability," while the MCA contains explicit exceptions to the prohibition of the ban on collective single-line ratemaking.

233. The result has been massive cancellations of joint routes by the rail carriers. Under collective ratemaking, routes had been kept generally open. "But now, in the wake of the recession and certain federal regulatory changes, . . . gentlemanly behavior is out." "Major Changes in Moving Rail Freight Raise Fears of Higher Rates for Shippers," *The Wall Street Journal*, 22 February 1983. See also "Curtailment of Antitrust Immunity Viewed as Divisive in Railroading," *Traffic World* (2 January 1984): 21:

> Cohesiveness of the American railway network, taken as a whole has been reduced since the passage of the Railroad Revitalization and Regulatory Reform Act of 1976 and the Staggers Rail Act of 1980, and *one cause of that decline is the curtailment of antitrust immunity for the collective determination and quotation of rates* applicable to movements over alternate interline routes, a subcommittee of the House Small Business Committee in Congress was told by a nationally prominent transportation educator in a recent hearing [emphasis added].

The massive cancellations of joint routes arising from the loss of antitrust immunity spawned considerable antitrust litigation. See "Lawyer Sees Destruction of Rail Joint-Rate System," *Traffic World* (21 March 1983): 78–79; "Small Railroad is Suing CSX in Rate Fight," *The Wall Street Journal*, 5 May 1983; and "Conrail to Pay Millions to Settle Antitrust Suit, Industry Sources Report," *Traffic World* (28 April 1986): 8.

234. Baker notes that the direct connectors doctrine resulted in a substantial increase in joint IA's, and "limitation or reduction in the number of joint routes applicable in connection with newly established specific joint rates," and problems for short-line railroads in monitoring and joining and proposals for interline traffic.

5. COMMUNICATING TO CUSTOMERS

235. Even those who would abolish collective ratemaking seem to agree. MAC states that "few shippers other than the smallest actually pay 'the rate,' as every

carrier has a discount or some variant on 'the rate.' " And " 'the rate' [the LTL class-rate structure] is the starting point for bilateral bargaining between carriers and most shippers." See MAC, "The Motor Carrier Market Place," p. 38.

236. See Tye, "Scenarios of the Motor Carrier Industry," for discussion of this revisionist position.

237. See MAC, pp. 17, 34.

238. MAC also notes that "in practice shippers use a small number of carriers for any given shipment/route . . . while a few large shippers may deal with as many as 150 or 200 carriers in a year" (MAC, p. 34). To the extent this is true, it is only because the system is held together by a set of joint-line tariffs that permit the shipper to deal primarily with the originating carrier.

239. See Study Commission, *Report*, pp. i, ii.

240. For a discussion of the advantages of a formal tariff system over unstructured spot prices, see Louis Lacoste, "The Structure of Railroad Fares and Rates in a Highly Competitive Freight Transportation Market," Kenneth D. Boyer and William G. Shepherd, eds. *Economic Regulation: Essays in Honor of James R. Nelson* (E. Lansing, Mich.: Michigan State University, 1981).

241. The sheer mass of the information on pricing in the motor carrier industry staggers the imagination. Peat, Marwick and Mitchell, *Motor Carrier Ratemaking Study: Task I—Report and Annotated Bibliography*, prepared for the Motor Carrier Ratemaking Study Commission, 24 May 1982, reported that one regional rate bureau published 90 to 100 million pages of tariff material in 1981 (see p. 7). Kenneth D. Boyer, "Equalizing Discrimination and Cartel Pricing in Transport Rate Regulation," *Journal of Political Economy* 89, no. 2 (1981): 274, reported, "Hundreds of billions of individual prices have been established and approved" in the rail and trucking industries. An early survey of carriers projected a 150 percent increase in tariff pages with individual carrier pricing, but the explosion in tariff publication suggests that this is a substantial understatement. See Joseph L. Cavinato and Gary B. Kogan, "An Assessment of the Impacts from Partial and Full Repeal of Section 10706 (Antitrust Immunity) upon the Motor Carrier Industry and Its Users," *ICC Practitioners Journal* 47 (1980): 427–49.

242. The Study Commission, *Report*, pp. iii, xii, 119, noted that shippers, particularly small ones, do not participate in collective ratemaking, and took this as evidence that the system failed to meet the needs of its users. A contrary interpretation is that the ability of small carriers and shippers to free ride on the collective ratemaking system reduces the minimum efficient scale of both buyers and sellers and is a benefit of the system.

243. While supporters of deregulation take a permissive view toward the increased transactions costs and view them as a necessary consequence of the benefits arising from price competition, such costs are real and should be minimized, especially when they threaten the political acceptability of deregulation. For a surprisingly large segment of the public, these transactions and information costs and the dislocations resulting from deregulation can be more acutely felt than the benefits of price competition in the transition to deregulation. See "Deregulation: A Puzzle to Consumers," *The New York Times*, (4 June 1983): 10.

244. Multisystems, Inc., "A Survey of LTL-Carrier Pricing Practices for Individual Shippers: The Aftermath of Deregulation," Oakland, Calif.: dated approximately January 1985.

245. For further discussion, see Study Commission, *Report*, pp. 111–18, and John W. McFadden, Jr., "A Description and Analysis of Rate Structures, Rate Levels and Competitive Conditions under Collective Ratemaking and Their Importance to the Public," before the Motor Carrier Ratemaking Study Commission, Kansas City, 5 March 1982.

246. Other designations, such as exceptions, use the class-rate system to determine a different rate than would apply. Like commodity rates, they are not part of the benchmark structure.

247. There are of course many class rates depending on geographic applicability and carrier participation, for example.

248. See any textbook on traffic management, such as Leon William Morse, *Practical Handbook of Industrial Traffic Management* (Washington, D.C.: Traffic Service Corporation, 1980), Chapter 5. See also *Statement of S.E. Somers, Jr.*, before the Motor Carrier Ratemaking Study Commission, 1 May 1982; and John P. Conner, "The Functional Machinery of Collective Ratemaking," before the Motor Carrier Ratemaking Study Commission, May 1982.

249. The New England Motor Rate Bureau publishes a separate classification system for commodities covered by its tariffs.

250. See Morse, Chapter 4.

251. William J. Augello, Executive Director/General Counsel, Shippers National Freight Claim Council, Inc., noted in "The Deregulation Disaster," Eleventh International Air Forum, 28 September 1982, pp. 3–4, that the big difference between transportation and other markets is that "a consumer need not enter into a written contract to purchase groceries . . . an effective and efficient network cannot be created without uniform, reasonable rules and regulations, particularly with respect to the terms and conditions of the contract of carriage."

252. Notably the Civil Aeronautics Board (CAB) recently published regulations designed to give all competitors equal access to vital marketing channels in the airline industry, such as computer reservation systems (CRS). The Department of Justice conducted an extensive investigation and concluded that certain airline-owned computer reservations systems were used and could be used to foreclose competition in the airline industry. See "Comments and Proposed Rules of the Department of Justice," 17 November 1983, in Docket No. 41686, before the Civil Aeronautics Board, *Advance Notice of Proposed Rulemaking—Computer Reservations Systems*. These conclusions led the Civil Aeronautics Board to implement rules that were designed to "deal with competitive abuses and consumer injury," such as "discrimination," "tying," "bias," and impeding "objective service information." *Federal Register*, Vol. 49, No. 159, pp. 32540–64, 15 August 1984. 14 CFR, Part 225.

253. See Mancur Olson, *The Logic of Collective Action* (Cambridge, Mass.: Harvard University Press, 1965).

254. Andrew F. Popper, *Shipper Antitrust Liability in a Rate-Deregulated Market: Fundamental Inquiries and Analysis* (Washington, D.C.: American University, 1979).

255. Steven J. Kalish, "Antitrust Considerations for Shippers in a Changing Environment," *Transportation Practitioners Journal* 52, no. 2 (Winter 1985): 185–97.

256. Shenefield, pp. 19–20. However, the Justice Department later approved

a collective arrangement, or shippers' council, to negotiate small shipment rates with carriers on behalf of NASSTRAC members. "First Shippers' Council Okayed by Justice Department: 1984 Start-up Planned," *Traffic World* (5 December 1983): 37–38.

257. During the hearings of the Study Commission, these transactions costs were the primary concern of shippers. As Velten, the representative of NAS-STRAC, stated in his testimony before the Ratemaking Study Commission (Tr. pp. 108–109):

> I think some of the answers you got this morning relative to rate bureaus continuing to function as publishing houses are very glib answers. I think the thing goes down the tubes without the rate bureaus because there's going to be such a plethora of rates that nobody is going to be able to keep up with them, certainly no shipper, because there will be a total lack of visibility.

As one shipper put it at the Akron hearing of the Study Commission,

> We have recently attempted to computerize some freight rates for one division consisting of four plants. We got the system in operation, and then the discounting came along. That just completely threw the system out . . . if that single line immunity is discontinued and every carrier starts to set their rates individually, we are going to have the most complicated mess that we have ever seen, and you will not be able to computerize any of it (Tr. p. 162, line 20 to p. 163, line 6).

Another shipper added that "if we get into a situation where every person has his own rate scale, his own method of calculating these rates, that would be chaos" (Tr. p. 165, lines 4–6). See also *Testimony of John K. Maser* on behalf of the National Industrial Traffic League before the Motor Carrier Ratemaking Study Commission, 18 November 1981, and Tr. pp. 74–77, 81–84, 99; and the testimony of other shipper witnesses before the commission (e.g., Washington hearing, Tr. pp. 124–28). Booz-Allen and Hamilton Inc. estimated that the loss of collective ratemaking would cost shippers $4 to $8 billion in increased administrative expenses. See *Impact on Transportation Management of Changes in the Collective Ratemaking System*, presented to the Motor Carrier Ratemaking Study Commission, July 1982. In a follow-up study three years later, most surveyed shippers stated that a "floating tariff system" was "extremely scary." Many shippers found it very useful to have a published rate standard against which individual carrier's offers were "represented by a single number for the most part, namely their discount." *Testimony of Paul O. Roberts*, before the Surface Transportation Subcommittee, U.S. Senate, September 1985.

258. Harbridge House, Inc., *Report on Harbridge House Survey of the Impact of Transportation Deregulation on Major U.S. Manufacturing Firms*. Boston, Mass. (June 1981): 2, found that most shippers expected to deal with fewer trucking companies as a result of deregulation.

259. *Report*, pp. 470–74. For a suggestion that the bureaus pursue such an alternative with the loss of immunity, see Paul S. Gardiner, "Rate Bureau Functions without Antitrust Immunity: A Suggested Strategy for Motor Freight Carriers," *ICC Practitioners Journal* 46, no. 5 (July/August 1979): 561–668.

260. MarTech Strategies, Inc., in a report to the Study Commission entitled "The Potential for Electronic Tariff Networks and Markets," September 1982, concluded that rate bureaus were building large data bases "to justify their existence" (p. 3–36). Concluding that "the institutions of collective ratemaking and rate bureaus could provide a disincentive on the part of motor carriers to pioneer new methods and seek out standards" (p. 3–45), the report averred that most of the services of rate bureaus could be provided without antitrust immunity by electronic systems supplied by private vendors.

261. Third-party systems in the airline industry have found that competing with carriers' propriety systems is made difficult by the fact that the largest systems refuse to participate. If the air carrier system is analogous, third-party systems might not compete effectively against the proprietary systems of the largest carriers.

262. See MarTech, pp. 3–37 to 3–41, where the need for tariff simplification is discussed.

263. See Conner.

264. Computerized tariff systems are a recent phenomenon. A survey conducted a few years back by Paul K. Sugrue, Manfred H. Ledford, and Nicholas A. Glaskowsky, Jr., "Computer Applications in the U.S. Trucking Industry," *Logistics and Transportation Review* 18, no. 2 (1982): 169–87, does not even mention such systems.

265. Notably the period prior to the restrictions on antitrust immunity for single-line ratemaking was marked by a flurry of effort by the rate bureaus to institute zip-coded tariffs in place of the previous rate groups. The revised tariffs were initially proposed by the Eastern Central Bureau (see "'ZIP Code Tariff' Proposed by ECMCA," *Transport Topics* (13 December 1982): 14, 18). Shippers, however, complained that tariff complexity would be worsened unless all the bureaus switched to the zip code system. See "Wanted: Adoption of Simple Uniform Rate System by Motor Rate Bureaus," *Traffic World* (25 April 1983): 19–20.

266. See *Official Airline Guides* v. *FTC*, 630 F.2d 920 (2nd Circuit, 1980). There the court ruled that the *Official Airline Guides* had no obligation to not discriminate among airlines as long as it was not in the airline business, supporting the idea that a third party might not need antitrust immunity as long as it simply reported independent carrier price offers and even if it were a monopoly.

267. As the Study Commission notes in *Report*, p. 139, "what appears to be a simple and objective fact-finding, i.e., representing actual distance," in fact incorporates many ratemaking functions which could perhaps not be conducted collectively in the absence of antitrust immunity.

268. There is also a controversy over the applicability of the copyright laws to tariffs. The ability to do so might be critical to the success of a third party because certain carriers might refuse to participate, as they have in the airline industry. See "RMMTB Bid to Copyright Zip Code-Based Tariff Assailed by Shippers," *Traffic World* (18 July 1983): 61–62.

269. Proponents of these systems essentially offer a "challenge/response" mechanism to justify forcing the market to make a desirable change by eliminating an existing alternative. See Study Commission *Report*, p. 485. Arnold Toynbee coined the phrase, which refers to the therapeutic role of chastening

crises in forcing the civilizations of the world to innovate. This philosophy comes awkwardly to proponents of a free market approach to transportation, as it implies that its proponents know more than buyers and sellers in the market.

270. See *Decision* of the ICC in *Ex Parte* No. 297 (Sub-No. 7), 20 May 1985.

271. Ironically, the Middle Atlantic Conference, for one, had taken the lead in proposing released rates in the past. As the *Annual Report 1981* noted, "The carriers had high hopes of being able to proceed with a small shipment tariff plan based on general released value provisions, however, those hopes were quickly dashed as the new Motor Carrier Act unfortunately removed the carriers' anti-trust immunity for collectively establishing any new released value rates or provisions."

272. The rationale for the prohibition apparently was born from admiration of the rate structure and tariff rules of United Parcel Service, which does not participate in collective ratemaking. See Darius W. Gaskins, Jr., and James M. Voytko, "The Surface Transportation Sector in a Competitive Era: Efficiency and Innovation in Pricing and Operations," *University of Florida Law Review* 32, no. 5 (Fall 1980): 859–76.

273. See "Shipper/Carrier Groups Seeking Immunity for Released Rates," *Transport Topics* (17 May 1982); "Trucking Industry Seeks Uniformity in Claims Liability for All Modes," *Traffic World* (18 July 1983): 27–28. William J. Augello, the Executive Director/General Counsel of the Shippers National Freight Claim Council, testified before the Study Commission on 19 March 1982 that the abolition was "ill-conceived, unjustified, and has produced unintended and undesirable results. . . . This issue has produced a rare occurrence in transportation—the unanimity of position by shippers and motor carriers."

274. Augello, *Testimony*, p. 4, points out two benefits of collective ratemaking in reducing transaction costs for released rates and the fallacy of the argument that computerization will solve these coordination problems without antitrust immunity:

1. Savings in management's time and effort required to negotiate reductions in claim liability and appropriate reductions in rate levels. Most shippers do business with hundreds of motor carriers throughout the country, and most carriers deal with thousands of shippers, many of whom they have never met face-to-face.
2. Uniformity in rate structures and liability standards thus created. When firms ship tens of thousands of pounds of product a month to all 50 states, via dozens of different carriers and modes, uniformity is essential. Preprinted bills of lading containing a uniform released rate statement is possible only if that released rate has industrywide application. Furthermore, many firms have computerized their invoicing and shipping documentation, thus compelling greater standardization of released rates and other shipping terms.

275. Strangely, the Study Commission, *Report*, p. 452, ignored the data which it cited and stated that "a properly designed and conducted classification system could determine class ratings based on a released commodity value. . . . [S]uch released rate classifications could be permissible inasmuch as they facilitate ratemaking and provide additional price-service options to shippers" (footnote

omitted). In light of the fact that the prohibition of collectively established re-leased value rates was precisely to force unilateral action by the carriers, the Study Commission's effort to have it both ways by suggesting that collective action should be reinstituted via classification without antitrust immunity is incomprehensible.

276. For a development of this theory, see Merton J. Peck, "Competitive Policy for Transportation," in *Perspectives on Antitrust Policy*, Almarin Phillips, ed. (Princeton, N.J.: Princeton University Press, 1965); Policy and Management Associates, "Regulatory Reform and Motor Carrier Tariff Complexity," submitted to U.S. Department of Transportation, October 1982. "Motor Carrier Freight Classification," and "The Potential for Motor Carrier Tariff Simplification," both presented to the Motor Carrier Ratemaking Study Commission, October 1982; Russell C. Cherry, "Rate Effects of Collective Ratemaking and the Meaning of Concentration in Regulated Motor Carriage," prepared for the Transportation Systems Center, U.S. Department of Transportation, July 1982; Trans-World Trucking Associates, "Patterns of Discrimination under Collective Motor Carrier Ratemaking Systems," presented to the U.S. Department of Transportation, 18 November 1981; Thomas M. Corsi and Merrill J. Roberts, "Patterns of Discrimination in the Collective Ratemaking System," *Transportation Research Forum Proceedings—Twenty-Third Annual Meeting* 23, no. 1 (1982): 621–30; and Christopher C. Barnekov, *Long Distance Freight Pricing in West Germany and Sweden*, prepared for U.S. Department of Transportation, January 1982.

277. See Gary Fauth, *The Role of Commodity Value in Motor Carrier Class Rate Structures* (Washington, D.C.: Department of Transportation, Project DTRS–57–81–C–00020, August 1981). Fauth conducted a study using 1976 data for seven rate bureaus. His results indicate that class revenue collected varies positively with commodity value, and that the elasticity of revenue with respect to value changes appears to be about 5 percent for LTL class rates and 2 percent for TL rates. Fauth concludes that elasticities of freight charges with respect to shipment value are higher than is necessary to recover loss and damage claims.

278. *Broemser Testimony*, pp. 2–3.

279. See Study Commission *Report*, p. 466. Leslie M. Goldner, "LTL-Carrier Pricing Practices for Individual Shippers: The Aftermath of Deregulation," *Traffic World* (11 February 1985): 83, reported that "(t)he trend is clearly moving towards more independent customer-specific pricing." The result has been a vast increase in the complexity of the tariff structure, contrary to the promises of the proponents of deregulation.

280. See the proposals of the ICC in *Ex Parte* No. MC–98 (Sub-No. 1), *Investigation into Motor Carrier Classification*, served 13 May 1981.

281. The situation prior to regulation, where every carrier had its own classification system, was hardly a model of simplicity. Morse, p. 38, describes the situation in the rail industry in 1887 when the ICC was created:

> Originally, each railroad published its own classifications, one for traffic moving locally on its own line and another for traffic handled jointly with other connecting lines. There were classifications that differed according to the direction of movement, and some railroads had separate classifications for their different divisions. One railroad had nine different clas-

sifications in effect at the same time, each with its own rules, packing requirements, minimum weights and ratings.

According to the author, the Commission's efforts to implement a uniform nationwide rail classification system continued until 1956!

282. See statement of William J. Augello, Executive Director/General Counsel, Shippers National Freight Claim Council, before the Study Commission, 19 March 1982, p. 8, when he reported that his organization unanimously supported retention of the classification system:

> We cannot envision a national transportation network without uniform bills of lading, uniform liability terms and burdens of proof, uniform packaging rules and specifications, uniform time limits and notification procedures, etc., all of which are presently published in the Classification.

283. Policy and Management Associates, Inc., a consulting firm retained by DOT in connection with support for its position in opposition to any antitrust immunity, noted:

> Some of the legal testimony is difficult for the layman to understand. For example, Department of Justice representatives suggested that publication of a single class rating is highly vulnerable to antitrust attack, while publication of a number regarding a particular characteristic (as in ICC *Ex Parte* No. MC–98 Sub-No. 1) would be fully acceptable. The fact is that the ICC's single number for, say, liability, represents a weighted aggregation of such subfactors as susceptibility to theft, likelihood of damage, value, and possibility of damage to other commodities. This is exactly the form of the single class rating based on a weighted aggregation of density, stowability, handling, and liability, except at a more particular level. It is not at all clear what permits the confident assertion that one violates the rule of reason and the other does not.

See Policy and Management Associates, "Motor Carrier Freight Classification," p. 41.

284. *Jay Foods, Inc.* v. *National Classification Committee and National Classification Board*, the U.S. District Court for the Eastern District of Virginia, Alexandria Division, in Civil Action No. 85–489-A, order dated 22 November 1985, stated that inclusion of exempt commodities in the classification manual did not constitute a *per se* antitrust offense. While the order appeared to extend to situations where classification was an ingredient in the pricing function but not the final determinant of the price charged, plaintiffs stipulated that classification was not used in ratemaking for the traffic at issue.

285. This is not to say that there is no effective rebuttal to the argument that elimination of collective ratemaking will lead to a desirable move toward tariff simplification. Indeed, we have already seen that the reverse is likely. See Paul O. Roberts, "Statement Addressing the Views of Other Parties Toward Motor Carrier Tariff Restructuring"; and Booz-Allen and Hamilton, "Review of Freight Tariff Modification Efforts," presented to the Study Commission, 8 October 1982. Furthermore, there is a long history of legitimate debate over the proper role of value-of-service considerations in ratemaking. See, for example, Kenneth D.

Boyer, "Equalizing Discrimination and Cartel Pricing in Transport Rate Regulation," *Journal of Political Economy* 89, no. 2 (April 1981): 270–86, and "How Similar Are Motor Carrier and Rail Rate Structures? The Value of Service Component," *Proceedings of the Transportation Research Forum* 19, no. 1 (1978): 523–31; J.E. Olson, "Price Discrimination by Regulated Motor Carriers," *American Economic Review* 62, no. 3 (June 1972): 395–402; A.S. DeVany and T.R. Saving, "Product Quality, Uncertainty, and Regulation: The Trucking Industry," *American Economic Review* 67, no. 4 (September 1977): 583–94; Kenneth D. Boyer, "Queuing Analysis and Value of Service Pricing in the Trucking Industry: A Comment," *American Economic Review* 70, no. 1 (March 1980): 174–80; and A.S. DeVany and T.R. Saving, "Competition and Value of Service Pricing in the Trucking Industry: Reply," *American Economic Review* 70, no. 1 (March 1980): 181–85; and Donald V. Harper, "Collective Pricing and Unreasonable Rate Discrimination in the Motor Carrier Industry," before the Study Commission, Kansas City, 5 March 1982.

286. The best illustrations of the tendency to equate the results of deregulation to improved efficiency regardless of the outcome are the recent evaluations of the results of airline deregulation. Skeptics were told that the desired result of deregulation was to eliminate the elements of value-of-service pricing induced by regulation and to make the rate structure more cost-based. When it appeared that the result of deregulation was a rate structure no more related to costs, a "new learning" emerged to defend price discrimination as a hallmark of a competitive market. See, for example, Robert H. Frank, "When Are Price Differentials Discriminatory?" *Journal of Policy Analysis and Management* 3, no. 2 (Winter 1983): 238–55. The process has already started for the motor carrier industry. See Richard Beilock, "Is Regulation Needed for Value of Service Pricing?" *Rand Journal of Economics* 16, no. 1 (Spring 1985): 93–102; and Denis A. Breen, "Antitrust and Price Discrimination," *The Antitrust Bulletin* 28, no. 1 (Spring 1983): 201–25.

287. See Breen. James T. Hong and Charles R. Plott, in "Rate Filing Policies for Inland Water Transportation: An Experimental Approach," *Bell Journal of Economics* 13, no. 1 (Spring 1982): 1–19, found in laboratory experiments designed to simulate the domestic barge industry that "rate filing policies cause higher prices, lower volume, and reduced efficiency, and they hurt the small participants." Although "plausible theoretical arguments can be made on both sides of the policy argument," in these particular experiments the inflexibility of the posted-price mechanism was a greater source of inefficiency than the lack of perfect information in the negotiated-price markets. Small, inefficient operators benefit from the poor information of buyers and are able to take advantage of price discrimination to stay in business. While the relative inefficiencies arising from the two sources is an empirical matter, the Hong and Plott study is useful in identifying the structural aspects of the two market forms that are relevant to the evaluation.

288. Shippers feel the strong need for publication of a clearly understood price schedule and service standards. An illustration of the difficulties when they are missing is the recent tendency of carriers to grant unpublished verbal discounts. After the carrier later went bankrupt, creditors submitted balance-due statements

to dismayed shippers, who were not legally entitled to a verbal discount. See "Bankrupt Truckers' Bills on Unpublished Discounts Subject of New ICC Probe," *Traffic World* (16 September 1985): 7–8, and "Shippers, Truckers Clash in Need for Phantom Truck Discount Rules," *Traffic World* (25 October 1985): 52.

Bibliography

"AAA Cooper Transportation 'Explains' Filing of Independent Action Rates." *Traffic World* (10 November 1980): 49–50

Adams, Walter. "Business Exemptions from the Antitrust Laws: Their Extent and Rationale." In Almarin Phillips, ed., *Perspectives on Antitrust Policy*. Princeton, N.J.: Princeton University Press, 1965.

"Administration Moving Antitrust Policy in New Directions." *The New York Times* (20 January 1985): 25.

Alchian, Armen A., and William R. Allen. *University Economics*. Belmont, Calif.: Wadsworth, 1968.

Alexis, Marcus. *Statement before the Subcommittee on Surface Transportation of the House Committee on Public Works and Transportation on the Motor Carrier Act of 1980* 10 June 1981.

———. "Regulatory Reform at the ICC." Paper presented at the Allied Social Sciences Annual Meeting, Atlanta, 29 December 1979.

Allen, Benjamin, and Maureen Schultheis. "Trade-offs Involved in Maintaining Railroad Rate Bureaus: An Evaluation of Shipper Support." *ICC Practitioners Journal* 47, no. 5 (May/June 1979): 538–48.

Allen, W. Bruce. "The Impact of Collective Ratemaking on Motor Carrier Rates: A Test." *International Journal of Transport Economics* 10, no. 1–2 (April/August 1983): 281–310.

Amnable, James. "The ICC, the IBT, and the Cartelization of the American Trucking Industry." *Quarterly Review of Economics and Business* 13 (1973): 36–43.

Areeda, Phillip. "Antitrust Laws and Public Utility Regulation." *Bell Journal of Economics and Management Science* 3, no. 1 (Spring 1972): 42–57.

Areeda, Phillip, and Donald F. Turner. "Predatory Pricing and Related Prices under Section 2 of the Sherman Act." *Harvard Law Review* 88 (1975): 697–733.

Asch, Peter, and J.J. Seneca. "Is Collusion Profitable?" *Review of Economics and Statistics* 58, no. 1 (February 1976): 1–12.

"A Symposium on Oligopoly, Competition, and Welfare." *Journal of Industrial Economics* 33, no. 4 (June 1985).

Augello, William J. "The Deregulation Disaster." Eleventh International Air Forum, 28 September 1982.

Baker, James N. *Speech before Meeting of American Short Line RR Association*, 3 November 1981.

Banfield, Edward C. "The Economist's Public Library." *The Public Interest* (Fall 1983): 141.

"Bankrupt Truckers' Bills on Unpublished Discounts Subject of New ICC Probe." *Traffic World* (16 September 1985): 52.

Barnekov, Christopher C. "Analysis of Evidence in *Ex Parte* No. MC–172, Withdrawal of Antitrust Immunity." ICC Staff Report, 6 August 1984.

———. *Long Distance Freight Pricing in West Germany and Sweden*. Prepared for U.S. Department of Transportation, January 1982.

Baumol, William J. "Use of Antitrust to Subvert Competition." *The Journal of Law and Economics* 28, no. 2 (May 1985): 247–65.

———. "Some Subtle Issues in Railroad Regulation." *International Journal of Transport Economics* 10, no. 1–2 (April/August 1983): 341–55.

Baxter, William F. *Statement before the Motor Carrier Ratemaking Study Commission*, 18 November 1981.

Beilock, Richard. "Is Regulation Needed for Value of Service Pricing?" *Rand Journal of Economics* 16, no. 1 (Spring 1985): 93–102.

Bohlander, George W., and Martin T. Farris. "Collective Bargaining in Trucking—The Effects of Deregulation." *Logistics and Transportation Review* 20, no. 3 (1984): 223–38.

Bohman, Ray, Jr. *Guide to Cutting Your Freight Transportation Costs under Trucking Deregulation*. Gardner, Mass.: Bohman Industrial Traffic Consultants, 1981.

Booz-Allen & Hamilton, Inc. "Review of Freight Tariff Modification Efforts." Presented to the Motor Carrier Ratemaking Study Commission, 8 October 1982.

———. *Impact on Transportation Management of Changes in the Collective Ratemaking System*. Washington, D.C., Motor Common Carrier Association, July 1982.

Boyer, Kenneth D. "Equalizing Discrimination and Cartel Pricing in Transport Rate Regulation." *Journal of Political Economy* 89, no. 2 (April 1981): 270–86.

———. "Queuing Analysis and Value of Service Pricing in the Trucking Industry: A Comment." *American Economic Review* 70, no. 1 (March 1980): 174–85.

———. "How Similar Are Motor Carrier and Rail Rate Structures? The Value of Service Component." *Transportation Research Forum Proceedings* 19, no. 1 (1978): 523–31.

Braeutigam, Ronald R. "Optimal Pricing with Intermodal Competition." *American Economic Review* 69, no. 1 (March 1979): 38–49.

Braeutigam, Ronald R., and Roger G. Noll. "The Regulation of Surface Freight Transportation: The Welfare Effects Revisited." *Review of Economics and Statistics* 66 (February 1984): 80–87.

Brander, James A., and Barbara J. Spencer. "Tacit Collusion, Free Entry and Welfare." *The Journal of Industrial Economics* 33, no. 3 (March 1985): 227–94.

Breen, Denis A. "Antitrust and Price Competition in the Trucking Industry." *The Antitrust Bulletin* 28, no. 1 (Spring 1983): 201–25.

———. "Regulatory Reform and the Trucking Industry: An Evaluation of the Motor Carrier Act of 1980." Bureau of Economics, Federal Trade Commission. Submitted to the Motor Carrier Ratemaking Study Commission, March 1982.

————. *Statement before the Motor Carrier Ratemaking Study Commission*, 18 November 1981.

Bridgeman, Lester M. "Antitrust Impact on Motor Carriers of the Proposed 'Kennedy Bill' Repeal of the Reed-Bulwinkle Act." *Transportation Journal* 19, no. 1 (Fall 1979): 19–39.

Broadcast Music, Inc. v. *CBS.* 441 U.S. 1 (1979).

Brodley, Joseph F. "Joint Ventures and Antitrust Policy." *Harvard Law Review* 95 (May 1982): 1521–88.

Broemser, Gary. *Testimony before the Motor Carrier Ratemaking Study Commission.* U.S. Department of Transportation, 18 November 1981.

Buchanan, Daniel H. "The Historical Approach to Rent and Price Theory." *Economica* (June 1929): 123–55.

Bullock, Kari, and Sumner J. LaCroix. "Welfare and Collusion: Comment." *American Economic Review* 72, no. 1 (March 1982): 256–58.

Bunce, Eliot. "A History of the Reed-Bulwinkle Act." Presented before the Motor Carrier Ratemaking Study Commission, February 1982.

Cartter, Allen M. *Theory of Wages and Employment.* Homewood, Ill.: Richard D. Irwin, 1959.

Case, Leland S. "Examination of Competition in the Truckload Intercity Motor Carrier Freight Industry." *Transportation Research Forum Proceedings* 20, no. 1 (1979): 116–25.

Cavinato, Joseph, and Gary B. Kogan. "An Assessment of the Impacts from Partial and Full Repeal of Section 10706(Antitrust Immunity) upon the Motor Carrier Industry and Its Users." *ICC Practitioners Journal* 47 (1980): 427–49.

Cherry, Russell C. "Rate Effects of Collective Ratemaking and the Meaning of Concentration in Regulated Motor Carriage." Prepared for the Transportation Systems Center, U.S. Department of Transportation. Arthur D. Little, Inc., July 1982.

————. "The Operating Ratio Effect and Regulated Motor Carriers." *Proceedings of a Workshop on Motor Carrier Economic Regulation.* Washington, D.C.: National Academy of Sciences, 1978.

Cherry, Russell C., and Carl Backman. "Market Structure and Concentration in the Regulated Trucking Industry." *American Economic Review* 71, no. 2 (May 1981): 385–88.

Cherry, Russell C., and Leslie K. Meyer. "A Comparison of Descriptive Statistics for 1976 and 1980 Continuous Traffic Study: A Report to the Motor Carrier Ratemaking Study Commission." Cambridge, Mass.: Arthur D. Little, Inc., 1982.

Chow, Garland. "An Economic Inquiry into the Options and Impacts of Rate Regulation on Motor Transportation Markets." Paper presented at the Third Dana/ATA Foundation Academic Symposium, Stanford University, 8–9 December 1981.

Chow, Garland, and Richard Gritta. "Motor Carrier Bankruptcy: An Industry Assessment of Financial Condition." *Transportation Research Forum Proceedings* 26, no. 1 (1985): 434–40.

Clapp, Joseph M. "Deregulation—Revolution? Evolution? Clearing Up Some Existing Confusion." *Traffic World* (1 July 1985): 28–33.

————. "Impact of the Motor Carrier Act of 1980: A Motor Carrier Perspective." Paper presented at the Transportation Research Board Annual Meeting, Washington, D.C., 19 January 1982.

Coburn, David H. "A Review of the Reed-Bulwinkle Act in the Context of Other Antitrust Exemptions." Presented before the Motor Carrier Ratemaking Study Commission, March 1982.

"Collective Ratemaking Backers Far Outnumber 'Antis' in MCRSC Record." *Traffic World* (20 December 1982): 22–23.

"Collective Ratemaking is Still Favored by Roadway with 'E-Z Rate' System." *Traffic World* (12 September 1983): 30.

"Commerce Secretary Baldridge Wants Elimination of Major Antitrust Law." *Traffic World* (18 March 1985): 75–76.

Connor, John P. "The Functional Machinery of Collective Ratemaking." *Statement before the Motor Carrier Ratemaking Study Commission*, May 1982.

"Conrail Plans to Resign from Rail Rate Bureaus Due to Change in the Law." *Traffic World* (16 November 1981): 26.

"Conrail to Pay Millions to Settle Antitrust Suit, Industry Sources Report." *Traffic World* (28 April 1986): 8.

Corsi, Thomas M., and Merrill J. Roberts. "Patterns of Discrimination in the Collective Ratemaking System."*Transportation Research Forum Proceedings* 23, no. 1 (1982): 621–30.

Crew, Eugene. "Rate Bureaus and the Rule of Reason." *Traffic World* (12 December 1983): 64–67.

Crew, Eugene, and Joel Linzner. "Joint Rates between Competitors—A True Antitrust Dilemma." *Traffic World* (2 May 1983): 77–82.

Crew, E.C. and Lester M. Bridgeman. "Do Antitrust Laws Provide a Feasible Alternative to Regulation?" *ICC Practitioners Journal* 47, no. 6 (September/October 1980): 673–97.

Cross, Robert G. "Problems of Air Carrier Management under the Jurisdiction of the Antitrust Laws." Paper presented at the 22nd annual meeting of the Transportation Research Forum, 5 November 1981.

"Curtailment of Antitrust Immunity Viewed as Divisive in Railroading." *Traffic World* (2 January 1984): 21.

Daughety, Andrew F. "Regulation and Industrial Organization." *Journal of Political Economy* 92, no. 5 (October 1984): 932–53.

Davis, Grant M. "The Collective Ratemaking Issue: Circa 1984." *Transportation Practitioners Journal* 52, no. 1 (Fall 1984): 60–68.

————. "Educator Sees Flaws in Report of Ratemaking Study Commission." *Traffic World* (9 May 1983): 35–40.

————. "Collective Ratemaking and Societal Benefits." Paper presented at the Third Dana/ATA Foundation Academic Symposium, Stanford University, December 1981.

————. "The Case for Single-Line Immunity." *ICC Practitioners Journal* 43, no. 6 (November 1975-October 1976): 740.

————. "Transportation Regulation: Another Dimension." *ICC Practitioners Journal* 42, no. 2 (January/February 1975): 164–74.

————. ed. *Collective Ratemaking in the Motor Carrier Industry: Implications to the American Public*. Danville, Ill.: Interstate Printers and Publishers, 1980.

Davis, Grant M., and John E. Dillard, Jr. "Collective Ratemaking—Does It Have a Future in the Motor Carrier Industry?" *ICC Practitioners Journal* 49, no. 6 (September/October 1982): 1112–29.

Davis, Grant M., and Eugene Shepard. *Motor Carrier Rate Structures*. New York: Praeger, 1979.

Davis, Grant M., and Linda J. Combs. "Some Observations Regarding Value of Service Pricing in Transportation." *Transportation Journal* 14, no. 3 (Spring 1975): 49–58.

Davis, Grant M., and Charles S. Sherwood. *Rate Bureaus and Antitrust Conflicts in Transportation: Public Policy Issues*. New York: Praeger, 1975.

Dempsey, Paul Stephen. "Rate Regulation and Antitrust Immunity in Transportation: The Genesis and Evolution of this Endangered Species," *The American University Law Review* 32, no. 2 (Winter 1983): 335–92.

"Deregulation: A Puzzle to Consumers." *The New York Times* (4 June 1983): 10.

DeVany, A. S., and T. R. Saving. "Competition and Value of Service Pricing in the Trucking Industry: Reply." *American Economic Review* 70, no. 1 (March 1980): 181–85.

———. "Product Quality, Uncertainty, and Regulation: The Trucking Industry." *American Economic Review* 67, no. 4 (September 1977): 583–94.

Dewey, Donald. "Welfare and Collusion: Reply." *American Economic Review* 72, no. 1 (March 1982): 276–81.

———. "Neglected Economic Issues in Collective Ratemaking." Paper presented at the Third Dana/ATA Foundation Academic Symposium, Stanford University, December 1981.

———. "Information, Entry and Welfare: The Case for Collusion." *American Economic Review* 69, no. 4 (September 1979): 587–94.

Dively, Dwight. "Applications of Regulatory Theory to the Trucking Industry." *Research in Law and Economics* 6 (1984): 211–26.

"DOJ Official Says Antitrust Immunity 'Much Ado About Nothing.'" *Transportation Antitrust Report* (November 1984): 8.

"D&TPTC Urged to Back Truck Industry Moves to Maintain Stability." *Traffic World* (8 November 1982): 50–51.

Eastern Central Motor Carriers Association. *Traffic Analysis Reports—Research, Economics and Cost: 1980 Composite*. Akron, Ohio: ECMCA, December 1982.

———. *Traffic Analysis Reports: 1980 Composite*. Akron, Ohio: ECMCA, October 1981.

Eisenberg, Barry. "Information Exchange among Competitors: The Issue of Relative Value Scales for Physicians' Services." *Journal of Law and Economics* 23, no. 2 (October 1980): 441–60.

Farris, M.T. "Discrimination in Transportation and Antitrust Laws." *ICC Practitioners Journal* 46, no. 4 (May/June 1979): 509–25.

Fauth, Gary. *The Role of Commodity Value in Motor Carrier Class Rate Structures*. Final Report prepared for the U.S. Department of Transportation. Kennedy School of Government, Harvard University, August 1981.

Feeney, J.D. *Remarks to the National Conference of State Rail Officials*. Seattle (9 July 1981).

———. *Remarks to the 4th AICCP Western Transportation Law Seminar*. Kansas City, 3 March 1981.

Felton, John Richard. "The Impact of Rate Regulation upon ICC-Regulated Truck Back Hauls." *Journal of Transport Economics and Policy* 15, no. 3 (September 1981): 253–67.

Ferguson, C.E. *Microeconomic Theory*. Homewood, Ill.: Richard D. Irwin, 1969.

Fessenden, John. *Collective Ratemaking: An Indivisible System*. Washington, D.C.: National Motor Freight Traffic Association, 1979.

"First Shippers' Council Okayed by Justice Department: 1984 Start-up Planned." *Traffic World* (5 December 1983): 37–38.

Flexner, Donald L. "The Scope of Antitrust Immunity and of Permissible Collective Activity in the Motor Carrier Industry." In *Competition in Transportation Sector*. Washington, D.C.: The Federal Bar Association, 1984.

Foley, Martin E. "Statement on Motor Carrier Collective Ratemaking." In *Transcript of Proceedings*. Akron, Ohio: The Motor Carrier Ratemaking Study Commission, 29 January 1982.

Folse, Parker C. "Antitrust and Regulated Industries: A Critique and Proposal for Reform of the Implied Immunity Doctrine." *Texas Law Review* 57 (May 1979): 751–828.

Food Transport Week 2, no. 8 (22 February 1982): 1.

Fraas, Arthur, and Douglas S. Greer. "Market Structure and Price Regulation: An Empirical Analysis." *Journal of Industrial Economics* (September 1977): 21–44.

Frank, Robert H. "When Are Price Differentials Discriminatory?" *Journal of Policy Analysis and Management* 3, no. 2 (Winter 1983): 238–55.

Freeman, James W. "Case Study: Impact of Motor Carrier Reform on Florida." Paper presented at the Transportation Law Institute, July 1981.

Frew, James R. "The Existence of Monopoly Profits in the Motor Carrier Industry." *Journal of Law and Economics* 24, no. 2 (October 1981): 289–315.

Friedlaender, Ann F., and Richard Spady. *Freight Transport Regulation: Equity, Efficiency and Competition in the Rail and Trucking Industries*. Cambridge, Mass.: MIT Press, 1981.

Friedman, James. *Oligopoly Theory*. Cambridge, England: Cambridge University Press, 1983.

Friedman, Jesse J. "What's Wrong with the Case Against Collective Ratemaking: Rejoinder to James C. Miller III." *Transportation Law Journal* 11, no. 2 (December 1980): 301–22.

———. "Collective Ratemaking by Motor Common Carriers: Economic and Public Policy Considerations." *Transportation Law Journal* 70 (October 1978): 33–53.

———. *Collective Ratemaking in Trucking: The Public-Interest Rationale*. Washington, D.C.: Author, October 1977.

Friedman, Thomas L. "The Rocky Road for Truckers." *The New York Times* (24 January 1982), Sec. 3, p. 1.

Gardiner, Paul S. "Rate Bureau Functions without Antitrust Immunity: A Suggested Strategy for Motor Freight Carriers." *ICC Practitioners Journal* 46, no. 5 (July/August 1979): 651–68.

Gaskins, Darius W., and James M. Voytko. "Managing the Transition to Deregulation." *Law & Contemporary Problems* 44, no. 1 (Winter 1981): 9–32.

———. "The Surface Transportation Sector in a Competitive Era: Efficiency and

Innovation in Pricing and Operations." *University of Florida Law Review* 32, no. 5 (Fall 1980): 859–76.

Gerschenkron, Alexander. Address to assembled faculty of Harvard University. As quoted in *The Public Interest* (Winter 1970): 118–19.

Gladwell, Daniel M. "The Barge Freight Call Session of the Merchants Exchange of St. Louis: An Innovation in Transportation Pricing." *Transportation Journal* 20, no. 1 (Fall 1980): 5–18.

Glaskowsky, Nicholas A. Jr., Brian F. O'Neil, and Donald R. Hudson. *Motor Carrier Regulation: A Review and Evaluation of Three Major Current Regulatory Issues Relating to the Interstate Common Carrier Trucking Industry*. Washington, D.C.: ATA Foundation, 1976.

Goldner, Leslie M. "LTL-Carrier Pricing Practices for Individual Shippers: The Aftermath of Deregulation." *Traffic World* (11 February 1985): 83–88.

Hamilton, Robert W. "Prospects for the Nongovernmental Development of Regulatory Standards." *The American University Law Review* 32, no. 2 (Winter 1983): 455–69.

Harbridge House, Inc. *Report on Harbridge House Survey of the Impact of Transportation Deregulation on Major U.S. Manufacturing Firms*. Boston, 2 June 1981.

Harkins, James. *Statement before the United States Senate Committee on Commerce, Science, and Transportation*, 9 September 1985.

Harper, Donald V. "Consequences of Reform of Federal Economic Regulation of the Motor Trucking Industry." *Transportation Journal* 21, no. 4 (Summer 1982): 35–58.

———. "Collective Pricing and Unreasonable Rate Discrimination in the Motor Carrier Industry." Presented before the Motor Carrier Ratemaking Study Commission. Kansas City, 5 March 1982.

———. "Entry Control and the Federal Motor Carrier Act of 1980." *Transportation Law Journal* 12 (1980): 51–73.

———. "The Federal Motor Carrier Act of 1980: Review and Analysis." *Transportation Journal* 20, no. 2 (Winter 1980): 5–33.

Hatley v. *American Quarter Horse Association*. 522 F.2d 646 (5th Circuit, 1977).

Hauser, Robert J., and Steven A. Neff. "The Pricing Efficiency of the Barge Freight Call Session." *Proceedings of the Transportation Research Forum* 25, no. 1 (1984): 331–36.

Hausman, Jerry A. "Information Costs, Competition, and Collective Ratemaking in the Motor Carrier Industry." *The American University Law Review* 32, no. 2 (Winter 1983): 377–92.

Hay, George, and Daniel Kelley. "An Empirical Survey of Price-Fixing Conspiracies." *Journal of Law and Economics* 17, no. 1 (April 1974): 13–38.

Hecker, Lawrence M. *Testimony before the Motor Carrier Ratemaking Study Commission*. Phoenix, 10 December 1981.

Heller, Walter W. "In a Fed Camp in the Rockies." *The New York Times* (26 August 1985): D6.

Henderson, James M., and Richard E. Quandt. *Microeconomic Theory*. New York: McGraw-Hill, 1958.

Hilton, George W. *Statement before the Motor Carrier Ratemaking Study Commission*. Phoenix, 10 December 1981.

——. "The Basic Behavior of Regulatory Commissions." *American Economic Review* 62, no. 2 (May 1972): 47–54.

——. "Barriers to Competitive Ratemaking." *ICC Practitioners Journal* 29, no. 9 (June 1962): 1083–98.

——. "Experience under the Reed-Bulwinkle Act." *ICC Practitioners Journal* 28, no. 10 (September 1961): 1207–19.

Hong, James T., and Charles R. Plott. "Rate Filing Policies for Inland Water Transportation: An Experimental Approach." *Bell Journal of Economics* 13, no. 1 (Spring 1982): 1–19.

Hoover, Harwood, Jr. "Pricing Behavior of Deregulated Motor Carriers." *Transportation Journal* 25, no. 2 (Winter 1985): 55–61.

Interstate Commerce Commission. *Ex Parte* No. MC–172. "Withdrawal of Antitrust Immunity for Collective Ratemaking on Shipments Weighing 1,000 Pounds or Less." 46 Federal Register 48,399. 12 October 1983.

——. *Ex Parte* No. MC–122 (Sub-No. 2). *Lease of Equipment and Drivers to Private Carriers: Policy Statement.* 17 February 1982.

——. *Ex Parte* No. MC–98 (Sub-No. 1). *Investigation into Motor Carrier Classification.* 364 ICC 906. 13 May 1981.

——. *Section 5b Application No. 2: Western Railroads Agreement.* 21 January 1981.

——. *Ex Parte* No. 297 (Sub-No. 5). *Motor Carrier Rate Bureaus: Implementation of P.L. 96–296.* 30 December 1980.

——. *Section 5b Application No. 2: Western Railroads Agreement.* 27 June 1980.

——. *Ex Parte* No. 297. *Rate Bureau Investigation.* 351 ICC 437. 23 January 1976.

——. *Ex Parte* No. 297. *Rate Bureau Investigation.* 349 ICC 811. 3 June 1975.

Interstate Commerce Commission, Office of Transportation Analysis. *Staff Report No. 10: Highlights of Activity in the Property Motor Carrier Industry.* March 1986.

Issues in American Trucking. Washington, D.C.: American Trucking Associations, 1981.

Jacobs, Leslie W. "Regulated Motor Carriers and the Antitrust Laws." *Cornell Law Review* 58, no. 1 (November 1972): 90–135.

"Justice Department, Shippers Convince ICC to Reject NFTB Single-Line Rates." *Traffic World* (17 September 1984): 8.

Kahn, Fritz. "Abolition of the Trucking Exemption: Pros and Cons." *ICC Practitioners Journal* 47, no. 2 (January/February 1980): 154–61.

Kalish, Steven J. "Antitrust Considerations for Shippers in a Changing Environment." *Transportation Practitioners Journal* 52, no. 2 (Winter 1985): 185–97.

Karr, Albert R. "Iowa Trucker Prospers After Deregulation Eases Rules on Routes." *The Wall Street Journal* (13 February 1984): 1.

Keenan, William Q. "Truck Rate Bureau Antitrust Immunities When Dealing with Independent Actions." *ICC Practitioners Journal* 48, no. 1 (November/December 1980): 20–23.

Keller, Roland H., II. "Welfare and Collusion: Comment." *American Economic Review* 72, no. 1 (March 1982): 256–67.

Kennedy, Edward M. "Senator Kennedy Releases New Trucking Industry Data Revealing High Market Concentration." Senate Office Press Release, 24 June 1979.

Kenworthy, William E. "Antitrust Considerations in Motor Carrier Ratemaking: Rate Bureau Operations and Alternatives." *Transportation Law Journal* 11 (1979): 65–89.

Kerwin, Cornelius M. "Assessing the Effects of Consensual Processes in Regulatory Programs." *The American University Law Review* 32, no. 2 (Winter 1983): 401–23.

Kim, Moshe. "The Beneficiaries of Trucking Regulation, Revisited." *Journal of Law and Economics* 27, no. 1 (April 1984): 227–41.

King, Michael L. "Transportation Official at GE Finds His Role Rises with Fuel Prices." *The Wall Street Journal* (31 December 1981): 1.

Lacoste, Louis. "The Structure of Railroad Fares and Rates in a Highly Competitive Freight Transportation Market." In Kenneth D. Boyer and William G. Shepherd, eds., *Economic Regulation: Essays in Honor of James R. Nelson*. E. Lansing, Mich.: Michigan State University, 1981.

LaMond, Annette M. *Competition in the General Freight Motor Carrier Industry*. Lexington, Mass.: Lexington Books, 1980.

Lande, Richard. "How Collective Ratemaking Improves the Canadian Economy." *Transportation Practitioners Journal* 52, no. 2 (Winter 1985): 198–200.

Landes, William M. "Harm to Competition: Cartels, Mergers, and Joint Ventures." In Eleanor M. Fox and James T. Halverson, eds., *Antitrust Policy in Transition: The Convergence of Law and Economics* (pp. 73–82). Washington, D.C.: American Bar Association, 1984.

"Law to Protect Multi-Employer Pensions is Causing Hardship for Many Businesses." *The Wall Street Journal* (5 March 1985): 1.

"Lawyer Sees Destruction of Rail Joint-Rate System." *Traffic World* (21 March 1983): 78–79.

Legg, William. *1985 Analysis of the Motor Carrier Industry*. Washington, D.C.: American Trucking Associations, 1985.

Levin, Richard C. "Railroad Rates, Profitability, and Welfare under Deregulation." *Bell Journal of Economics and Management Science* 12, no. 1 (Spring 1981): 1–26.

———. "Railroad Regulation, Deregulation, and Workable Competition." *American Economic Review* 71, no. 2 (May 1981): 394–98.

———. "Allocation in Surface Freight Transportation: Does Rate Regulation Matter?" *Bell Journal of Economics and Management Science* 9, no. 1 (Spring 1978): 18–45.

Lidell, Florence W. *1981 Financial Analysis of the Motor Carrier Industry*. New York: Citibank, 1982.

Mabley, Robert E., and Walter D. Strack. "Deregulation—A Green Light for Trucking Efficiency," *Regulation* (July/August 1982): 36–56.

MacAvoy, Paul, and John W. Snow, eds. *Regulation of Entry and Pricing in Truck Regulation*. Washington, D.C.: American Enterprise Institute for Public Policy Research, 1977.

McFadden, John W., Jr. "A Description and Analysis of Rate Structures, Rate Levels and Competitive Conditions under Collective Ratemaking and Their Importance to the Public." Presented before the Motor Carrier Ratemaking Study Commission, Kansas City, 5 March 1982.

McGibbon, James R., and Douglas E. Rosenthal. *Antitrust Primer for Motor Carrier Executives*. Washington, D.C.: American Trucking Associations, 1982.

Machalaba, Daniel. "More Companies Push Freight Haulers to Get Better Rates, Service." *The Wall Street Journal* (18 December 1985): 1.

———. "Trucking Association, Powerful for Decades, Has a Load of Trouble." *The Wall Street Journal* (24 February 1984): 1.

"Major Changes in Moving Rail Freight Raise Fears of Higher Rates for Shippers." *The Wall Street Journal* (22 February 1983)

Management Analysis Center, Inc. "The Motor Carrier Marketplace Without Collective Ratemaking." Report prepared for the Motor Carrier Ratemaking Study Commission, Washington, D.C., September 1982.

———. "Ratemaking Analogies." Report prepared for the Motor Carrier Ratemaking Study Commission, Washington, D.C., August 1982.

———. "Statistical Overview of the Trucking Industry." Report prepared for the Motor Carrier Ratemaking Study Commission, August 1982.

———. "Developments Expected by Participants." Report prepared for the Motor Carrier Ratemaking Study Commission, Washington, D.C., July 1982.

Mann, H. Michael, "Collective Ratemaking: A Victim of Traditional Antitrust Doctrine?" *The American University Law Review* 32, no. 2 (Winter 1983): 393–99.

MarTech Strategies, Inc. "The Potential for Electronic Tariff Networks and Markets." Presented to the Motor Carrier Ratemaking Study Commission, September 1982.

Mas-Collel, Andrew. "Noncooperative Approaches to the Theory of Perfect Competition: Presentation." In Andrew Mas-Collel, ed., *Noncooperative Approaches to the Theory of Perfect Competition*. New York: Academic Press, 1982.

Maser, John K. *Statement on behalf of the National Industrial Traffic League (NITL)*. Washington Hearing of Study Commission, 18 November 1981.

Meeks, James E. "Legal Issues and Consequences of Changes in Motor Carrier Ratemaking Regulations." Paper presented at the Third ATA/Dana Academic Symposium, Stanford University, 9 December 1981.

Meyer, John R., and William B. Tye. "The Regulatory Transition." *American Economic Review* 75, no. 2 (May 1985): 50.

Michalson, George D. *Statement before the National Commission for the Review of Antitrust Laws and Procedures*, 18 October 1978.

Middle Atlantic Conference. *Bulletin Nos. 1–19: Individual Tariffs Containing Threshold, Volume, and Aggregate Tender Discount Rates or Charges*. Riverdale, Md.: Middle Atlantic Conference, October 1981–February 1982.

———. *Individual Carrier Discount Tariff Index and Profile*. Riverdale, Md.: Middle Atlantic Conference, 29 September 1981.

———. *Continuing Traffic Study, Report No. 24: Five Year Trends in Characteristics of Traffic Study Years 1975 through 1979*. Riverdale, Md.: Middle Atlantic Conference, October 1980.

———. *Ex Parte No. MC–98 (Sub-No. 2). Proposed Rulemaking on Released Rates in Conjunction with a Small Shipments Tariff: Initial Statement of Middle Atlantic Conference*, 21 July 1978.

Miller, James C., III. "First Report Card on Trucking Deregulation." *The Wall Street Journal* (8 March 1982).

———. *Testimony before the Motor Carrier Ratemaking Study Commission*, 18 November 1981.

———. "Collective Ratemaking Reconsidered: A Rebuttal." *Transportation Law Journal* 11, no. 2 (December 1980): 291–300.

———. "Economic Regulation of Trucking." In *Report to the President and the Attorney General*, Vol. 2 (pp. 181–95), edited by the National Commission for the Review of Antitrust Laws and Procedures. Washington, D.C.: U.S. Government Printing Office, 1979.

———. *Perspectives on Federal Transportation Policy*, 3rd ed. Washington, D.C.: American Enterprise Institute for Public Policy Research, 1975.

Moore, Thomas Gale. "Keep on Deregulating Trucking." *The Wall Street Journal* (12 July 1985).

———. "Rail and Truck Reform—The Record So Far." *Regulation* (November / December 1983): 33–41.

———. "It's a Success, but Truck Deregulation Remains a Long Haul." *The Wall Street Journal* (26 July 1983).

———. *Testimony before the Motor Carrier Ratemaking Study Commission*. Boston, 19 March 1982.

———. "The Beneficiaries of Trucking Regulation." *Journal of Law and Economics* 21, no. 2 (October 1978): 327–43.

———. *Trucking Regulation: Lessons from Europe*. Washington, D.C.: American Enterprise Institute for Public Policy Research, 1976.

———. "Deregulating Surface Freight Transportation." In Almarin Phillips, ed., *Promoting Competition in Regulated Markets* (pp. 55–98). Washington, D.C.: Brookings Institution, 1975.

Morse, Leon William. *Practical Handbook of Industrial Traffic Management*. Washington, D.C.: Traffic Service Corporation, 1980.

Motor Carrier Act of 1980. U.S. Code, Public Law 96–296 Supp. 2245, 1 July 1980, 94 Stat. 793, 49 U.S.C. 10101.

Motor Carrier Ratemaking Study Commission. *Collective Ratemaking in the Trucking Industry: A Report to the President and the Congress of the United States* and various transcripts of hearings. Washington, D.C.: U.S. Government Printing Office, June 1983.

Multisystems, Inc. "A Survey of LTL-Carrier Pricing Practices for Individual Shippers: The Aftermath of Deregulation." Oakland, Calif., January 1985.

"'NASSTRAC' Executive Backs Packwood Bill but Urges More Shipper Protection." *Traffic World* (9 April 1984): 38.

National Academy of Sciences. *Motor Carrier Economic Regulation*. Washington, D.C.: NAS, 1982.

National Commission for the Review of Antitrust Laws and Procedures. *Report to the President and the Attorney General*, Vols. 1 and 2 (22 January 1979).

———. "Staff Paper on Trucking." Washington, D.C., 6 October 1978.

National Cooperative Research Act of 1984. Public Law 98–462, 98 Stat. 1815, 15.

National Motor Freight Traffic Association, Inc. *National Motor Freight Classification*. Washington, D.C.: NMFTA (3 April 1981).

Nelson, James C. "The Emerging Effects of Deregulation of Surface Freight Transport in the United States." *International Journal of Transport Economics* 10, no. 1–2 (April/August 1983): 219–36.

Nicholson, Walter. *Microeconomic Theory—Basic Principles and Extension*. Hinsdale, Ill.: Dryden Press, 1978.

Noll, Roger. "Antitrust Exemptions: An Economic Overview." *Report to the President and the Attorney General*, Vol. 2 (pp. 167–80), edited by the National Commission for the Review of Antitrust Laws and Procedures. Washington, D.C.: U.S. Government Printing Office, 1979.

Olson, J. E. "Price Discrimination by Regulated Motor Carriers." *American Economic Review* 62, no. 3 (June 1972): 395–402.

Olson, Mancur, *The Logic of Collective Action*. Cambridge, Mass.: Harvard University Press, 1965.

Paul, Bill. "Trucks' Rates on Small Loads Stir Big Fight." *The Wall Street Journal* (28 July 1983).

Peat, Marwick and Mitchell. *Motor Carrier Ratemaking Study: Task 1—Report and Annotated Bibliography*. Prepared for the Motor Carrier Ratemaking Study Commission, 24 May 1982.

Peck, Merton J. "Competitive Policy for Transportation." In Almarin Phillips, ed., *Perspectives on Antitrust Policy*. Princeton, N.J.: Princeton University Press, 1965.

Policy and Management Associates. "Regulatory Reform and Motor Carrier Tariff Complexity." Presented to the Motor Carrier Ratemaking Study Commission, October 1982.

———. "The Potential for Motor Carrier Tariff Simplification." Presented before the Motor Carrier Ratemaking Study Commission, October 1982.

———. "Motor Carrier Freight Classification." Submitted to the Motor Carrier Ratemaking Study Commission, August 1981.

Popper, Andrew F. "The Antitrust System: An Impediment to the Development of Negotiation Models." *The American University Law Review* 32, no. 2 (Winter 1983): 283–334.

———. "Did the Motor Carrier Act Alter Antitrust Immunity for Collective Ratemaking?" *Your Letter of the Law* 26, no. 6 (March 1981): 25–55.

———. *Shipper Antitrust Liability in a Rate-Deregulated Market: Fundamental Inquiries and Analysis*. Washington, D.C.: American University, 1979.

———. "Collective Ratemaking: A Case Analysis of the Eastern Central Region and an Hypothesis for Analyzing Competitive Structure." *Transportation Law Journal* 10 (1978): 365–88.

Posner, Richard A. "Effects of Railroad Rate Bureaus on Economic Efficiency." *Ex Parte* No. 290 (Sub-No. 2). *Railroad Cost Recovery Procedures*, 16 July 1980.

———. "Information and Antitrust: Reflections on the *Gypsum* and *Engineers* Decisions." *Georgetown Law Journal* 67, no. 3 (February 1979): 1187–1203.

———. "A Program for the Antitrust Division." *University of Chicago Law Review* 38 (1971): 516–19.

"Pricing Executive Sees End of Motor Carrier Collective Ratemaking." *Traffic World* (11 February 1985): 34.

Pustay, Michael W. "Regulatory Reform of Motor Freight Carriage in the United

States." *International Journal of Transport Economics* 10, no. 1–2 (April/August 1983): 259–80.

Railroad Revitalization and Regulatory Reform Act of 1976. U.S. Code, Public Law 94–210, Supp. 2718, 5 February 1976.

Rakowski, James. "Motor Carrier Size and Profitability." *Transportation Journal* 16, no. 4 (Summer 1977): 36–45.

"Rate Commission's Darby Says Study is On Schedule." *Transport Topics* (9 August 1982): 3.

Reed-Bulwinkle Act. 62 Stat. 472 (1948) (codified as amended at 49 U.S.C. 10706).

Regular Common Carrier Conference. *Quarterly Operating Results of the Motor Common Carriers of General Freight: Second Quarter 1985*. Alexandria, Va.: Regular Common Carrier Conference, 1985.

"Report of Arthur Anderson & Company." *Reports and Studies on Behalf of Motor Carrier Rate Bureaus, I.C.C. Ex Parte No. MC–128, Revenue Need Standards in Motor Carrier Increase Proceedings*, Vol. 1 (4 January 1980).

"RMMTB Bid to Copyright Zip Code-Based Tariff Assailed by Shippers." *Traffic World* (18 July 1983): 61–62.

Roberts, Merrill J., Thomas Corsi, and Leaford Williams. "Patterns of Discrimination under Collective Motor Carrier Ratemaking System." Report prepared for the Office of Regulatory Policy, U.S. Department of Transportation, 7 August 1981.

Roberts, Paul O. "Statement Addressing the Views of Other Parties Toward Motor Carrier Tariff Restructuring." Presented to Motor Carrier Ratemaking Study Commission, 8 October 1982.

Rose, J. C. "Surface Transportation and Antitrust Laws: Let's Give Competition a Chance." *ICC Practitioners Journal* 44, no. 4 (May/June 1977): 431–45.

Rose, Nancy L. "The Incidence of Regulatory Rents in the Motor Carrier Industry." *Rand Journal of Economics* 16, no. 3 (Autumn 1985): 299–318.

Scherer, F. M. *Industrial Market Structure and Economic Performance*, 2nd ed. Boston: Houghton-Mifflin, 1980.

———. *Industrial Market Structure and Economic Performance*. Chicago: Rand-McNally, 1973.

Schwarzer, William W. "Regulated Industries and Antitrust Laws—An Overview." *ICC Practitioners Journal* 41, no. 5 (July/August 1974): 543–52.

Seiden, Elliot M. *Statement before the Motor Carrier Ratemaking Study Commission*, 19 March 1982.

"Senate MC [Motor Carrier] Act Oversight Hearing is Rerun of Last Year's Review." *Traffic World* (26 September 1983): 115.

Shenefield, John H. *Statement before the Committee on Commerce, Science and Transportation of the U.S. Senate Concerning S.1400, the Trucking Competition and Safety Act of 1979*, 3 December 1979.

———. *Statement before the Subcommittee on Antitrust and Monopoly, U.S. Senate*, 27 October 1977.

Shephard, Robert J., Jr. *Statement before the Motor Carrier Ratemaking Study Commission*, 18 November 1981.

Sherwood, Charles S. "The Operational Reality of Independent Rate Making: Some Empirical Findings." *Transportation Journal* 15, 2 (Winter 1975): 5–12.

"Shipper Carrier Groups Seeking Immunity for Released Rates." *Transport Topics* (17 May 1982).

"Shipper Group Alters Ratemaking Stand: Supports Abolition." *Transport Topics* (16 May 1983).

"Shippers End Support for Collective Rates." *Transport Topics* (28 November 1983): 1.

"Shippers, Truckers Clash in Need for Phantom Truck Discount Rules." *Traffic World* (25 October 1985).

Silberman, Irwin H. *Statement before the Surface Transportation Subcommittee, U.S. House of Representatives,* 6 November 1985.

————. *Analysis of the Financial Performance of the General Freight Motor Common Carrier Industry.* Submitted to the Motor Carrier Ratemaking Study Commission, July 1982.

Sloss, James. "Regulation of Motor Freight Transportation: A Quantitative Evaluation of Policy." *Bell Journal of Economics and Management Science* 1, no. 2 (Autumn 1970): 327–59.

Somers, S. E., Jr. *Statement before the Motor Carrier Ratemaking Study Commission,* 1 May 1982.

Spychalski, John C. "Antitrust Standards and Railway Freight Pricing: New Round in an Old Debate." *American Economic Review* 71, no. 2 (May 1981): 104–109.

Staggers Rail Act of 1980. U.S. Code, Public Law 96–148, Supp. 1946, 14 October 1980.

Steptoe and Johnson. "Overview of the Case for Collective Ratemaking in the Post 1980 Competitive Environment." Presented before the Motor Carrier Ratemaking Study Commission, 8 December 1982.

Stigler, George J. *The Theory of Price.* New York: Macmillan, 1966.

Sugrue, Paul K., Manfred H. Ledford, and Nicholas A. Glaskowsky, Jr. "Computer Applications in the U.S. Trucking Industry." *Logistics and Transportation Review* 18, no. 2 (1982): 169–87.

Swan, Alison B. *Testimony before the Motor Carrier Ratemaking Study Commission,* 10 December 1981.

Taylor, Reese H. *Statement before the Subcommittee on Surface Transportation of the House Committee on Public Works and Transportation on Implementation of the Motor Carrier Act,* 23 June 1982.

Telser, Lester G. "Cooperation, Competition, and Efficiency." *Journal of Law and Economics* 28, no. 2 (May 1985): 271–95.

Thibodeau, Robert E., and James P. Farrell. "A Price Index for Interstate Motor Common Carriers." *Transportation Research Forum Proceedings* 22, no. 1 (1981): 156–63.

Thompson, F. S. "How to Improve Profits with an Innovative Pricing System." *Transport Topics* (28 June 1982): 7.

Thompson, Stephen J. "Trucking Rate Bureaus." *Congressional Research Service,* Report No. 79–57 E. Washington, D.C.: Library of Congress (26 February 1979).

Thurow, Lester C. "Let's Abolish the Antitrust Laws." *The New York Times* (19 October 1980).

Transportation Policy Associates. *Transportation in America*. Washington, D.C. (November 1985): 5.

Trans-World Trucking Associates. "Patterns of Discrimination under Collective Motor Carrier Ratemaking Systems." Presented to the U.S. Department of Transportation, 18 November 1981.

Trantum, Thomas A. *Testimony before the Motor Carrier Ratemaking Study Commission*. Boston, 19 March 1982.

"Trucking Industry Seeks Uniformity in Claims Liability for All Modes." *Traffic World* (18 July 1983): 27–28.

Tye, William B. "On the Application of the 'Williamsonian Welfare Tradeoff' to Rail Mergers." *The Logistics and Transportation Review* 21, no. 3 (September 1985): 239–48.

———. "Scenarios of the Motor Carrier Industry without Collective Ratemaking." *Transportation Practitioners Journal* 52, no. 4 (Summer 1985): 493–511.

———. "Some Subtle Pricing Issues in Railroad Regulation: Comment" and "Rejoinder." *International Journal of Transport Economics* 11, no. 2–3 (August/December 1984): 207–16, 219–20.

———. "Status Review on Regulation of Trucking and Collective Ratemaking." In J. Rhoads Foster *et al.*, eds., *Boundaries between Competition and Economic Regulation*, Washington, D.C.: Institute for the Study of Regulation, 1983.

———. "Fundamental Elements of a Marketing Audit for a More Competitive Motor Carrier Industry." *Transportation Journal* 22, no. 3 (Spring 1983): 5–22.

———. "Review of 'Regulatory Reform and the Trucking Industry: An Evaluation of the Motor Carrier Act of 1980.' " Paper submitted to the Motor Carrier Ratemaking Study Commission, May 1982.

———. "Preserve the Antitrust Immunity—A Defense of Collective Ratemaking." *Transport Topics* (12 April 1982).

———. "Pricing Under the Motor Carrier Act of 1980." *Proceedings: Seminar on Transport Pricing, Costing, and User Charges*. Transportation Research Forum, Washington Chapter, Washington, D.C. (April 1982): 6–7.

———. *Statement before the Motor Carrier Ratemaking Study Commission*, 19 March 1982.

———. "Implications of Motor Carrier Regulatory Reform for Carrier Planning and Marketing." *Transportation Research Record 804: Surface Regulatory Reform: Rail, Truck, and Intermodal*. Washington, D.C.: Transportation Research Board, National Academy of Sciences, 1981.

———. "Motor Carrier Act of 1980 Requires New Marketing Strategy in Trucking." *Traffic World* (16 March 1981): 32–33.

Tye, William B., A. Lawrence Kolbe, and Miriam Alexander Baker. "The Economics of Revenue Need Standards in Motor Carrier General Increase Proceedings." *Transportation Journal* 20, no. 4 (Summer 1981): 1–25.

Tye, William B., Paul O. Roberts, and Joseph G. Altonji. "Load Factors of Motor Carriers in the Interstate Highway System: Consequences for Regulatory Policy." In *Motor Carrier Economic Regulation*. Washington, D.C.: National Academy of Sciences, 1978.

U.S. Department of Justice. *Merger Guidelines* (14 June 1984). Reprinted in *An titrust and Trade Regulation*, Special Supplement, pp. S-5–S-16. 49 Federal Register 26,823, 29 June 1984.

———. "Comments and Proposed Rules of the Department of Justice." 17 November 1983, Docket No. 41686. Presented before the Civil Aeronautics Board. *Advance Notice of Proposed Rulemaking—Computer Reservations Systems.*

U.S. General Accounting Office. "Effects of Regulatory Reform on Unemployment in the Trucking Industry." Gathersville, Md.: GAO, 1982.

U.S. Senate. "Comments and Proposed Rules of the Department of Justice." Docket No. 41686. Presented before the Civil Aeronautics Board, 17 November 1983. *Advance Notice of Proposed Rulemaking—Computer Reservations Systems.*

———. Committee on the Judiciary. *Federal Restraints on Competition in the Trucking Industry: Antitrust Immunity and Economic Regulation Draft Report.* 96th Congress, 2nd session, Washington, D.C.: U.S. Government Printing Office, April 1980. Committee Print 37.

———. *Motor Carrier Reform Act of 1980: Report Together with Additional and Minority Views of the Senate Committee on Commerce, Science and Transportation.* 96th Congress, 2nd session, 24 March 1980. S. Rept. 96–641.

———. *Report of the Task Group on Antitrust Immunities.* Washington, D.C.: U.S. Government Printing Office, 1977.

Velten, Richard G. *Statement on behalf of the National Small Shipments Traffic Conference (NASSTRAC).* Washington Hearing of Study Commission, 18 November 1981.

Voytko, James M. *Testimony Before the Motor Carrier Ratemaking Study Commission.* Boston, 19 March 1982.

"Wanted: Adoption of Simple Uniform Rate System by Motor Rate Bureaus." *Traffic World* (25 April 1983): 19–20.

Waring, Dabney T. "No Protection for the Inefficient Carrier in Collective Ratemaking." Paper presented before the Motor Carrier Ratemaking Study Commission, Kansas City, 5 March 1982.

West, Gene T. "The Challenge of the Eighties! What a Motor Carrier is Doing." *Traffic World* (1 July 1985): 48–55.

Williams, Kevin M. *Antitrust Compliance Manual for Motor Carriers.* Washington, D.C.: Regular Common Carrier Conference, American Trucking Associations.

Wilner, Frank. "Creating a Linkage between Rate and Costs: A Survival Tactic for Small Carriers under Deregulation." *ICC Practitioners Journal* 48 (November/December 1980): 65–81.

Wilson, George W. *Testimony before the Motor Carrier Ratemaking Study Commission.* Boston, 19 March 1982.

Winship, H. D., Jr. "New Procedures in Motor Carrier Restructuring Proceedings: Initial Statement on Behalf of Georgia Highway Express." Presented before the Interstate Commerce Commission, 8 March 1976.

Winston, Clifford. "The Welfare Effects of ICC Rate Regulation Revisited." *Bell Journal of Economics and Management Science* 12, no. 1 (Spring 1981): 232–44.

" 'Zip Code Tariff' Proposed by ECMCA." *Transport Topics* (13 December 1982): 14, 18.

Index

About the Author

William B. Tye is a Principal of Putnam, Hayes & Bartlett, Inc. (PHB), an economics and management consulting firm which specializes in antitrust and regulation. After receiving his Ph.D. in economics at Harvard University in 1969, he taught economics and management at the U.S. Air Force Academy for three years. Returning to Cambridge, Massachusetts, he became a transportation consultant at Charles River Associates Incorporated and joined PHB in 1980.

Dr. Tye has supervised and participated in numerous studies of economics and management in the motor carrier industry, specializing in antitrust, marketing, and finance. His research papers have been published by *Transportation Research Record, Journal of Transport Economics and Policy, Journal of Policy Analysis and Management, Logistics and Transportation Review, Transportation, Transportation Practitioners Journal, Research in Transportation Economics, Transportation Journal, Motor Freight Controller, Proceedings of the Transportation Research Forum, Transportation Research, Rand Journal of Economics, International Journal of Transport Economics,* and *American Economic Review.* He has appeared before the Interstate Commerce Commission as an expert witness in numerous proceedings and served as National President of the Transportation Research Forum in 1983.